EXPLORING

IDAHO GEOLOGY

TERRY MALEY

FIRST EDITION

Mineral Land Publications
P. O. Box 1186
Boise, Idaho 83701
(208) 343-9143

Front cover photo courtesy Brian McGrath

Copyright ©1987 by Terry S. Maley

Library of Congress Catalog Card Number:
86-090540

ISBN: 0-940949-00-8

Typesetting by B & J Typesetting Co., Boise, Idaho.

The Yankee Fork Dredge, a large capacity bucket-line dredge, is situated along the Yankee Fork River west of Sunbeam.

PREFACE

Geology is the science which deals with the origin, structure and history of the earth. This also includes the study of past life as recorded in the rocks. The main purpose of this book is to aid the reader in understanding the origin and character of Idaho's spectacular scenic landforms. Another major objective is to focus on geologic features of particular scenic, economic, or scientific interest. In geologically recent times, Idaho has experienced major earthquakes, catastrophic floods, huge glacial ice sheets and volcanic eruptions.

Idaho is one of the few states with excellent examples of almost every type of geologic landform, structure, rock type and mineral deposit. Idaho's oldest rocks are more than 2500 million years old and contain a record of all the events that transpired during that vast period of geologic time. By visiting the localities discussed in this book, it is possible to develop a broad background in field geology which could be useful almost anywhere on earth.

Major breakthroughs in the understanding of almost every aspect of Idaho's geology have occurred during the last 15 years. This book includes the latest developments on the origin of the Idaho Batholith, basaltic and rhyolitic volcanism, Precambrian rocks, the Snake River Plain, accreted terrane of west-central Idaho, the Basin and Range and the Idaho-Wyoming thrust belt.

For those interested in finding and collecting valuable earth resources, *Exploring Idaho Geology* also contains detailed information on discovering valuable gems and minerals, gold panning, claim staking and fossil collecting.

The first several chapters give a basic introduction to geology with Idaho examples. A detailed glossary of scientific terms used in the book is included to help the beginner.

Acknowledgments

Although many friends and relatives offered help and encouragement on this book, my wife Louise, also a geologist, deserves special mention for her contribution. She substantially influenced every aspect of the book including planning, organization, content, revision and editing of manuscripts and photographs and was an enthusiastic companion on field trips.

Contributing Authors

I would like to extend my appreciation to my friends and colleagues who contributed chapters for the book. As a group they have more than 90 years of combined experience in their specialties of geology and mining engineering. I particularly appreciate their constant encouragement and help on the project. Obviously their contribution to the book goes well beyond the chapters they authored.

Lawrence L. Dee   — Snake River Gold
The Gooding City of Rocks

Robert E. DeTar   — Hot Springs of Idaho

R. David Hovland   — Phosphate Resources in Southeastern Idaho
Borah Peak Earthquake

Steven W. Moore   — Borah Peak Earthquake
Phosphate Resources in Southeastern Idaho

Ted R. Weasma   — Fossils of Idaho

CONTENTS

Cave formed in granite by case hardening of the outer shell
and removal of the core by weathering and erosion.

Part 1

INTRODUCTION TO GEOLOGY

Vertical set of joints in the Quiet City of Rocks.

GEOLOGIC TIME SCALE

The earth is generally considered to be about 4.6 billion years old, originating about the same time as other planets in our solar system. The oldest rocks found on earth have been dated at 3.8 billion years. Consequently, the geologic time scale runs from the present time to 3,800 million years ago. Because the oldest rocks found in Idaho have been dated at 2.5 to 2.7 billion years, we have a record of events in Idaho for a large part of the geologic time scale.

The present geologic time scale was originally developed by correlation of fossils based on relative age relationships. With the advent of radioactive dating techniques, the subdivisions of the time scale were assigned absolute ages. For example we now know that the Triassic Period began 245 million years ago.

Radioactive Dating

In radioactive dating we compare the amount of radioactive elements present with the amount of their radioactive decay products present. We can compute how much time has elapsed since the rocks formed on the basis of the known rate of radioactive decay. Radioactive elements are useful for determining age because the rate of decay is nearly constant. The decay rate for isotopes is given in terms of half life. The half life is the time it takes for a specified amount of a radioactive isotope to be reduced by one-half. Igneous rocks are dated more successfully than sedimentary or metamorphic rocks.

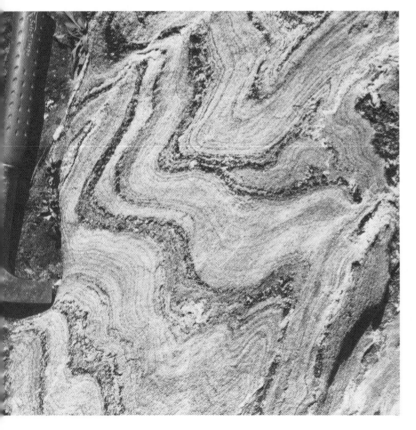

Strongly metamorphosed, pre-Belt sedimentary rock which may be more than two billion years old. The character of the folds indicate the rock behaved like a plastic when it was deformed under great heat and pressure.

Geologic Time Scale

Era	Period		Epoch	Time (Million Years)	Event
CENOZOIC	Quaternary		Holocene	0.01	Great Rift Flows Bonneville Flood Worldwide Glaciation
			Pleistocene	1.6	
	Tertiary	Neogene	Pliocene	5.3	Columbia River Basalt
			Miocene	23.7	Quiet City of Rocks
		Paleogene	Oligocene	36.6	Challis Volcanism
			Eocene	57.8	
			Paleocene	66.4	Early Primates Extinction of Dinosaurs
MESOZOIC	Cretaceous				Idaho Batholith Accreted Terrane Overthrust in Eastern Idaho
	Jurassic			144	Early Birds and Mammals
	Triassic			208	Opening of Atlantic Ocean
PALEOZOIC	Permian			245	
	Carboniferous	Pennsylvanian		286	Early Reptiles
		Mississippian		320	
	Devonian			360	Early Trees
	Silurian			408	Early Land Plants
	Ordovician			438	Early Fishes
	Cambrian			505	
PRECAMBRIAN	Proterozoic			570	Multicelled Organisms Deposition of Belt Supergroup Oldest Rocks in Idaho
	Archean			2500	Early Bacteria and Algae
				3800	Oldest Earth Rocks

MINERALS

Minerals are naturally-occurring, inorganic (not derived from living things) compounds or elements. They have a definite chemical composition or range of compositions and a crystalline structure. Some substances are still considered minerals even though they are not covered by the definition given above. Among these are opal, a non-crystalline solid, and mercury, a liquid.

More than 2,500 minerals have been recognized. Their names are derived from languages such as Greek and Latin. Some are named for geographic localities in which they were first found and others are named after properties such as color, crystal form, density or change. However, most commonly, they have been named after people.

Common Minerals

These 2,500 minerals do not occur in equal abundance; some are relatively common, whereas, most of them are rare. Only 10 elements occur abundantly in nature and they represent about 99 percent of the total mass of the earth's surface. Thus the abundant minerals are composed of the abundant elements. Of the elements comprising the continental rocks, oxygen and silicon make up 75 percent of the elements. Seven metals, aluminum, iron, calcium, sodium, potassium, magnesium, and titanium make up the rest. Another interesting fact is that oxygen atoms are relatively large and make up approximately 94 percent of the volume of the continental crust. Because of the abundance of oxygen and silicon, the minerals (silicates) composed of these elements are the most common in the earth's crust. Most of the silicates also contain varying amounts of one or more of the seven metals in addition to silicon and oxygen. Although silicates make up most of the common minerals, a few non-silicates are abundant.

Rock-Forming Minerals

Rocks are aggregates of one or more minerals. For example, limestone is composed primarily of the mineral calcite. Granite typically contains three minerals: feldspar, quartz and mica. Certain minerals are so common in rocks they are called the rock forming minerals. The minerals listed below make up most of the earth and are so few in number that most beginning amature prospectors or mineral collectors should be able to identify them. The important rock-forming minerals include quartz, potassium feldspar (orthoclase), plagioclase feldspar, muscovite mica, biotite mica, hornblende, augite, olivine, garnet, chlorite and clay. With the exception of olivine, all of the rock-forming minerals are common in Idaho.

Crystals

When crystalline minerals grow without interference, they have smooth, flat crystal faces that are related directly to the internal atomic structure of the mineral. Each mineral is assigned to one of six crystal systems. These systems are based on the number, position and relative lengths of the crystal axes. Crystal axes are imaginary lines extending through the center of the crystal. The six crystal systems include isometric or cubic, tetragonal, hexagonal, orthorhombic, monoclinic and triclinic.

Any given mineral crystal will grow in such a manner so as to form certain typical shapes or crystal habits. Crystal habits are used to identify minerals because they indicate the forms or combination of forms a mineral is likely to have. Cubic, columnar and tabular are examples of crystal habits.

Mineral Identification

After a little practice the common rock-forming minerals can be identified on sight. However, some may require an examination of the various chemical and physical properties. The properties most useful in mineral identification include hardness, streak, color, specific gravity, fracture, cleavage, luster and shape or form. Some of the more important rock-forming minerals are discussed below.

The feldspar group constitutes the most important group of the rock-forming minerals. They are so abundant that they make up 60 percent of the earth's crust. Feldspars are common in igneous, metamorphic and sedimentary rock.

Orthoclase is the common potash (potassium) feldspar. It is transparent to translucent with colors of white, gray, flesh-red, yellow, pink, or colorless. In the Idaho Batholith, orthoclase tends to be flesh colored or pink.

Plagioclase feldspars are common in igneous rocks and some metamorphic rocks. Colors are white, yellow and gray. In much of the Idaho Batholith, plagioclase tends to be chalky white in color.

Quartz is the second most common mineral and is widely distributed. Pure quartz is composed of silicon dioxide. It forms six-sided crystals with pyramidal ends. Colors include white, colorless, rose, purple, yellow, and smoky gray. Among the common crystalline varieties of quartz are amethyst (purple), milky quartz, rose quartz and smoky quartz. Very fine-grained varieties include agate, chalcedony, chert, flint and jasper. Some sedimentary rocks such as sandstone and quartzite are composed almost entirely of quartz.

Mica has a perfect basal cleavage (also called micaceous cleavage). Micas are one of the easiest minerals to identify because they consist of stacks of sheets or books of easily-parted plates. Muscovite and biotite are the most common micas. Muscovite is the white, transparent mica and is most common in granites, and pegmatites. Biotite is the black mica and is common in both igneous and metamorphic rocks.

The mineral *calcite* is composed of calcium carbonate. Calcite occurs primarily in sedimentary rocks and some metamorphic rocks such as marble. Calcite is the most abundant constituent of limestone. Many of the limestone formations in eastern Idaho consist of more than 90 percent calcite. Calcite has the property of reacting with cold dilute hydrochloric acid by effervescing or fizzing. Dolomite is calcium magnesium carbonate and reacts only mildly with acid.

ROCKS

Rocks are naturally-formed, consolidated material composed of grains of one or more minerals. Geologists group rocks into three categories depending on their origin: igneous, sedimentary and metamorphic.

Igneous rocks are formed from solidification of molten material. Sedimentary rocks are formed by the accumulation of fragmental material derived from preexisting rocks of any origin as well as the accumulation of organic material or precipitated material. Metamorphic rocks occur as a result of high pressure, high temperature and the chemical activity of fluids changing the texture and (or) mineralogy of preexisting rocks.

Rock Colors

Perhaps the most apparent feature of rocks to the observer is the coloration. Although most rocks have a rather drab appearance, some have very distinctive and, in some cases, beautiful colors. Shades of red, green, gray and brown may be caused by iron-bearing minerals. Very light-colored rocks are generally lacking in iron-bearing minerals. The coloration of sedimentary rocks reflects the environmental conditions that existed during deposition.

Purple and Red Rocks

Purple, maroon and red rocks are stained by the mineral hematite (iron oxide). Hematite results from the decomposition and oxidation of iron-rich minerals such as magnetite, ilmenite, biotite, hornblende and augite. A rock composed of only several percent hematite may be stained a deep red.

Green Rocks

Green sedimentary rocks are typically formed in a reducing environment where oxygen is not available. For sedimentary rocks, this would normally mean deposition in deeper water than red rocks. In a reducing environment, iron combines with silica compounds to form iron silicate minerals. Then low-grade metamorphism will convert the iron silicates to the green mineral chlorite. Chlorite in sedimentary rocks indicates a deep-water depositional environment. Where chlorite-rich strata alternate with hematite-rich strata, a change in sea level probably occurred.

Black Rocks

Higher-grade metamorphism (high heat and pressure) will convert the hematite in red rocks and the chlorite in green rocks to the black minerals magnetite and biotite. An abundance of these minerals will yield a gray to dark gray mineral. Traces of black organic matter will also darken a rock to a gray or dark gray.

Weathered Surfaces

Many rocks have a different color on the weathered surface than on a fresh break. Weathering of disseminated pyrite (iron sulfide) in rocks will convert them to brown or yellow iron hydroxide and iron sulfate.

IGNEOUS ROCKS

Magma

Igneous rocks are those rocks that have solidified from an original molten state. Temperatures within the earth are so hot that many rocks and minerals are able to exist in a molten condition called magma. This molten rock exists deep below the earth's surface in large pools called magma chambers. Many magmas or portions of magmas are lighter than the surrounding rock and tend to rise toward the surface of the crust; also, the high pressure at depth facilitates the upward movement of magma. Molten materials that extrude through the surface of the earth are called eruptive, extrusive or volcanic rocks. Those magmas that crystallize and solidify at depth, never reaching the earth's surface before consolidation, are called intrusives or plutonic rocks. Of course after consolidation, plutonic rocks may be exposed at the earth's surface by the process of erosion.

The crystal size of igneous rocks is very diagnostic of their origin. Volcanic or extrusive rocks have a very small average grain size which is generally too small to discern with the naked eye. Extrusive rock has a very high component of glass because it was quickly frozen from the molten stage before crystals had time to grow. The more deeply-buried plutons cool more slowly and develop a coarse texture composed of large crystals. Therefore, large mineral crystals of more than one inch in diameter indicate formation at a depth of 6 to 12 miles.

Mafic and Felsic Magmas

Magmas are thought to be generated in the outer 60 to 180 miles of the earth where temperatures are hot enough to cause melting. Magmas rich in magnesium, iron and calcium are called mafic. Those rich in sodium, potassium and silicon are called felsic. Those that are transitional between mafic and felsic are called intermediate. Felsic magmas are generated mostly within the continental crustal regions where the source of parent rocks are abundant; whereas, mafic magmas may be derived from parent materials rich in magnesium, iron and calcium which occur beneath the crust. Mafic magmas, coming from a deep hot source, are about 1,200 degrees centigrade when they reach the earth's surface; whereas, felsic magmas are much cooler — about 700 degrees centigrade upon reaching the earth's surface.

Origin of Basalt

Most basalt originates at spreading centers such as the mid-oceanic ridge system. Basalt magma originates from partial melting of mantle material. The fluid magma rises through fissures formed by tensional forces of two diverging plates.

Origin of Andesite and Granite

Intermediate and felsic magma in Idaho are believed to have originated where a cool slab of oceanic lithosphere of basalt and overlying sedimentary rock descended beneath the continental crust of the western United States. The descending plate of lithosphere becomes hotter with increasing depth. Water trapped in the descending plate also lowers the melting temperature so that partial melting of basalt takes place. While the basaltic magma rises through the overriding continental crust, the magma absorbs some of the more silica rich rocks to become intermediate in composition. Also, the very hot basaltic magma chambers in the continental crust could melt the surrounding felsic rocks and create granitic magmas.

Emplacement of Magma

Bodies of intrusive rocks exist in almost every shape and size. Regardless of shape or size, they all come under the general term pluton. Most of them appear to be emplaced in the surrounding country rocks (host rocks) by the process of forceful injection. By forceful injection, the body is intruded along zones of weakness, such as fractures, by pushing

Granitic intrusion in dark country rock. Rotated xenoliths ripped off the country rock are indicative of forceful intrusion. Photo taken near Shoup.

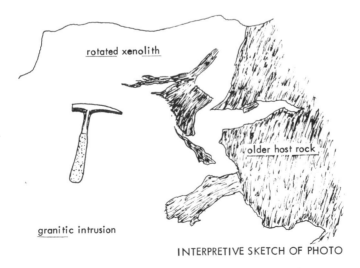

INTERPRETIVE SKETCH OF PHOTO

apart the surrounding rock. A pluton is also emplaced by melting rock around it and prying out blocks of the country rock. The surface between the pluton and the country rock is the intrusive contact. Magma is also aided in its upward movement because it is generally less dense than the surrounding rock. When the magma stops moving it begins to crystallize. Those plutons that reach shallow to intermediate depths tend to be porphyritic, that is, large crystals are contained in a finer crystalline groundmass.

Types of Plutons

Dikes are small tabular plutons which cut across layering in the host rocks. Dikes may range from one inch to tens of feet thick. They are much longer than wide and can commonly be traced a mile or more. Dikes are generally intruded along fractures and tend to have the composition of pegmatite, aplite (white, sugar-textured dikes) and basalt. In almost every roadcut through the Idaho Batholith of central Idaho, aplitic and pegmatitic dikes can be seen.

Sills are also tabular bodies of the same approximate size and shape range as dikes. However, sills are concordant or parallel to the layers of the surrounding host or country rock. The Purcell sills are examples of such plutons in northern Idaho.

The largest plutons consist of granite and diorite and are found in the cores of mountain ranges. The Idaho Batholith is a good example. A batholith is defined as a pluton with a surface exposure in excess of 40 square miles. If the exposure is less than that, the pluton is called a stock. It is commonly believed that buried batholiths underlie large areas of widespread silicic volcanics in Idaho. Many of the large batholiths such as the Idaho Batholith are known to be a composite of many granitic plutons.

Pegmatites

Pegmatite bodies have a relatively larger grain size than the surrounding igneous rocks. Individual crystals are known to reach more than 30 feet in length. A pegmatite may have the composition of a granite, diorite or gabbro. All three types are exposed in the large granitic plutons of Idaho. However the granitic pegmatites are by far the most common. In practically every exposure of granitic rock in the state, there are one or more granitic pegmatite dikes ex-

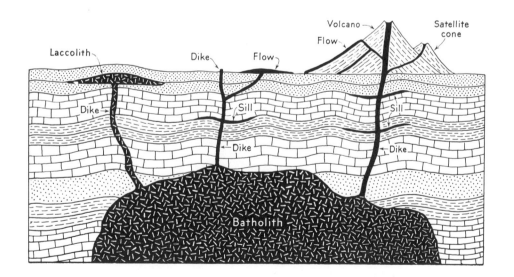

Cross section showing the various types of plutons found in the vicinity of a batholith.

Large basalt dike in granite exposed in roadcut near Boise.
Note dilation offset of older thin dike.

posed. Although most of these pegmatites do not exceed 10 feet in thickness; an uncommonly large pegmatite more than 300 feet along its smallest dimension is exposed in the City of Rocks near the town of Oakley.

The extremely large crystal size (generally 2 to 8 inches), is attributed to both slow cooling and low liquid viscosity. Pegmatites are the last portion of a pluton to crystallize. These residual fluids are much richer in certain elements than the original magma. High amounts of silica and ions of elements that are necessary to crystallize sodium plagioclase and potassium feldspar must be abundant in the fluids. The fluids are also rich in certain elements that could not be used in the crystal structure of the previously crystallized minerals. Water is also very abundant which promotes slower cooling and a lower temperature of crystallization. Many pegmatites were intruded along existing fractures.

Most Idaho pegmatites are composed of orthoclase feldspar, quartz and muscovite. Careful inspection will also reveal small red garnets, black tourmaline and bluish-green aquamarine. Aquamarine is generally only found in the tertiary plutons.

Common Igneous Rocks

Igneous rocks are classified on the basis of their texture and composition. Although more than several hundred names have been given to igneous rocks, only a few major divisions are discussed below.

Granite is the most common coarse-textured rock. It is formed at great depths within the earth and has crystals ranging from microscopic to more than one inch in size. Granite typically contains quartz, feldspar, mica and hornblende. Granites are generally light in color and may have a salt and pepper appearance. The feldspar may cause it to be white, gray, pink or yellowish brown. Most of the large

Refolded fold in rhyolite. Fold was formed by movement of the viscous rhyolitic lava prior to solidifying.

Classification of Igneous Rocks

Texture	Composition		
	Quartz, Feldspar Hornblende, Biotite Light Colored	Intermediate	Feldspar, Augite Dark Colored
Coarse Grained	Granite	Diorite	Gabbro
Fine Grained	Rhyolite	Andesite	Basalt
Glassy	Pumice	Obsidian	
Pyroclastic or Fragmental	Air – Fall Tuffs Ash – Flow Tuffs		

bodies of plutonic rocks in Idaho have typical granitic texture and composition. Potassium feldspar and plagioclase feldspar make up most of the rock, though quartz may represent up to 25 percent of the bulk composition. The black minerals are commonly hornblende and biotite mica. Muscovite is also common in some granites.

Gabbro is a dark, coarse-grained igneous rock. It is generally composed of plagioclase feldspar and augite. Gabbro is generally dark green or dark gray in color. Idaho has relatively little gabbro compared to granite.

Pumice is lava that solidified while gases were released from it. It is essentially a frozen volcanic froth. Because of the abundance of gas cavities, pumice is so light in weight that it can float in water. Pumice is generally light gray or tan and has the same chemical composition as obsidian, rhyolite and granite.

Diorite is a coarse- to fine-grained plutonic rock and has a mineral composition that places it midway between granite and gabbro. It has little quartz or potassium feldspar. Diorite tends to be a gray rock due to the high amounts of plagioclase feldspar and iron-rich minerals.

Andesite is much finer grained than diorite but has the same mineral composition. Andesites are more common than rhyolites, but less common than basalts.

Rhyolite is a volcanic rock with the same composition as granite. The major difference is its fine-grain size or glassy texture. Rhyolite is generally light colored and may be gray, white, tan or various shades of red. It has a characteristic streaked texture called flow banding. Flow banding is caused by slow flowage of highly viscous lava.

Obsidian forms when magma of a rhyolitic composition cools so fast that crystallization of the minerals is not possible. Thus volcanic glass is essentially a frozen liquid. It is a lustrous, glassy black or reddish-black rock. Obsidian has a conchoidal fracture giving it very sharp edges. Because of this property, it was commonly used to make tools and weapons by early man. One of the best-known obsidian flows occurs at Obsidian Cliffs in Yellowstone National Park.

Basalt is the fine-grained compositional equivalent of gabbro. It is by far the most abundant volcanic rock. For example, the volume of basalt in the Columbia Plateau is estimated to be 74,000 cubic miles. Basalt is normally coal black to dark gray when not weathered. Common constituent minerals include pyroxene, calcic plagioclase and olivine. Basalt commonly has small cavities called vesicles. Basalt flows are characterized by columnar jointing which causes polygonal vertical columns that look like giant fence posts stacked on end. Most of the large basalt flows are extruded from large fissures in the earth's crust. Basalts are very common throughout Idaho, especially western and southern Idaho.

Porphyritic Texture

Some fine-grained rocks such as basalt, rhyolite and, most commonly, andesite have a mixed texture of large and small grains. This texture is called porphyritic and is characterized by large crystals called phenocrysts surrounded by a groundmass (background) of smaller crystals.

Pyroclastic Rocks

In addition to the fluid lava extruded from a volcano, a great amount of lava is blown out the vent by violent gas explosions. All material driven out explosively is called pyroclastic. Large fragments such as spindle-shaped volcanic bombs fall near the vent. However, the dust-size fragments called ash can be carried hundreds of miles by prevailing winds. Volcanic ash is composed of fragments of volcanic glass and small crystals. When air-fall ash deposits consolidate, they are called ash-fall tuffs. Excellent examples of most of these volcanic products can be observed at Craters of the Moon National Monument.

One type of pyroclastic rock very common in southern and east-central Idaho is the welded ash-flow tuff. This material consists of a very hot mixture of fragments of pumice, cinders, crystals and glass shards, many of which are more than one inch in size. They flow out of the vent and downslope somewhat like a lava flow, but riding on a cushion of hot gases. When the deposit settles and comes together, the angular fragments are so hot they weld together. Unlike rhyolite flows, a single ash flow tuff unit may extend up to 100 miles. These tuffs make distinctive rim formers above the lake-bed deposits in the Snake River Plain.

Volcanic Cones

Volcanoes are vents in the earth's crust through which molten rock and other volcanic products are extruded. There are three types of volcanic cones: cinder cones, shield volcanoes (lava domes), and composite cones (stratovolcanoes). All three types are common in southern Idaho.

Cinder cones are formed entirely of pyroclastic material, mostly of cinders. These cones consist of a succession of steeply-inclined layers of reddened scoriaceous cinders around a central crater. They are generally less than 1,000 feet in height and are susceptible to erosion because there is generally nothing holding the mass together. This type of cone has the steepest flanks of the three types of volcanic cones. Hundreds of cinder cones are distributed throughout the Snake River Plain, generally aligned along frac-

tures in the crust. These cones disrupt the otherwise flat, featureless plain.

Shield volcanoes are built almost entirely of basaltic lava flows. They have gently-rounded profiles with a circular outline. This type of cone is the most stable and least susceptible to erosion.

Composite or stratovolcanoes are composed of alternating sheets of lava and pyroclastic material. These volcanic mountains are cone shaped and may be as much as 12,000 feet high. The alternating pyroclastic layers and lava layers indicate that the pyroclastic material was produced during periods of explosive activity, whereas the lava eruptions occurred at times of quiescence.

Calderas are nearly circular basin-shaped depressions in the upper part of volcanoes. They are much larger than craters and are generally more than 6 miles in diameter. There are two types: explosive calderas and collapse or subsidence calderas. Most of those in Idaho are thought to have formed by collapse caused by the sudden withdrawal of supporting lava. Such calderas are common in southern and east-central Idaho.

Spindle Bomb

Breadcrust Bomb

Bombs or projectiles of lava are blown out of a volcanic vent and partly solidified while in the air.

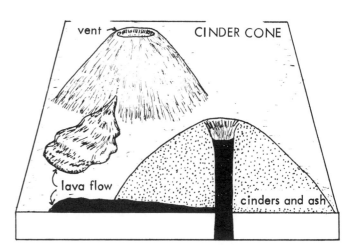

Block diagram of a cinder cone.

— 13 —

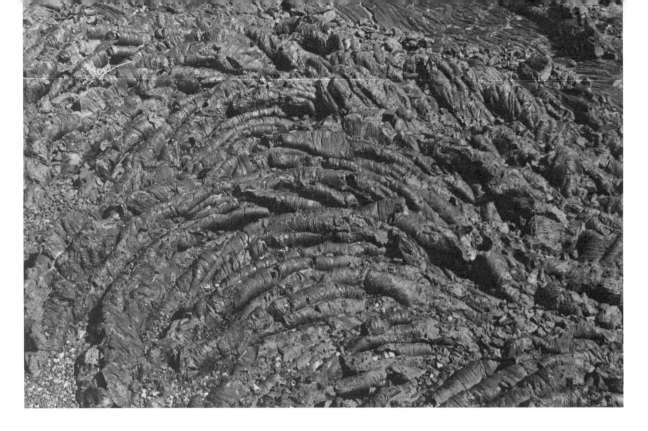

Pahoehoe lava; note the smooth, ropy surface.

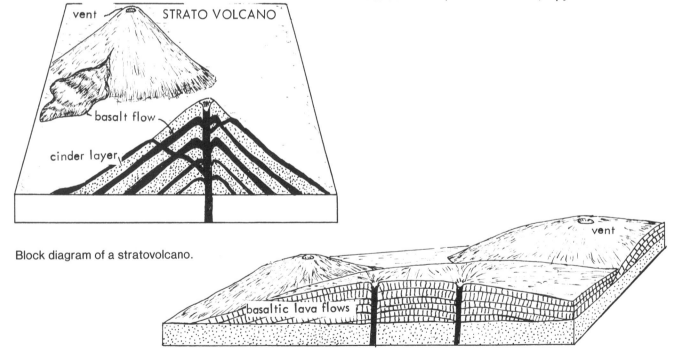

Block diagram of a stratovolcano.

Block diagram of shield volcanoes.

SEDIMENTARY ROCKS

Sedimentary rocks are derived from preexisting igneous, sedimentary and metamorphic rocks. These rocks contain many clues as to their origin and the conditions that existed while they formed. Sedimentary rocks make up 75 percent of the rocks at the earth's surface but only 5 percent of the outer 10 miles of the earth. Sediment, as distinguished from sedimentary rock, is a collective name for loose, solid particles and is generally derived from weathering and erosion of preexisting rock. After formation, sediments are transported by rivers, ocean waves, glaciers, wind or landslides to a basin and deposited. Lithification is the process of converting loose sediment into sedimentary rock and includes the process of cementation, compaction and crystallization.

Sedimentary rock is formed by lithification of sediments, precipitation from solution and consolidation of the remains of plants or animals. Coal is an example of sedimentary rock formed from the compression of plant remains.

Rounding of Rock Particles

Rounding occurs during the transportation process by one or more of the erosional agents. Current and wave action in water are particularly effective in causing particles to hit and scrape against one another or a rock surface. The larger the particle the less distance it needs to travel to become rounded. For example, the boulders of the melon gravel deposited by the Bonneville flood were rounded after 3 to 6 miles of transportation.

Deposition of Sediment

Sorting of sediment by size is also effectively accomplished by moving water. A river sorts sediment by first depositing cobbles, then pebbles, sand, silt and clay. The larger the size of sediment, the greater the river's energy necessary to transport it. Deposition is the term used to describe the settling of transported sediment.

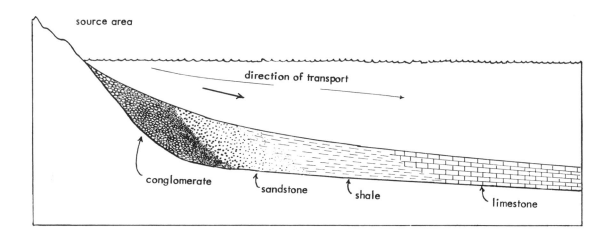

Sediment deposits become thinner away from the source. The grain size also becomes finer the greater the distance from the source area.

Lithification of Clastic Rock

Clastic or detrital sedimentary rock is composed of fragments of preexisting rock. The grains are generally rounded and sorted during the transportation process. Clastic sediment is generally lithified by cementation. Cementation occurs when material is chemically precipitated in the open spaces of the sediment so as to bind the grains together into a hard rock. Common cements include calcite, silica and iron oxides. A matrix of finer-grained sediments may also partly fill the pore space.

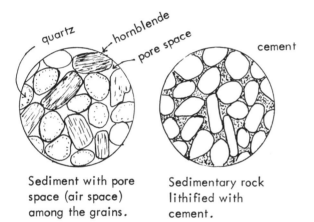

Sediment with pore space is converted to solid rock (lithified) when the pores are filled with cement.

Common Types of Sedimentary Rock

Conglomerate is the coarsest-grained sedimentary rock formed by the cementation of gravel-sized sediments. The gravel is generally rounded; however, it probably did not travel very far. Conglomerates are generally deposited by a river.

Sandstone is a medium-grained sedimentary rock formed by the cementation of sand-sized sediments, with silt and clay forming the matrix. Sandstones may be deposited by rivers, wind, waves or ocean currents.

Shale is a fine-grained sedimentary rock composed of clay- and silt-sized fragments. Shale is noted for its thin laminations parallel to the bedding. Compaction is very important in the lithification of shales. Before compaction, shale may consist of up to 80 percent water in the pore spaces.

Chemical Sedimentary Rocks are formed by material precipitated from solution. Examples include rock salt, gypsum and limestone.

Organic Sedimentary Rocks consist mostly of the remains of plants and animals. Coal is an organic rock formed from compressed plant remains.

Limestone is a sedimentary rock composed of mostly calcite. Some limestones are chemical precipitates, whereas others consist mostly of clastic grains of calcite or shells of marine invertebrates. The calcite grains in limestone recrystallize readily so as to form new and larger crystals.

Sedimentary Structures

Sedimentary Structures in sedimentary rock are formed either during the deposition process or shortly after deposition. One of the most important structures is bedding. An important principle of geology holds that sedimentary rocks are deposited in horizontal layers. The bedding plane is the nearly flat surface separating two beds of rock. Bedding planes originate by a change in grain size, a change in grain composition or a pause in deposition during the depositional process.

Mud Cracks are sedimentary structures that are abundant in many of the formations of the Belt Supergroup as well as in many Paleozoic marine sedimentary formations in Idaho. Mud cracks are polygonal cracks formed in clay- and silt-sized sediments. They are caused by the exposure of lake bottoms, river bottoms and tidal flats to the sun after being beneath water. The cracks are caused by the sun drying and shrinking the upper several inches of the exposed mud flat.

Ripple marks are small ridges, generally less than one inch high and 2 to 8 inches wide. The ridges are developed by moving water and form perpendicular to the direction of water movement. If the profiles of

Classification of Sedimentary Rock

Origin		Particle Size/Composition	Rock Name
Detrital or Clastic		Boulder, Cobble, Pebble ($>$ 2mm) Sand (1/16 – 2mm) Silt and Clay ($<$ 1/16mm)	Conglomerate Sandstone Shale
Chemical	Inorganic	Calcite Dolomite Halite	Limestone Dolomite Salt
	Biochemical	Calcite Plant Remains	Limestone Coal

the ripple marks are symmetrical, they are caused by waves; if the profiles are assymetrical, they are caused by currents. The steep sides occur in the down-current direction.

Sedimentary Rocks of Idaho

Sedimentary rocks of Idaho were generally deposited in marine environments; however, a significant part are of continental origin. Most Precambrian and Paleozoic strata are marine; Mesozoic strata include both marine and continental deposits; all Cenozoic formations are continental. Marine deposits are noted for being thick and distributed over a large area. Most of the marine rocks in Idaho were deposited in the Cordilleran geocline (formerly called geosyncline). A geocline is a large regional area generally on the continental shelf and slope that slowly subsides as sediments accumulate over a long period of geologic time. Even though a layer of sediments more than 50,000 feet thick may form, most of the material is deposited in shallow water such as in the intertidal zone.

METAMORPHIC ROCKS

Metamorphic rocks are those that have transformed from preexisting rock into texturally or mineralogically-distinct new rocks by high temperature, high pressure or chemically-active fluids. One or more of these agents may induce the textural or mineralogical changes. For example, minute clay minerals may change into coarse mica. Heat is probably the most important single agent of metamorphism. Metamorphism occurs within a temperature range of 100 to 800 degrees centigrade. Heat weakens bonds and accelerates the rate of chemical reactions. Two common sources of heat include friction from movement and intrusion of plutons. Pressure changes are caused primarily by the weight of overlying rock. Where there are more than 30,000 feet of overlying rock, pressures of more than 40,000 psi will cause rocks to flow as a plastic. Pressure may also be caused by plate collision and the forceful intrusion of plutons.

Chemically-active fluids (hot water solutions) associated with magma may react with surrounding rocks to cause chemical change. Directed pressure is pressure applied unequally on the surface of a body and may be applied by compression or shearing. Directed pressure changes the texture of a metamorphic rock by forcing the elongate and platy minerals to become parallel to each other. Foliation is the parallel alignment of textural and structural features of a rock. Mica is the most common mineral to be aligned by directed pressure.

Types of Metamorphism

There are two types of metamorphism: contact metamorphism and regional metamorphism. Contact metamorphism is the name given when country rock is intruded by a pluton (body of magma). Changes to the surrounding rocks occur as a result of penetration by the magmatic fluids and heat from the intrusion. Contact metamorphism may greatly alter the texture of the rock by forming new and larger crystals. In contact metamorphism, directed pressure is not involved so the metamorphosed rocks are not foliated.

Regional Metamorphism

Most metamorphic rocks are caused by regional metamorphism. This type of metamorphism is caused by high temperature and directed pressure. These rocks are typically formed in the cores of mountain ranges, but may be later exposed at the surface by erosion. Typical rock types include foliated rocks such as slates, phyllites, schists and gneisses.

Common Metamorphic Rocks

Marble is a coarse-grained rock consisting of interlocking calcite crystals. Limestone recrystallizes during metamorphism into marble.

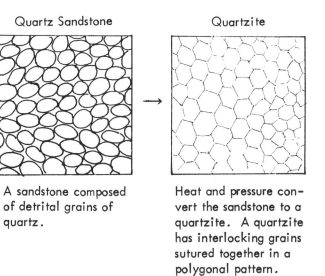

Quartz Sandstone | Quartzite

A sandstone composed of detrital grains of quartz.

Heat and pressure convert the sandstone to a quartzite. A quartzite has interlocking grains sutured together in a polygonal pattern.

Quartz sandstone may be metamorphosed to quartzite by heat and pressure.

Quartzite forms by recrystallization of quartz-rich sandstone in response to heat and pressure. As the grains of quartz grow, the boundaries become tight and interlocking. All pore space is squeezed out; and when the rock is broken, it breaks across the grains. Quartzite is the most durable construction mineral. Although both marble and quartzite may be white to light gray, they may be readily distinguished because marble fizzes on contact with dilute hydrochloric acid, whereas quartzite does not. Also, marble can be scratched with a knife, whereas quartzite cannot.

Slate is a low-grade metamorphic equivalent of shale. It is a fine-grained rock that splits easily along flat, parallel planes. Shale, the parent rock, is composed of submicroscopic, platy clay minerals. These clay minerals are realigned by metamorphism so as to create a slaty cleavage. In slate, the individual minerals are too small to be visible with the naked eye.

Phyllite is formed by further increase in temperature and pressure on a slate. The mica grains increase slightly in size but are still microscopic. The planes of parting have surfaces lined with fine-grained mica that give the rock a silky sheen.

A *schist* is characterized by coarse-grained minerals with parallel alignment. These platy minerals, generally micas, are visible to the naked eye. A schist is a high-grade, metamorphic rock and may consist entirely of coarse, platy minerals.

A *gneiss* is a rock consisting of alternating bands of light and dark minerals. Generally the dark layers are composed of platy or elongate minerals such as biotite mica or amphibolite. The light layers typically consist of quartz and feldspar. A gneiss is formed under the highest temperatures and pressures which cause the minerals to segregate into layers. In fact, slightly higher temperatures than necessary to convert the rock into a gneiss would cause the rock to melt. If temperatures become sufficiently high, the rock begins to melt and magma is squeezed out into layers within the foliating planes of the solid rock. The resulting rock is called a migmatite — a mixed, igneous and metamorphic rock.

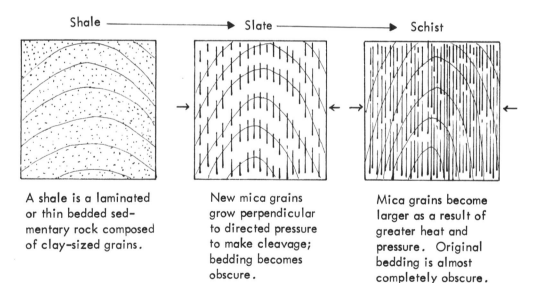

Shale ——→ Slate ——→ Schist

A shale is a laminated or thin bedded sedimentary rock composed of clay-sized grains.

New mica grains grow perpendicular to directed pressure to make cleavage; bedding becomes obscure.

Mica grains become larger as a result of greater heat and pressure. Original bedding is almost completely obscure.

A shale may be progressively metamorphosed to a slate and then to a schist by heat and pressure.

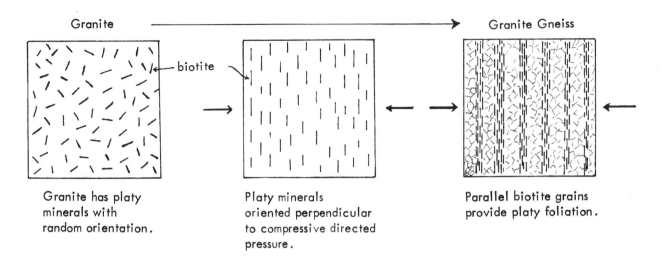

Granite has platy minerals with random orientation.

Platy minerals oriented perpendicular to compressive directed pressure.

Parallel biotite grains provide platy foliation.

Granite is converted to granitic gneiss by the heat and pressure of high-grade metamorphism.

Origin of Metamorphic Rocks

Rock Type	Metamorphic equivalent under increasing temperature and pressure →			
Shale	Slate	Phyllite	Schist	Gneiss
Sandstone	Quartzite			
Limestone	Marble			
Basalt	Schist		Amphibolite	
Granite		Granite	Gneiss	

STRUCTURAL GEOLOGY

The crust of the earth is constantly moving. However, with the exception of faults accompanied by earthquakes, this rate of movement is far too slow to notice. In the mountain ranges of Idaho, movement generally occurs at a much higher rate than it does in the more stable interior of the continent.

The movement of a part of the crust creates a stress. A stress is a force that is applied to a body of rock in such a way as to change its shape or size. The body of rock affected may range from microscopic to continental in size. The adjustment to the body of rock is called strain. Strain, then, is the adjustment of the rock unit in response to stress. Stress may be (1) compressive, which shortens the rock body, (2) tensional, which elongates the rock body, or (3) shear, where the forces are parallel but in opposite directions.

In solid material like rock, stress can cause three types of strain or deformation: plastic, elastic and fracture. In plastic deformation, the rock is molded or changed in shape under stress and does not return to its original shape when the stress is released. For example, silly putty changes shape when squeezed between your fingers and does not return to its original shape when the pressure is released. This is an example of plastic deformation. In elastic deformation the rocks may partly return to their original form after stress is released. If the rock responds to stress by cracking or fracturing, it breaks. Common examples of fractures are faults and joints. Typically, rocks initially yield to stress plasticaly and then fracture. In most cases the movement of rock is very slow, generally several millimeters or less per year.

Strike and Dip

Strike and dip are two terms used to describe the extent and direction of tilting of fractures and layering (bedding and foliation) of rock. This is determined by relating the inclined surface to an imaginary horizontal plane.

Strike is the compass direction of a line formed by the intersection of an inclined plane (tilted bedding or fault plane) with an imaginary horizontal plane. Dip has two components: the angle of dip is measured downward from the horizontal plane to the bedding; the direction of dip is the compass direction in which the angle of a dip is measured. The dip would be the direction a ball would follow down a tilted surface. The dip angle is always measured at right angles to the strike. Geologists use the symbols $_{40}\curlyvee$ to denote strike and dip, the strike is the long line and the short line indicates the direction of dip. A small number beside the symbol indicates the angle of dip. In this case the tilted bed is dipping 40 degrees from the horizontal. Geologists use a specially designed compass called a Brunton to take these measurements.

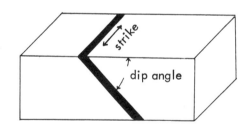

Block diagram shows relationship of strike and dip to a horizontal plane.

Folds

Folds are bends in rock layers generally caused by compression. Typically there are a series of arches (upfolds) and troughs (downfolds). This type of deformation is plastic so the rocks were probably buried deeply in the earth's crust when the folding occurred. High temperatures and pressures deep in the crust allow rocks to deform as a plastic rather than break. On the other hand fractures such as faults and joints occur near the surface where the rock is cold and brit-

Large open fold in shale.

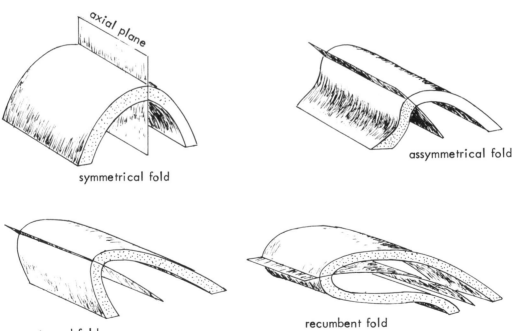

axial plane

symmetrical fold

assymmetrical fold

overturned fold

recumbent fold

Different types of anticlinal folds shown with axial planes.

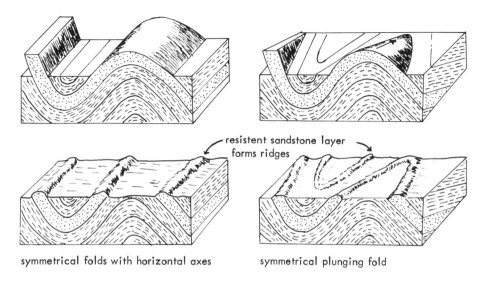

resistent sandstone layer
forms ridges

symmetrical folds with horizontal axes

symmetrical plunging fold

Symmetrical folds with horizontal axes and plunging axes both before and after erosion.

tle. Therefore you can see that the type of deformation, plastic or fracture, indicates the level in the crust where the deformation occurred.

Several terms are necessary to describe and interpret a series of folds. An anticline is an upfold or arch and where layers dip away from the axis (or hinge line). A syncline is a downfold or arch. Synclines and anticlines are typically plunging folds. In a plunging fold the axes are not horizontal. In a dome, the beds dip away from a central point and in a structural basin the beds dip towards a central point. Folds exist in all sizes from microscopic to more than a half mile in height. basic types of folds include:

    open folds – caused by mild compressional stress
    isoclinal folds – caused by intense compressional
        stress; limbs of the fold are parallel.
    overturned folds – the limbs dip in the same direc-
        tion
    recumbent fold – overturned to such a degree that
        the limbs are nearly horizontal.

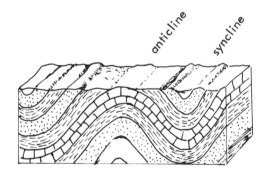

anticline   syncline

An open symmetrical anticline and syncline. The oldest rocks are found in the core of the anticline and the youngest rocks are found in the core of the syncline.

Two sets of fractures in granite intersecting at right angles.
Photo taken in the Quiet City of Rocks area.

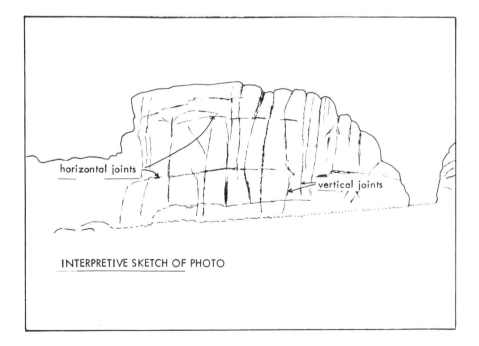

horizontal joints

vertical joints

INTERPRETIVE SKETCH OF PHOTO

Fractures

If a rock is brittle, it may rupture or break under stress. Most rock near the earth's surface is brittle so almost every exposure of bedrock is cut by fractures. There are two types of fractures in rock: joints and faults. A joint is a fracture along which no movement has taken place. Joints are generally caused by tensional forces. A fault is a fracture or break in the rock along which movement has taken place. The rupture and subsequent movement may be caused by tensional, compressional or shear forces.

Joints

Joints are fractures in rock where no displacement has occurred along the fracture surface. Columnar jointing is a specialized type of jointing common to volcanic flows. Hexagonal columns form in response to contraction of a cooling lava flow. Exfoliation (or sheeting) is another specialized type of joint generally caused by expansion parallel to the weathering surface. Where closely-spaced joints are parallel, they make up a joint set. These joints may be spaced

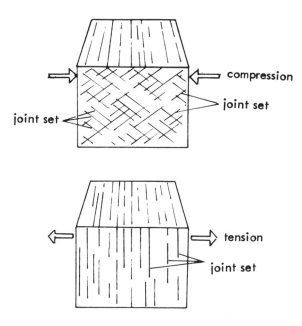

Block diagram shows how joints form as a consequence of directed pressure or tension.

from several inches to tens of feet apart. Typically rock exposures exhibit two or more joint sets. The study of joints is important for site evaluations for dams because jointing can affect the permeability and strength of the rock. Joints are also important as a plumbing system for hot water systems and the emplacement of mineral deposits.

Faults

Faults are fractures in rock along which movement has taken place parallel to the fracture plane. Many faults are active, that is, movement has taken place during historical times. Where faults are exposed in bedrock the geologist looks for evidence of displacement or offset features to determine the amount of displacement and the relative direction of movement. Fault planes or zones vary considerably in thickness. Some are just a thin crack in the rock, whereas others may consist of a brecciated and sheared zone up to 1,000 feet wide. Faults also range in length from several feet or less to hundreds of miles. For example the San Andreas fault extends about 620 miles through western California, slowly moving Los Angeles toward San Francisco. The current rate of movement averages about one inch per year so it will take about 25 million years to make Los Angeles a western suburb of San Francisco. During the 1906 earthquake that devastated much of San Francisco, bedrock along the fault was displaced as much as 15 feet. This was determined by measuring the amount of displacement along features such as roads and fences offset by the fault. The total displacement along the fault is probably about 300 miles since movement began about 30 million years ago.

The three major types of faults include normal or gravity faults, reverse or thrust faults and strike-slip or transcurrent faults.

A normal fault is one along which the hanging wall has moved down relative to the footwall. The fault plane of normal faults typically dips at an angle of 60 degrees from the horizontal. The normal fault is the most common type of fault that you can expect to see in the field. The largest and most impressive

Exfoliation of granite in the Quiet City of Rocks area southeast of Oakley.

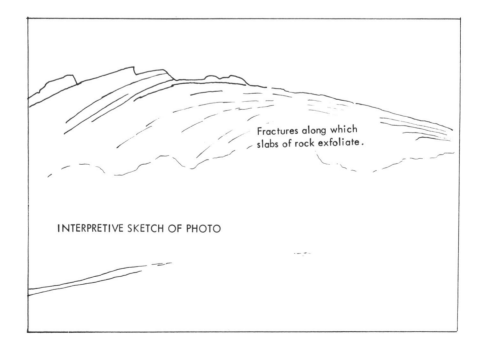

Fractures along which
slabs of rock exfoliate.

INTERPRETIVE SKETCH OF PHOTO

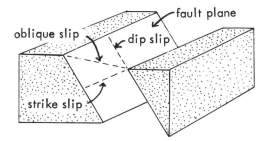

The types of slip on a fault plane.

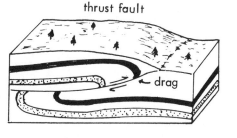

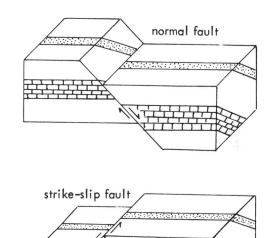

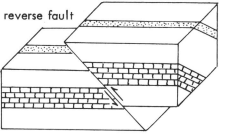

Types of faults.

group of normal faults are those that form the fault blocks that make up the Basin and Range Province of eastern Idaho. Normal faults are caused by rupture in response to tensional forces. Because the rock is pulled apart rather than pushed together, the broken area has much space available for ore solutions to move in and precipitate. Most lode or vein deposits are formed in normal fault zones.

In a reverse fault, the hanging wall moves up relative to the footwall. The fault plane is typically inclined 30 degrees from the horizontal, but may vary significantly from this. Reverse faults are not nearly as common as gravity or normal faults.

A thrust fault is a type of reverse fault that is characterized by a low angle of inclination of the fault plane. In fact the fault plane is commonly horizontal or subhorizontal. Both reverse and thrust faults are caused by rupture in response to compressional forces. Eastern Idaho has many exceptional examples of large thrust faults where the upper plate has moved from west to east tens of miles placing older rocks over younger rocks.

A strike-slip fault is one along which the movement has been parallel to the strike of the fault plane and is caused by rupture in response to shear forces. If an observer looks along the strike of a left-lateral, strike-slip fault, the relative movement has been such that the left-hand side has moved towards the observer. Along a right-lateral, strike-slip fault, the block on the right has moved towards the observer.

PLATE TECTONICS

The theory of plate tectonics has revolutionized the thinking of geologists. This is a unifying theory that explains many seemingly unrelated geologic processes. Plate tectonics was first seriously proposed as a theory in the early 1960's although the related idea of continental drift was proposed much earlier.

The Plates

The outer part of the earth is broken into rigid plates approximately 62 miles thick. These outer plates are called lithosphere and include rocks of the earth's crust and upper mantle. Below the rigid lithosphere is the asthenosphere, a zone around the earth that is approximately 90 miles thick and behaves like a plastic because of high temperature and pressure. The lithosphere plates move over the plastic asthenosphere at a rate of an inch or more per year. Eight large plates and a few dozen smaller plates make up the outer shell of the earth.

The internal heat of the earth is the most likely cause of plate movement; this heat is probably generated by the decay of radioactive minerals.

The entire surface of the earth is moving, and each plate is moving in a different direction than any other. We now believe that plate movement is responsible for the highest parts of the continents and the deepest trenches in the oceans. Such movements also cause catastrophic events like earthquakes, volcanoes and tsunamis.

Plate Boundaries

Plate boundaries are of three types: a diverging plate boundary is a boundary between plates that are moving apart; a converging plate boundary is one

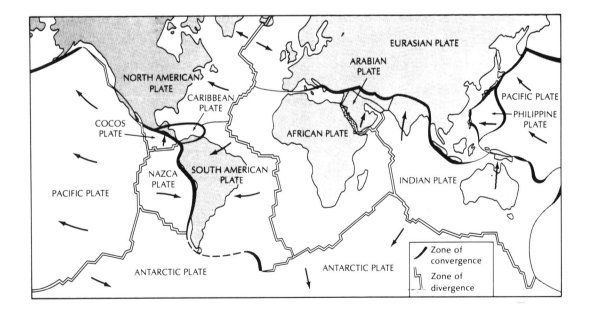

Map showing the earth's lithospheric plates, zones of convergence and divergence. Arrows indicate the direction of plate movement.

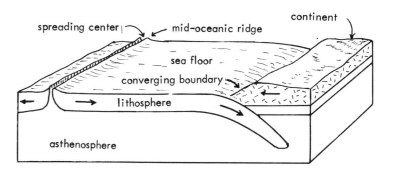

Plate motion away from a spreading center toward a converging boundary.

where plates are moving towards each other; and a transform plate boundary is one at which two plates move past each other.

Diverging Boundaries

Diverging boundaries occur where plates are moving apart. Most of these boundaries coincide with the crests of the submarine mid-oceanic ridges. These ridges form by ascending hot mantle material pushing the lithosphere upward. When heat rises, molten rock moves upward and the expansion from the heart and pressure causes the ridge plate to bow upward and break apart at the spreading centers. Tension cracks form parallel to the ridge crest and molten rock from magma chambers in the mantle is intruded through the fractures. Magma errupts into submarine volcanoes and some of it solidifies in the fissure. New crust forms in rifts at the spreading cen-

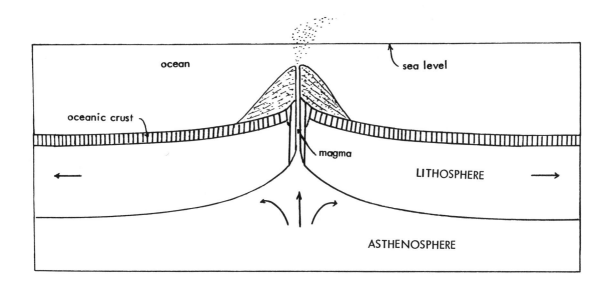

Cross section of a spreading center at a mid-oceanic ridge. Hot asthenosphere moves upward beneath the ridge crest. Magma is then forced into fissures between the two lithospheric plates.

ters. As new magma is extruded, it accretes to both sides of the plates as they are pushed or pulled apart. As the plates continue to pull apart, new tension fractures form and fill with magma. This cycle repeats itself again and again.

Transform Boundaries

The transform boundary occurs where two plates slide past one another. The San Andreas Fault is one of the best known land exposures of a transform boundary.

Converging Boundary

A converging boundary where plates move toward each other is responsible for the origin of most of Idaho's igneous rock as well as most of the major structural features of the state. Where one plate is covered by oceanic crust and the other by continental crust, the less dense continental plate will override the denser oceanic plate. The older the oceanic plate, the

colder and more dense it is. Where two plates collide, the dense plate is subducted below the younger and less dense plate margin. At this boundary, a subduction zone forms where the oceanic plate descends into the mantle beneath an overriding plate. As the oceanic plate descends deeper into the earth it is heated progressively hotter. Also the friction caused by the two plates grinding past each other leads to greater temperatures.

At the subduction zones, submarine trenches form, representing the deepest parts of the ocean basins. Earthquakes continuously occur at the plate margins where the overriding plate is grinding and abrading the subducted layer. The subducted plate causes earthquakes all along its downward path as it slowly moves into the earth's mantle. By measuring the depth and position of the earthquakes, geologists are able to determine almost exactly the position and orientation of the subducting plate.

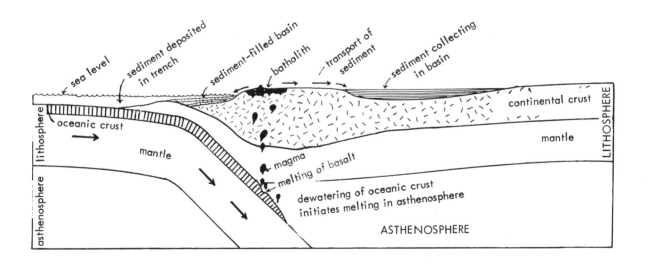

A converging plate boundary occurs where one plate is subducted under another plate. Igneous activity and sedimentation associated with the plate boundary are shown.

— 30 —

Age of Ocean Basins

The youngest rocks are found at the spreading centers, and become progressively older in both directions away from the spreading centers. The oldest rocks in the ocean basins are approximately 150 million years old as compared to the oldest rocks on the continents of 3.8 billion years.

Physical Properties of Oceanic Rocks

Rocks forming the ocean basins are dark, iron-rich and have a higher specific gravity than those forming the continents. Rocks of the continents tend to be low in density, light colored and rich in silica and aluminum. Because of the lower density of continental rocks, they are floating on the denser oceanic-type rocks.

Generation of Magma, Volcanoes and Batholiths

When the plate reaches a certain depth, the heat and pressure melts the lighter minerals within it. This light molten rock or magma coalesces at depth and floats upward through the more dense rock towards the surface of the earth. Where these globs of molten rock break through the oceanic crust, they form chains of volcanic islands. The Aleutian Islands are a well-known example.

The portion of the magma that manages to break through the surface forms volcanoes like Mount St. Helens and is classified as volcanic or extrusive rock. The portion that does not break through the earth's surface, but instead solidifies within the earth's crust, is classified as intrusive igneous or plutonic rock.

Where an oceanic plate is subducted below a continent, the rising globs of magma melt and absorb portions of the silica-rich, low specific gravity continental rocks. Where magma manages to break through the continental crust, the extrusive products are much more siliceous than their oceanic counterparts.

Geologists have found that rocks intruded through continental rocks have strontium isotope values much different than those intruded through oceanic rocks. Consequently, we are able to determine, on the basis of strontium isotope ratios, whether or not a particular intrusion passed through continental rocks.

Rocks in the vicinity of a subduction zone are drastically changed by the intense heat and pressure. If these rocks do not melt, they become metamorphic rocks. Also rocks in the continental crust in the path of a rising magma chamber are metamorphosed by the heat and pressure exerted by the upward-moving molten rock.

Mantle Plumes

Mantle plumes are believed to form where convection currents in the earth's mantle cause narrow columns of hot mantle rock to rise and spread radially outward. One of the most convincing theories for the origin of the Snake River Plain proposes that a hot mantle plume tracked across the plain from west to east and was the source for most of the volcanism in the Snake River Plain. This hot mantle plume is now thought to underlie the caldera at Yellowstone Park. Many of the volcanic islands of the Pacific Ocean may have originated from a mantle plume. The best known examples are the Hawaiian Islands.

EARTHQUAKES

An earthquake is a shaking of the ground caused by a sudden release of energy stored in the earth's crust. This occurs when stresses build up in certain parts of the crust until suddenly a rupture (fault) occurs and energy waves are sent out through the earth. Volcanic activity can also cause earthquakes. These energy waves sent out by an earthquake are called seismic waves. The movement of the seismic waves through the ground during an earthquake causes the ground to shake.

The focus of an earthquake is the point within the earth where seismic waves originate. The focus is normally centered on the part of a fault that has the greatest movement. The epicenter of an earthquake lies on the earth's surface, directly above the focus.

Seismic Waves

Earthquakes that originate beneath the ocean generally cause great waves of water called tsunamis or seismic sea waves. These waves travel at speeds of up to 500 miles per hour and may reach 200 feet in height when they reach land. Earthquake waves (seismic waves) are detected and recorded with an instrument called a seismograph. A seismogram is the record of an earthquake made by the seismograph. The seismogram shows the duration and the severity of the shock.

There are two types of seismic waves: body waves (P waves and S waves) which move through the earth's interior and surface waves (L waves) which move along the earth's surface. The time intervals between first arrivals of P, S, and L waves are used to calculate the distance between a seismograph and an epicenter. At least three stations are necessary to determine the location of earthquakes.

Measuring an Earthquake's Size

The size of an earthquake is directly related to the amount of energy released at its focus. Two parameters are used to show the size of an earthquake: magnitude (energy released), and intensity (damage caused). The American seismologist, Charles F. Richter, devised the Richter scale to measure the total amount of energy released by an earthquake. This scale, which is recorded by seismographs, is quantitative and measures a quake independently of its effects. The Richter Scale uses numbers from 1 on up to describe magnitude. Each number represents an earthquake ten times stronger than the next lower number. For example, an earthquake with a magnitude of 5 is ten times stronger than an earthquake with a magnitude of 4.

An earthquake with a magnitude of 7 or higher is a major quake. The strongest earthquake on record had a magnitude of 9.5 on the revised Richter Scale (Chile, 1960). The 1906 San Francisco earthquake registered 7.9 on the revised Richter Scale and the 1983 eastern Idaho earthquake had a magnitude of 6.9.

The intensity of an earthquake is an approximate indication of how much the earth shook at a given place near the earthquake. It is expressed in terms of the damage it caused and is measured on the modified Mercalli Scale. Damage decreases as distance from the epicenter increases.

Effects of Earthquakes

Ground motion is the shaking of the ground that causes buildings to vibrate. Large structures such as office buildings, dams and bridges may collapse. Fire may cause much damage after an earthquake. Broken gas lines and fallen electrical wires cause fires, while broken water lines hinder the capability of controlling fires. Landslides are commonly caused by earthquakes. For example, in 1920 more than 100,000 people were killed in China by collapse of a cliff. Displacement of the land surface occurs along a fault line. Both streams and roads were vertically offset by the Idaho earthquake.

ORIGIN OF MOUNTAINS

Mountains are the most conspicuous landforms in Idaho. Any isolated mass of rock may be called a mountain because no minimum height or shape is required. Mountains may be formed by volcanoes, by erosional processes and by structural processes such as faulting and folding.

Volcanic Mountains

There are many volcanic mountains in southern Idaho, particularly within the Snake River Plain Province. These mountains generally consist of individual cones of cinder and extrusive igneous rock. The volcanic material was extruded through a central vent in the earth's crust and piled up on the surface to form a cone. In Idaho, volcanic mountains tend to be smaller than other types of mountains, generally less than 1,000 feet high. They also tend to be isolated and erratically distributed, although they are commonly aligned along rifts or fissures such as the Great Rift of the Snake River Plain. Volcanic mountains are generally dome to conical shaped and are symmetrical in plan view. As a general rule, volcanic mountains consisting mostly of cinders and tuffaceous material are the most susceptible to erosion of all mountains.

Erosional Mountains

Erosional mountains are found in regions of crustal uplift such as the central Idaho uplands. They are characterized by steep gorges, precipitous slopes and youthful streams. Idaho's erosional mountains have primarily been carved by glaciers and running water and are the result of hundreds of thousands of years of erosion in the intervening valleys.

Structural Mountains

Structural mountains were created by structural activity such as folding and faulting. The Basin and Range Province of eastern Idaho is an outstanding example of mountains created by faulting. In the Basin and Range Province, large elongate blocks of the earth's crust were moved up relative to the intermontane valleys along large normal faults.

WEATHERING

Weathering causes the disintegration of rock near the surface of the earth. Plant and animal life, atmosphere and water are the major causes of weathering. Weathering breaks down and loosens the surface minerals of rock so they can be transported away by agents of erosion such as water, wind and ice. There are two types of weathering: mechanical and chemical.

Mechanical Weathering

Mechanical weathering is the disintegration of rock into smaller and smaller fragments. Frost action is an effective form of mechanical weathering. When water trickles down into fractures and pores of rock, then freezes, its volume increases by almost 10 percent. This causes outward pressure of about 30,000 pounds per square inch at –7.6 Fahrenheit. Frost action causes rocks to be broken apart into angular fragments. Idaho's extreme temperature range in the high country causes frost action to be a very important form of weathering.

Exfoliation is a form of mechanical weathering in which curved plates of rock are stripped from rock below. This results in exfoliation domes or dome-like hills and rounded boulders. Exfoliation domes occur along planes of parting called joints, which are curved more or less parallel to the surface. These joints are several inches apart near the surface but increase in distance to several feet apart with depth. One after another these layers are spalled off resulting in rounded or dome-shaped rock forms. Most people believe exfoliation is caused by instability as a result of drastically reduced pressure at the earth's surface allowing the rock to expand.

Exfoliation domes are best developed in granitic rock. Yosemite National Park has exceptional examples of exfoliation domes. Idaho has good examples in the Quiet City of Rocks near Oakley as well as in many parts of the granitic Idaho Batholith. In fact, these characteristic rounded forms make rock exposure of the granitic Idaho Batholith easy to identify.

Another type of exfoliation occurs where boulders are spheroidally weathered. These boulders are rounded by concentric shells of rock spalling off, similar to the way shells may be removed from an onion. The outer shells are formed by chemical weathering of certain minerals to a product with a greater volume than the original material. For example, feldspar in granite is converted to clay which occupies a larger volume. Igneous rocks are very susceptible to mechanical weathering.

Chemical Weathering

Chemical weathering transforms the original material into a substance with a different composition and different physical characteristics. The new substance is typically much softer and more susceptible to agents of erosion than the original material. The rate of chemical weathering is greatly accelerated by the presence of warm temperatures and moisture. Also, some minerals are more vulnerable to chemical weathering than others. For example, feldspar is far more reactive than quartz.

Differential weathering occurs when some parts of a rock weather at different rates than others. Excellent examples of differential weathering occur in the Idavada silicic volcanic rocks in the Snake River Plains. Balanced Rock and the Gooding City of Rocks are outstanding examples of differential weathering.

Spheroidal weathering of granitic outcrop.

RUNNING WATER

Running water is the most powerful agent of erosion. Continents are eroded primarily by running water at an average rate of 1 inch every 750 years. The velocity of a stream increases as its gradient increases but velocity is also influenced by factors such as degree of turbulence, position within the river, the course of the stream, the shape of the channel and the stream load.

River Cycles

Stages in the cycle of river erosion are labeled as youth, maturity and old age. Each stage has certain characteristics that are not necessarily related to age in years — only phases in development. Typically, rivers tend to have old-age-type development at their mouths and youthful development at their upper reaches. So the three stages may grade imperceptibly from one to another and also from one end of the stream to the other.

The youthful stage is characterized by rapid downcutting, high stream gradient, steep-sided valleys with narrow bottoms and waterfalls. The mature stage is characterized by a longer, smoother profile and no waterfalls or rapids.

Gradient is normally expressed as the number of feet a stream descends each mile of flow. In general, a stream's gradient decreases from its headwaters toward its mouth, resulting in a longitudinal profile concave towards the sky.

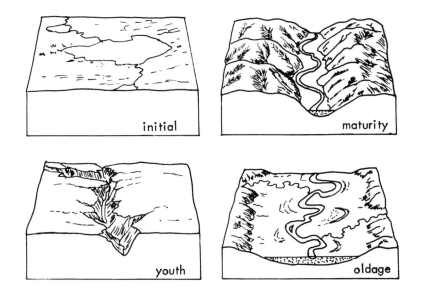

Stream evolution described in stages of a life cycle. The initial cycle is characterized by swamps. Youth involves rapid downcutting and V-shaped valleys. The mature stage has a flood plain caused by lateral cutting. Old age is characterized by a broad flood plain and ox-bow lakes.

Base Level

The base level of a stream is defined as the lowest level to which a stream can erode its channel. An obstacle such as a resistent rock across a stream can create a temporary base level. For example, if a stream passes into a lake, it cannot erode below the level of the lake until the lake is destroyed. Therefore different stretches of a river may be influenced by several temporary base levels. Of course the erosive power of a stream is always influenced by the ocean which is the ultimate base level below which no stream can erode. Many streams in Idaho eventually reach the ocean through the Columbia River.

If the base level is raised in some manner such as by a landslide blocking a stream, the stream's velocity is reduced and it can no longer carry as much material. Sedimentary material will then be deposited in the lake formed by the landslide. Conversely, if the base level is lowered, the stream will begin eroding its channel downward.

Transportation of Material

Running water transports material in 3 ways: solution, suspension and by rolling and bouncing on the stream bottom. Dissolved material is carried in suspension. About 270 million tons of dissolved material is delivered yearly to the oceans from streams in the United States. Particles of clay, silt and sand are generally carried along in the turbulent current of a stream. Some particles are too large and heavy to be picked up by water currents, but may be pushed and shoved along the stream bed.

Waterfalls

Waterfalls are a fascinating and relatively rare occurrence. Waterfalls may be caused in several ways. For example, where a relatively resistant bed of rock overlies less resistant rock, undermining of the less resistant rocks can cause a falls. Waterfalls are short-lived features in the history of a stream as they are created by a temporary base level. As time passes, falls may slowly retreat upstream, perhaps as rapidly as several feet per year. There are many spectacular waterfalls in Idaho, including the 212-foot-high Shoshone Falls in the Snake River Canyon just north of Twin Falls.

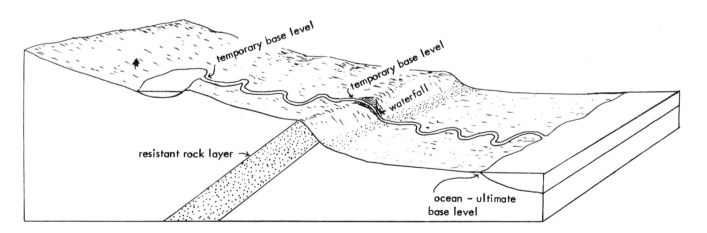

Block diagram showing a river flowing from the uplands to the ocean. Downcutting of the stream towards ultimate base level (sea level) is temporarily halted by dams and resistant layers of rock.

GROUND WATER

Ground water is the water that lies below the surface of the ground and fills the pore space as well as cracks and other openings. Porosity is the percentage of a rock's volume that is taken up by openings. Most sedimentary rocks such as sandstone, shale and limestone can hold a large percentage of water. Loose sand may have a porosity of up to 40 percent; however, this may be reduced by half as a result of recrystallization and cementation. Even though a rock has high porosity, water may not be able to pass through it. Permeability is the capacity of a rock to transmit a fluid such as water. For a rock to be permeable, the openings must be interconnected. Rocks such as sandstone and conglomerate have a high porosity because they have the capacity to hold much water.

Water Table

In response to gravity, water seeps into the ground and moves downward until the rock is no longer permeable. The subsurface zone in which all openings of the rock are filled with water is called the zone of saturation. The upper surface of the zone of saturation is called the water table. The zone that exists between the water table and the ground surface is called the zone of aeration. In order to be successful, a well must be drilled into the zone of saturation. The velocity at which water flows underground depends on the permeability of the rock or how large and well connected the openings are.

Springs occur where water flows naturally from rock onto the surface of the land. Springs may seep from places where the water table intersects the land surface. Water may also flow out of the ground along fractures.

Aquifers

An aquifer is a body of saturated rock through which water can easily move. Aquifers must be both permeable and porous and include such rock types as sandstone, conglomerate, fractured limestone and unconsolidated sand and gravel. Fractured volcanic rocks such as columnar basalts also make good aquifers. The rubble zones between volcanic flows are generally both porous and permeable and make excellent aquifers. In order for a well to be productive,

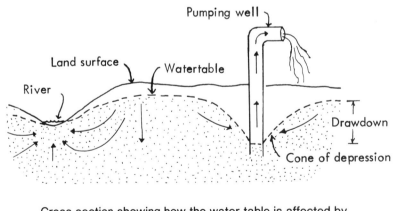

Cross section showing how the water table is affected by wells and topography. Arrows show movement of ground water beneath a sloping water table in uniformly permeable rock.

it must be drilled into an aquifer. Rocks such as granite and schist are generally poor aquifers because they have a very low porosity. However, if these rocks are highly fractured, they make good aquifers. A well is a hole drilled into the ground to penetrate an aquifer. Normally such water must be pumped to the surface. If water is pumped from a well faster than it is replenished, the water table is lowered and the well may go dry. When water is pumped from a well, the water table is generally lowered into a cone of depression at the well. Ground water normally flows down the slope of the water table towards the well.

Snake River Plains Aquifer

The Snake River Plain north of the Snake River is a remarkable aquifer of great resource and economic significance. It is not a single homogeneous geologic formation. Rather it consists of a volcanic pile of the Quaternary Snake River Group basalts. In eastern Idaho, these basalts may be about 1 mile thick. The individual flows are 20 to 30 feet thick with the upper 3 to 6 feet consisting of a very permeable rubble zone.

Interbedded alluvial sediments are also found between many of the flows. In the eastern Snake River Plain, the Snake River lies near the southern edge of the plain, about 40 to 50 miles southeast of the ranges of central Idaho. The rivers in the ranges north of the plain all disappear into the surface of the Snake River Plain near the mountain front. The Little Lost River is a typical example. For about 100 miles downstream from Milner Dam in the vicinity of Twin Falls an estimated total volume of approximately 200 billion cubic feet of water (1.4 cubic miles) enter the Snake River from gigantic springs on the north side of the canyon. This is the well-known Thousand Springs area.

Groundwater flows to the southwest through the Snake River Plains aquifer which is consistent with the overall tilt to the southwest of the basalt strata. The channel of the Snake River cuts through the aquifer. Consequently the gravity and weight of the water in the basalt layers north of the river drives the huge springs.

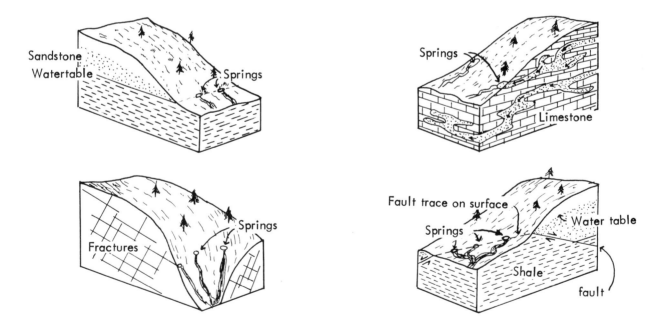

Illustrations above show how springs may form under different geologic conditions.

Large spring flowing from the north wall of the Snake River
canyon in the Thousand Springs area.

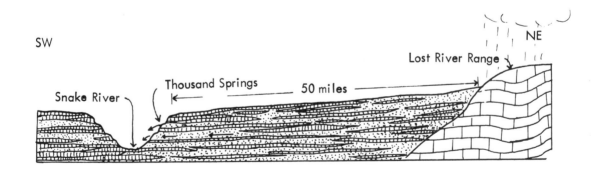

Cross section along the northern Snake River Plain showing
water transported from the Lost River Range through
aguifers in permeable beds underlying the plain and surfac-
ing again at Thousand Springs.

MASS MOVEMENT

Mass movement is the movement of surface material caused by gravity. Landslides and rockfalls are examples of very sudden movements of this type. Of course geological agents such as water, wind and ice all work with gravity to cause a leveling of land.

Water aids in the downslope movement of surface material in several ways. Water adds weight to the soil; it fills pore spaces of slope material and it exerts pressure which tends to push apart individual grains. This decreases the resistance of the material to movement. Landslide is a general term that is commonly broken down into the more specialized terms such as slump, rockslide, debris slide, mudflow and earthflow.

Slump

A slump is a downward and outward movement of rock or unconsolidated material moving as a unit or series of units. Large blocks of material move suddenly downward and outward along a curved plane.

Rockslide

Rockslides are the most catastrophic type of landslide. They involve a sudden rapid slide of bedrock along planes of weakness. Rockslides are very common in the oversteepened canyons and drainages of Idaho, particularly in those areas like the Salmon River Canyon where more than 5,000 feet of elevation may exist between the ridge tops and the canyon bottoms.

Debris Slide

A debris slide is a small sudden downslope movement of unconsolidated material. This type of slide produces a hummocky surface of low relief.

Mudflow

A mudflow is a mass of saturated rock particles of all sizes. This type of landslide is caused by a sudden flood of water from a cloudburst in semi-arid country or a sudden thaw. The flood waters carry the soil and

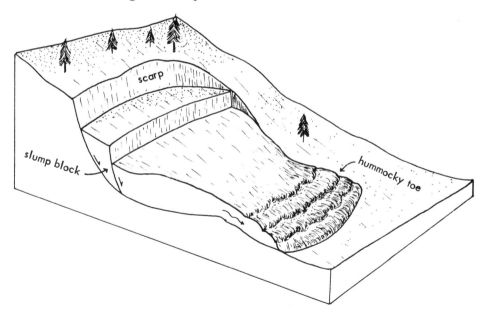

Block diagram of an earth flow where movement is a combination of slip and flow.

rocks from a large slope area and washes them to a gulch or canyon. Then the water and debris move down the canyon and spread out on the gentle slopes below. Mudflows are very common in the semi-arid areas of southwestern Idaho.

Earthflow

An earthflow is a downslope movement of soil which has been saturated with water to the extent that the debris moves as a fluid. While flowing, either slowly or rapidly, the mass generally remains covered by a blanket of vegetation. Typically a steep scarp is developed where the moving debris has pulled away from the upper slope. A hummcky lobe forms at the toe or front of the earthflow.

Talus

A talus slope is developed by an accumulation of rock fragments at the foot of a cliff or ridge. Rock fragments break loose from the cliff above, roll down the slope and pile up in a heap of rock rubble. Individual talus forms as a half-cone with the apex pointing upwards. In most cases a series of half cones coalesce around the base of a mountain.

Horseshoe Bend Hill Slide Area

Earthflows are a very common occurrence on the Horseshoe Bend Hill area between Boise and Horseshoe Bend. From the highway you can easily see earthflows of less than one year old as well as those much older. The more recent flows show fresh brown crescentric cracks where the fresh earth is exposed. The older flows are more difficult to identify because vegetation has grown over the scarp areas. Most of the slides occur during the spring when the ground surface is saturated with water. Placement of this major north-south highway over an active slide area has resulted in a section of highway constantly deformed and broken by the slowly-moving land surface.

Warm Springs Mesa Slide

Warm Springs Mesa is situated immediately south of Table Rock in east Boise. The entire Warm Springs Mesa is a 300-acre landslide. The construction of Warm Springs Avenue along the toe of the landslide has caused an oversteepened natural slope. There has been sliding along this oversteepened slope for years and debris is constantly falling on Warm Springs Avenue. Although geologists have long cautioned against development until study of the effect of increased water in the sediment is completed, development of the subdivision has not stopped.

A number of investigators has determined that the combination of the oversteepened slopes coupled with ground water causes the sliding. The additional ground water derived from the new residential uses is also believed to have had an adverse impact on the sliding activity.

The Warm Springs Mesa slide originated in an area next to Table Rock. Perhaps an earthquake suddenly dislodged the material and caused a sudden movement of a large earth mass downslope in a southwest direction some 1,200 feet towards the Boise River. The surface of the landslide is now revegetated but has the typical hummocky rolling topography of a landslide area. Numerous large boulders of sandstone are exposed chaotically over the surface but are particularly abundant on the oversteepened south slope. The large sandstone boulders are derived from the sedimentary rock (Glenns Ferry Formation) that is now exposed at Table Rock. From an airplane perspective, one can readily envision both the source and the total extent of the fan-shaped slide deposit.

As one drives along Warm Springs Avenue near the toe of the slide, undisturbed river gravels predating the slide are exposed in the road cuts just to the north of the road. These Boise River gravels were overriden by the slide.

Other Idaho Landslides

Landslides are a common sight in the mountainous areas of Idaho. Once you know what to look for they can be readily identified by the presence of a rupture in the vegetative cover exposing fresh earth or by a hummocky lower surface.

CAVES IN IDAHO

Caves in Idaho generally fall into one of three types: corrosion caves, solution caves and lava caves. Corrosion caves are formed by erosive action of water, waves or currents on a relatively soft rock. These caves generally occur at the edge of a river or lake.

Corrosion Caves

Corrosion caves are generally shallow and not as impressive as lava caves or solution caves. Archeologists, however, have found that early man commonly camped in small corrosion caves while hunting or fishing in the vicinity of water bodies. Rock shelters are also formed by erosion recessing the lower rocks in a cliff and leaving an overhanging rock shelter. Many of these rock shelters have yielded valuable information on the culture and migration patterns of early man in Idaho.

Solution Caves

Solution caves are formed by slightly acidic ground water circulating through fractures in limestone. This water is capable of dissolving great quantities of solid rock. As time passes, the openings become larger and larger until they may be large enough for a man to pass through. Cone-shaped forms called stalactites are deposited by underground water. Stalactites are composed of calcium carbonate and look like icicles hanging from cave roofs. Stalagmites are similar in composition and origin to stalactites but are formed from ground water dripping on the cave floor. The best examples of solution caves are found in the Paleozoic carbonate rocks in eastern Idaho.

Lava Caves

Lava caves, also known as lava tubes, form in the central portion of a lava flow. Immediately after the

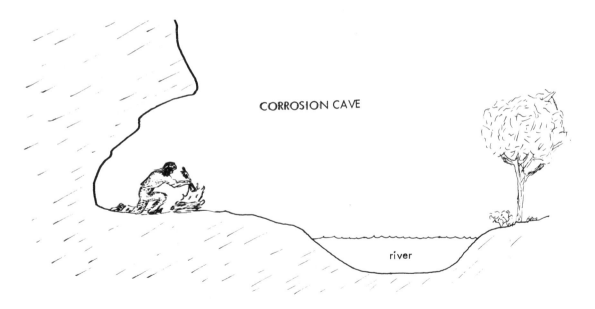

CORROSION CAVE

river

Cross section of a corrosion cave and the stream that formed it. Corrosion caves, along Idaho's rivers were very commonly used as rock shelters by early man.

— 43 —

flow is extruded, the outer margins of the flow cool and freeze in place, including the bottom, sides and top. Although the outer margin of the flow has solidified into basaltic rock, the central core is still molten and continues to flow towards the flow front. When the source of lava is cut off, the lava flows out the end of the tube and leaves a cave. These caves are typically 10 to 20 feet in diameter. They are characterized by both stalactites and stalagmites formed by lava dripping off the roof of the tube. Basalt flows on the Snake River Plain have many excellent examples of these caves. Many such caves are found where a thin portion of the roof collapses and leaves a precarious entrance to the cave.

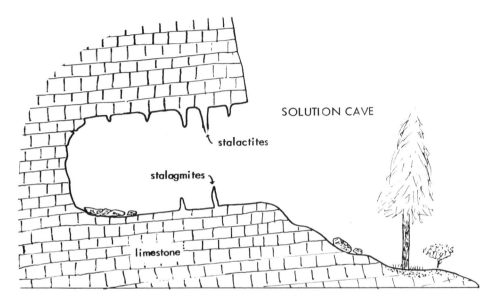

Cross section of a solution cave in limestone. Limestone is readily dissolved by acidic ground water.

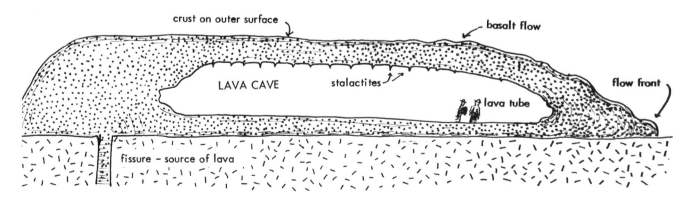

Longitudinal section of a lava flow containing a lava cave.

GLACIATION IN IDAHO

A glacier is a large, slow-moving mass of land ice that moves under its own weight. It is formed by the accumulation, compaction and recrystallization of snow. For a glacier to form, more snow must accumulate than is melted. Two types of glaciation are recognized and both have affected Idaho. Alpine glaciation of smaller areal extent is found in mountainous regions; whereas continental glaciation has covered a large part of the continent with a huge ice sheet. Both types of glaciation have dramatically changed the landscape.

Great Ice Age

The Great Ice Age was a period of recurring glaciations that affected northern Idaho. This ice age began about a million years ago and marked the beginning of a long period of colder climate. Mountain glaciers formed in all the high country. These glaciers were so extensive that almost a third of the present land surface of the earth was covered with ice. About 20,000 years ago the last great ice sheet retreated from the northern United States. During the later stages it went through a succession of retreats and minor advances. The part of the ice sheet that affected northern Idaho lingered in Canada until about 6,000 years ago when it finally melted. Evidence of this ice age is now widespread throughout the high country of Idaho. Traces of glacial erosion and deposition can be found in most of the mountainous areas.

Glacial Erosion

Slow-moving glaciers plowed up soil and loose rock and plucked and gouged boulders from outcrops. This material, caught in the glacier, was used as an abrasive to grind down, polish and scratch the exposed outcrops in its downward path. In this way glaciers soften landscapes by wearing down hilltops and filling in valleys. In mountainous areas, glaciers confined to valleys (valley glaciers) scooped out and widened the valleys leaving a U-shaped cross profile.

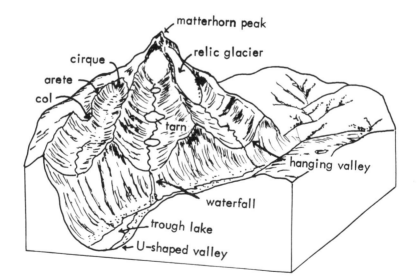

Erosional features left by valley glacier when the ice disappears.

Stream erosion normally leaves a V-shaped valley so that the presence of a U-shaped valley is strong evidence that the valley was shaped by a glacier.

A glacial cirque is a steep-sided, rounded, bowl-shaped feature carved into a mountain at the head of a glacial valley. In the cirque, snow accumulates and eventually converts to glacier ice before heading down the glacial valley. A horn is the sharp peak that remains after cirques have cut back into a mountain on several sides. Sharp ridges called arêtes separate adjacent glacially-carved valleys. The Sawtooth Mountains of Idaho offer exceptional examples of glacial erosional features such as U-shaped valleys, cirques, horns and arêtes as well as smaller features such as polished and striated bedrock.

Glacial Deposition

As glaciers move down valley, rock fragments are scraped and plucked from the underlying bedrock and the canyon walls. Most of these rock fragments are angular. When the material picked up and transported by the glacier is deposited, it is called till. Glacial till consists of unsorted fragments ranging from clay size to boulder size, all mixed together with no layering. Glaciers can easily carry any size rock fragment including boulders as large as a house. An erratic is a huge, ice-transported boulder that is not related to bedrock in the vicinity.

A moraine is a body of till deposited by a glacier. Ridge-like piles of ice left at the sides of a glacier are called lateral moraines. Medial moraines are developed where two glaciers come together and their lateral moraines merge and continue downglacier as a single long ridge of till. An end moraine is piled up along the front edge of ice at the downslope terminous of a glacier. Valley glaciers tend to leave an end moraine with the shape of a cresent ridge. There are two types of end moraines: a terminal moraine is an end moraine marking the farthest advance of a glacier; a recessional moraine is an end moraine developed while the terminous of a receding glacier is temporarily stationary. Redfish Lake near Stanley is a glacial lake. The lake occupies a U-shaped, glacially-carved valley and the water is contained on the sides by lateral moraines and on the north end near the lodge by a terminal moraine.

As the ice of a glacier melts, ground moraine is deposited at its base. This blanket of till extends over

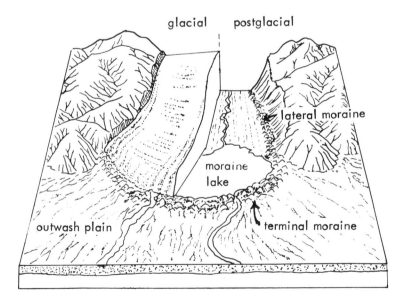

Depositional features shown with and without ice.

Looking west down Trail Creek drainage towards Sun Valley. This is an excellent example of a U-shaped valley.

larger areas that were covered by an ice sheet. Oval-shaped hills consisting of thick ground moraine deposits are called drumlins. Drumlins have their long axis parallel to the direction of ice movement.

Streams that drain glaciers are heavily loaded with sediment, especially during the summer months. These outwash streams form a braided pattern and their deposits are layered as are all stream deposits. Thus, outwash deposits can be distinguished from till which is unsorted.

Eskers are long, sinuous ridges of water-deposited material up to 30 feet in height. They are deposited in tunnels either within or under glaciers where the meltwater loaded with sediment flows under and out of the ice.

Large blocks of ice are commonly buried within the thick deposits of outwash in front of a retreating glacier. When the ice block melts, a depression called a kettle is formed. These depressions may be later filled with water and become permanent lakes.

Pleistocene Ice Age in Idaho

Glaciation began in the northern hemisphere more than two million years ago. However it was not until about 100,000 years ago that glaciers formed in southern British Columbia began moving southward following major south-trending valleys.

Central and northern Idaho were exposed to glaciation during Early and Late Pleistocene time. Northern Idaho was first covered by a continental ice sheet, and later carved by mountain glaciation. Evidence of Pleistocene glaciation can be seen in mountainous areas at elevations as low as 5,000 feet above sea level.

In northern Idaho, the continental ice sheet moved from the Canadian ice fields towards the south into northern Idaho. This ice sheet probably extended no further south than the north end of Coeur d'Alene Lake. As climatic changes affected the sources of ice in the Canadian ice fields, the ice sheet may have receded and again moved north through several episodes. The continental ice sheet, originating in the Canadian ice fields, invaded northern Idaho repeatedly. Slow advances were followed by retreat as the climate warmed or cooled. During the melting phases, deposits of sand and gravel accumulated at the margins of the ice lobe. These deposits are commonly called recessional moraines. The grinding of the moving ice sheet left scratched, grooved and polished surfaces on much of the bedrock in northern Idaho.

During maximum glaciation, the ice was thick enough to pass over the highest peaks of the Selkirk and Cabinent Ranges at elevations of more than 6,000 feet. This required an ice sheet to be more than 4,500 feet thick in the vicinity of Sandpoint. The ice may have been more than 2,000 feet thick at the southern end of Lake Pend Oreille during maximum glaciation.

Alpine Glaciation in Idaho

From 7,000 to 25,000 years ago, alpine glaciation was widespread in the higher elevations of the state. At least two periods of major glaciation are evident in Idaho. The last stage of alpine glaciation occurred about 4,000 years ago. This glacial action was relatively minor as glaciers existed only in the highest mountains of the State.

Glacial Lakes and Floods

Large quantities of glacial meltwater had a dramatic effect on the landscape. Much rock debris was transported by water and deposited in valleys. Many floods were caused by glacial ice impounding water and then bursting. Huge catastrophic floods were caused in such a manner and drastically eroded the landscape.

During and immediately following the ice age, the streams of Idaho carried much more water than they do now. Larger streams and rivers could transport a much greater sediment load, mostly of glacial debris. At this time, the abundance of water caused large lakes to form in closed basins. One of the largest of these lakes was ancient Lake Bonneville, once covering more than 20,000 square miles with a maximum depth of more than 1,000 feet. The Great Salt Lake is a remnant of this lake. Lake Bonneville rose until the water broke through Red Rock Pass in southeastern Idaho. This huge flood swept over the pass, down the Portneuf River to the Snake River. The flood waters roared across the Snake River Plains, and for the most part, followed the Snake River into Oregon. The remarkable depositonal and erosional features caused by this flood are discussed in another part of this book.

Ancient glacial Lake Missoula was created by an ice lobe forming a dam near the Idaho-Montana border. By melting or erosion this dam was suddenly removed and great floods were released throughout the northwest. Glacial debris left by the retreat of the great glaciers dammed streams and formed many modern lakes in Northern Idaho, including Hayden, Spirit and Twin Lakes. Pend Oreille Lake was formed in a similar fashion by glaciers eroding the lake basin and glacial debris damming the south end.

Floods from glacial Lake Missoula passed through the northern part of Pend Oreille Lake. Ice dams forming glacial Lake Missoula failed many times causing floods to move across northern Idaho. These catatrophic floods flowed south and southwest scouring great channels in the Columbia Plateau in the eastern and central parts of the State of Washington. This area is commonly called the channeled scablands. Three terraces along the Clark Fork and Pend Oreille River valleys were formed by the three floods from glacial Lake Missoula.

Part 2

MAJOR ROCK TYPES AND PHYSIOGRAPHIC PROVINCES

PRECAMBRIAN ERA

Although the Precambrian Era represents more than three billion years, relatively little is known of this vast span of time as compared to the last 20 or 30 million years. Very little evidence of fossil plant and animal life can be found in Precambrian rocks because plants and animals had not yet developed hard parts necessary for fossilization. Without fossils it is difficult to date rocks, correlate geologic events and fully understand depositional environments. Furthermore, the older a rock is, the greater the chance it will be deeply buried, removed by erosion, or metamorphosed or deformed by geologic events. Such deformation would obscure important original textures and mineralogy of the rock.

Radiometric Dating

Absolute age dating using radioisotopes has been very useful in determining the ages of Precambrian rocks during the last few decades. Isotope ages are obtained by quantitative chemical analyses of radioactive minerals and their decay products. Large errors in the ages of older rocks are possible due to contamination and other problems. Radiometric dating is also an expensive process.

Pre-Beltian Rocks

Pre-Belt rocks in Idaho range in age from 2,760 to 1,450 million years old. Many older, strongly-deformed schists, gneisses and quartzites are commonly referred to as pre-Beltian rocks. Because these rocks are believed to be 1,600 million years old or older, most have experienced one or more metamorphic events, drastically changing the original character of the rock. Only by reliable age dating and overlap relationships by Belt rocks can these older rocks be established as pre-Belt.

Pre-Belt rocks are thought to exist in several localities. The Green Creek Complex in the Albion Range of Cassia County was dated at 2.46 billion years by Armstrong and Hill and dated at 2.7 billion years by Small (1968). An area in Fremont County has the southern extension of pre-Belt metamorphic rocks that crop out over large areas in southern Montana. Metamorphosed sedimentary rocks of micaceous quartzites and schists in the Salmon River Mountains west of Shoup are intruded by an augen gneiss dated at 1.5 billion years (Maley, 1974; Armstrong, 1975). Pre-Belt rocks near Pocatello in Bannock County include the Bannock Formation, the Pocatello Formation and the Blackrock Limestone. They are separated from the overlying Cambrian rocks by an unconformity.

Precambrian sedimentary rocks are known at a number of other places in Idaho, but so far they cannot be correlated positively with the north Idaho rocks. For example, in Lemhi County, the Lemhi and Swauger Quartzites are many thousands of feet thick. In east-central Idaho, the extensive Yellowjacket Formation and the Hoodoo Quartzite are examples. Farther south, in the vicinity of Sun Valley, several thick quartzite units are known in the Pioneer Range east of Sun Valley. These formations include the Hyndman Formation and the East Fork Formation.

PRE-BELT ROCKS

Many probable pre-Belt rocks have been tentatively identified and are scattered throughout Idaho. Gneissic rocks on the western border zone of the batholith in the vicinity of McCall contain sedimentary rock. Strontium isotope data indicate that the Mesozoic granitic rocks were contaminated by crustal rocks as many as 2.5 billion years ago. Possible pre-Belt gneisses in northern Idaho, south of the Kaniksu Batholith have been dated at 1,540 million years (Reid, Morrison and Greenwood, 1973). Large anorthosite exposures and aluminous schists in the Boehls Butte area in northern Idaho, not typical of Belt strata, have zircon Pb/Pb dates of 1625 and 1665 million years (Reid, Morrison and Greenwood, 1973).

Augen Gneisses Near Shoup

The augen gneiss in central Idaho may be a large 1,500 million year old plutonic complex of batholithic proportions occupying the same east-west position of the much better known Cretaceous batholith. Because large exposures of the augen gneiss occur on both sides of the Cretaceous batholith, it is possible that the Cretaceous batholith penetrated upwards along a zone of crustal weakness similar to that followed by this Precambrian 1,500 million year old batholith. This fascinating gneiss may be examined just east of Shoup along the Salmon River. If you drive up the Panther Creek road, you can see large ellipsoidal microcline crystals up to 6 inches long in the road cuts.

Salmon River Arch

On the basis of four whole rock Rb-Sr dates, Armstrong (1975) applied a tentative 1,500 million year old date to the augen gneiss near Shoup in the Salmon River Mountains. He further proposed that the quartzites, argillites and schists intruded by the Augen gneisses represent a pre-Belt basement complex that underlies a large region in central and south-central Idaho. This basement complex of pre-Belt rocks, older than 1,500 million years old, forms the Salmon River Arch.

The arch remained above sea level throughout the remainder of the Precambrian and on through the Paleozoic. The arch served as a source of sediments. It also represented the southern edge of the Belt basin. During the Cambrian and Ordovician the Arch also supplied sediments to the miogeocline.

Augen Gneisses Near Elk City

The highly metamorphosed possible pre-Belt complex near Shoup is somewhat similar to the augen gneisses, amphibolites and metasedimentary rocks in the vicinity of Elk City. In fact Reid and others (1970) published a 1,500 million year old date for the augen gneisses near Elk City. West of Elk City and to the east between Elk City and Shoup along the Salmon River canyon, many probable pre-Belt rocks of a high metamorphic grade are exposed.

Oldest Rocks in Idaho

Armstrong (1975) has proposed that the oldest rocks in Idaho may be found in the gneissic domes of the Albion Range in south-central Idaho. These old rocks, called the Green Creek Complex, were first dated at 2.46 billion years old and dated shortly thereafter at 2.7 billion years old. Armstrong dated an amphibolite in the complex at 2,550 million years old plus or minus 72 million years. So far these are the oldest dates for rocks in Idaho.

PRECAMBRIAN IN EAST-CENTRAL IDAHO

Precambrian and Lower Ordovician Rocks in East-Central Idaho

Precambrian sedimentary rocks of east-central Idaho are exposed over an area that extends 150 miles from the Snake River Plain and is about 50 miles wide. These rocks are primarily dark, fine-grained, micaceous, feldspathic quartzites in the northern third of the area. They are tentatively correlated with the Yellowjacket Formation.

Deep Water Environment of Deposition

The east-central Idaho rocks differ from the Belt rocks because the grain size of most Belt rocks is medium silt or finer, whereas the Lemhi Range rocks are composed of fine- to medium-grain feldspathic or micaceous sand. Shallow-water features such as mud cracks, ripple marks and salt casts are rare in Lemhi Range rocks. Also, only a few occurrences of stromatolites, which are common in Belt limestones and dolomites, have been found.

Metamorphism and Thrusting

Both groups show low-grade regional metamorphism that increases with depth. Stratigraphic problems are plentiful because thrust faults have overturned about half of the rocks and at least some of the strata have been transported as much as 100 miles to the east along a flat detachment surface.

Tentative Correlation

Correlation of the Precambrian rocks of east-central Idaho with those of the Belt Supergroup is tenuous at best. It appears likely that the two groups were deposited under different conditions: the Belt Supergroup in the Belt basin and the east-central Idaho rocks in the Belt miogeocline. However, there are some tentative correlations possible between the two groups on the basis of similar lithology.

BELT SUPERGROUP

Belt Basin

Sedimentary rocks of the Belt Supergroup formations range from about 850 to 1,450 million years old. In the northwestern United States and in adjacent parts of Canada, these Precambrian rocks occupy the so-called "Belt basin," an area that covers most of the Idaho panhandle as well as adjacent parts of eastern Washington, western Montana and southern Canada.

The Belt basin is not strictly a basin but is rather the only re-entrant of a sea that existed off the west coast of North America. Because much of the Belt basin is now covered by younger rocks, the outer limits of the basin cannot be accurately established. On the western and southwestern parts of the basin, the Belt strata have been strongly metamorphosed. Because the mineralogy and texture has been changed so drastically, it is difficult to correlate these rocks with other Belt strata to the east. In fact, it is possible that some of the high-grade metamorphic belt rocks may be pre-Belt age. The degree of metamorphism also increases with depth.

Belt Island

Based on isopach maps, many formations had a large source of sediments from the south — perhaps a Belt island. Ruppel (1973) has proposed that rocks in the Belt seaway were a clastic section of the Cordilleran miogeocline thrust into the Belt seaway. Evidence for a Belt island and a Belt seaway include a westward coarsening in grain size and an increase in feldspar content of highly-feldspathic quartzites. These rocks indicate a granitic source to the west which would be the Belt island. There is no Precambrian Z sedimentation in the Belt basin because of uplift at that time. Precambrian Z sedimentation occurred between 800 and 570 million years ago. Middle Cambrian quartzites disconformably overlie the Belt rocks and cover the entire Belt basin. Belt rocks were uplifted during the East Kootenay

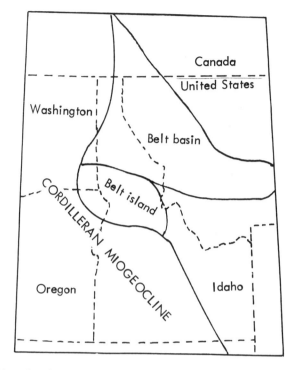

Map showing the position of the Belt basin during the depositional period (modified after Harrison and Ruppel).

orogeny and were exposed to major erosion for the first time. This orogeny started 850 million years ago.

Metamorphism of the Belt

Belt rocks in the west and southwest are strongly metamorphosed; whereas, those in the upper part of the section and the eastern part of the basin are only slightly metamorphosed. However, most of the Belt rocks in Idaho are metamorphosed to Greenschist facies (low-grade metamorphism).

Rock Types

The sedimentary Belt rocks have a fine-grain size predominately of clay and silt size with only a very small percent of the sand-sized component. The rock

Ripple marks in Precambrian Belt rocks.

types include quartzites, dolomites and limestones. Fossil algal forms are found in some of the carbonate rocks. These forms, called stromatolites represent the only evidence of life in the Belt rocks. Because most of the rocks have been metamorphosed at least slightly, the terms argillite and quartzite are commonly used rather than claystone, shale, siltstone and sandstone. Because of similar grain size, composition and color, the Belt rocks tend to be similar in appearance throughout the basin. The Belt rocks were intruded by sheets of mafic igneous rocks known as the Purcell sills of Late Precambrian age. Purcell lavas also covered parts of the Belt basin. Anomalously high amounts of copper (100 or ppm) occur in almost all formations of the Belt; however, the greenish-colored strata are highest in copper.

Age of the Belt Rocks

The age of the formations of the Belt Supergroup ranges from 1,450 to 850 million years. Belt rocks accumulated in a shallow continental basin and adjoining continental margin. They were deposited on crystalline rocks of a continental crust ranging in age from 2,760 to 1,450 million years. During 600 million years, a maximum of 12 miles of sediments were deposited.

Major Stratigraphic Divisions

Belt rocks are separated into four major stratigraphic Divisions: the Missoula Group with 30,000 feet of strata; the Helena-Wallace Formations with 10,000 feet of strata; the Ravalli Group with 6,600 feet of strata; and the Prichard Formation with 23,000 feet of strata.

Shallow Water Depositional Environments

Sediments collected in the Belt basin exhibit substantial evidence of shallow-water environment of the Belt Supergroup. These include fossil stromatolitic algae, mud cracks, small-scale cross-bedding, ripple marks, salt crystal casts, flute casts, groove casts, load casts, and mud-chip breccia. Mud-chip breccias are thin layers of dried mud ripped up by moving currents and redeposited and buried in new sand and silt. All of these features are indicative of a shallow water environment of deposition or deposition above sea level such as on a tidal flat.

There was a prolonged gradual subsidence which kept pace with sedimentation. Most of the sedimentation took place on flood plains, tidal flats and as bank deposits on the advancing front of a subsiding delta or shallow marine water. Before metamorphism, the Belt rock types were clays, silts, sands, and limes. These sediments were lithified by compaction and natural cementation into shales, siltstones, sandstones and limestones. Metamorphism converted these rocks into argillites, siltites, quartzites and dolomites.

Stromatolites

Fossil forms of ancient algae or former marine plant life are called stromatolites. These stromatolites are similar to the modern blue-green algae; and in the outcrop they consist of alternating bands of light and dark-colored mineral matter arranged in swirling patterns. Fossilized algae have nearly spherical or ellipsoidal structures ranging from the size of a football to a large reef.

All the algal forms are collectively called stromatolites or, when forming massive rock, they are

Mud-chip breccia in the Belt Supergroup originally formed by burial of mud crack layers in beach sands.

— 55 —

called stromatoliths. The genus name for many of the forms in this area is *Collenia*. *Collenia* lived in protected intertidal flats of the ancient Precambrian Beltian sea.

The algae probably grew many miles from shore but in water ranging from the tidal zone to 100 feet deep. The water had to be shallow enough so as to allow sunlight to reach the algae. Blue green algae, like the stromatolites, took carbon dioxide from sea water and sunlight and released oxygen as a waste product through the process of photosynthesis. This process was not only a major factor in producing an oxygen-rich atmosphere which made it possible for oxygen-consuming life forms to exist on earth, but also caused large quantites of calcium carbonate to be deposited on the sea bed. When carbon dioxide is removed from the seawater by algae, it generates a chemical reaction that forms fine particles of calcium carbonate.

Purcell Sills

The Purcell sills intruded the Belt Supergroup rocks in northern Idaho, western Montana, eastern Washington and adjacent Canada. They were generally intruded along and parallel to the foliation (planes of parting) in the metamorphosed Belt rocks. The foliation lies at a low angle to the Prichard argillites. The sills are also concordant with bedding in some outcrops. Ranging in thickness from less than a 3 feet to more than 2,300 feet, these sills extend for tens of miles.

Precambrian igneous activity in the Belt basin was dominated by the intrusion of Purcell sills and sheets. These sills are widespread throughout the lower Belt and make up a significant part of the lower Belt (Prichard section). These sills have been dated at 1,433 million years and are the source for the oldest date of the Belt rocks. Diabase sills and dikes ranging from 750 to 830 million years old are slightly younger than the youngest Belt rocks.

Normal Faults

The Belt rocks were tilted, faulted and uplifted by an estimated 20,000 feet from their original position in the earth's crust. Three grabens are superimposed on the Belt rocks. These include the Purcell trench, the Libby trough and the Rocky Mountain trench in western Montana. In the vicinity of Alberton, Montana, approximately 67,000 feet of Belt strata are exposed; however, neither the top nor the base is exposed.

Thrust Faults

Belt rocks have been telescoped large distances by thrust faults. Harrison and others (1980) proposed that many listric faults exist across the 500 miles of Belt terrane from Spokane, Washington westward to Glacier National Park. The maximum age of thrusting is believed to be 100 million years in the west and 50 million years in the east. These thrusts show eastward transport of about 110 miles and clockwise rotation. The thrusting is believed to be in response to plate actions that began about 200 million years ago on the western continental margin.

PALEOZOIC SEDIMENTARY ROCKS

Marine sedimentation, initiated in the Late Precambrian, continued through the Paleozoic in Idaho. The seas tended to be deeper than those of Belt time; however, during most of the Paleozoic, much of Idaho was above sea level. A maximum of 30,000 feet of sedimentary deposits accumulated in Idaho during the Paleozoic. The sedimentary record of the Paleozoic is much easier to understand than that of the Precambrian because the units are more distinctive lithologically, more restricted in distribution and contain fossils so that the strata can be dated.

Late Precambrian Through Devonian Miogeocline

Stewart (1972) believes a continental separation occurred along the western edge of the North American plate about 850 million years ago. From Late Precambrian through Devonian time, shallow-water shelf sediments were deposited on the eastern Idaho miogeocline; whereas, in southwestern Idaho, shelf to slope deposits of the eugeocline were deposited. The Cambrian, Ordovician and Silurian epicontinental seas covered almost the entire U.S. except for the central continental arch.

Precambrian to Devonian

From Precambrian to Devonian, the continent had low relief. Sediments were derived from the continental interior and accumulated on the continental margin so as to create a broad continental shelf. There was an offshore volcanic island arc riding on oceanic crust. Consequently, volcanic rocks and deep oceanic sediments occurred in deep water and thicken as a wedge from east to west. In the miogeoclinal rocks to the east, carbonates and quartzites are dominant in a thick sequence of pelagic carbonates, chert, shale and siliceous volcanic rock.

Cambrian Sedimentary Rocks

Cambrian sedimentary rocks have been mapped in several areas of Idaho. In the vicinity of Bannock and Bear Lake Counties, seven formations of Cambrian age are recognized. From oldest to youngest, they include the Brigham Quartzite and the Bloomington Formation. These rocks are coarse grained indicating deposition near shore, whereas the other formations are limestones indicating the shoreline was much farther away. In northern Idaho, limestone, shales and quartzites bearing Cambrian fossils have been mapped on the east side of Pend Oreille Lake. In Cassia County, Cambrian-age sedimentary rocks occur along the southern border of the state. In Custer County, the Bayhorse dolomite and the Garden Creek phyllite are considered to be Precambrian because they underlie rock of Early Ordovician age. Shorelines fluctuated constantly during the Cambrian leaving much of Idaho above water at times.

Ordovician Sedimentary Rocks

In Southeastern Idaho the Ordovician sedimentary rocks are similar to the Cambrian deposits, both in kind and distribution. Three major formations, including the Seven Peak Formation, the Fish Haven Dolomite and the Garden City Limestone have a combined thickness of approximately 2,500 feet.

In central Idaho (Custer and Blaine Counties) the Ordovician sedimentary rocks are much thicker and more widespread. Five formations, aggregating more than 10,000 feet, include the Phi Kappa Formation, an argillaceous quartzite, the Ramshorn Slate, Kinnikinnic Quartzite and Saturday Mountain Formation. In the northwestern side of the Cassia Mountains, south of Twin Falls, 1,500 feet of dolomitic limestones are exposed.

During the Ordovician there were major fluctuations in the shoreline, depth of water and character of the deposits. Although evidence of small uplifts is shown by small deposits of conglomerate, the predominance of fine-grained material indicates the surrounding relief was low. Sufficient time had passed since the Precambrian uplift for the land above sea level to have been deeply weathered and worn down to low relief by erosion.

Silurian Sedimentary Rocks

During Silurian time, the seas receded and left even more land above sea level than during the Ordovician. As a result, Silurian rocks are relatively rare in Idaho. In fact, during Late Silurian to Early Devonian, the entire state may have been below sea level. Silurian rocks are shales and sandstones, suggesting a low relief for the lands above sea level. Silurian sedimentary rocks have been observed in the southwestern part of Custer County where the Trail Creek Formation of shales and sandstones is exposed. Silurian rocks are also known in southeastern Idaho and Custer County where the laketown Dolomite ranges from 1,000 to 2,500 feet thick.

Devonian Sedimentary Rocks

At the beginning of the Devonian period, the entire state of Idaho may have been above sea level because no formation of Early Devonian age has been identified in the state. In Middle Devonian time the seas again invaded eastern Idaho.

In southwestern Idaho, the Jefferson Dolomite and the three Forks Limestone have a combined thickness of 1,100 feet. These two formations plus the Grand View Dolomite have a combined thickness of more than 3,000 feet in the Bayhorse region and the Lost River Range. They consist mainly of limestone with some shale and sandstone. The Three Forks Limestone is an important marker bed because it weathers to an easily-recognizable bright yellow color and has well-preserved fossils. The Milligen Formation of south-central Idaho is believed to be Devonian in age.

During Late Devonian, the passive continental margin in what is now central Nevada and south-central Idaho was subjected to compressive mountain building. The Antler Mountains rose in response to compression and subsequent uplift. Young siliceous and volcanic rocks of the western eugeocline were thrusted over older slope and shelf carbonate sediments to the east. This thrust, which moved approx-

imately 90 miles from west to east across Nevada and southern Idaho is called the Roberts Mountain Thrust. Some geologists believe that the Antler Orogeny was caused by the collision of an eastward-moving island arc against the western margin of the North American continent.

The clastic wedge deposited to the east includes conglomerate, greywacke and shale of the Muldoon Formation; whereas, the clastic wedge to the west includes argillite, chert and limestone of the Wood River and Milligen Formations. The present position of the Atlanta lobe of the Idaho Batholith may have been the region of uplift.

Mississippian, Pennsylvanian and Permian Sedimentary Rock

In east-central Idaho the break between Devonian and Mississippian rocks is not clearly understood. The transition from one period to the next may have taken place without interruption in the deposition of sediments. Furthermore, the stratigraphic record shows continuous marine deposition beginning in the Late Devonian and continuing through the remainder of the Paleozoic. Conglomerate lenses and broken fossils indicate rapid deposition at the western edge of the sea.

Sedimentary rocks of Mississippian, Pennsylvanian and Permian ages are the most abundant Paleozoic rocks in Idaho. The seas of the Late Paleozoic were parts of seaways that extended far beyond the boundaries of the state, in some cases extending from Alaska to Mexico. These Idaho seas are considered to be a part of the miogeocline because of the lack of volcanic rocks and the presence of thick sequences of shallow-water sediments. Paleozoic formations cropping out in East-Central Idaho include the Milligen Formation, the White Knob Limestone, the Wood River Formation and the Copper Basin Formation.

The Milligen Formation, thought to be Devonian to Late Mississippian age, is several thousand feet thick. It is a dark-colored, carbonaceous argillite. Although the beds of coal in this formation have no economic value, they represent some of the oldest coal in the United States.

The White Knob Limestone, a blue-gray limestone with some sand and clay layers, may be as much as 10,000 feet thick. This Early Mississippian through Permian age formation contains chert nodules and fossils.

The Wood River Formation is a calcareous, cross-bedded sandstone, approximately 2,800 feet thick. It contains shale and limestone layers and typically has a basal conglomerate unit.

The Copper Basin Formation interfingers with the above three formations and resembles them in many ways. Limestone, argillite, siltstone, sandstone and conglomerate are all represented in this formation having a combined thickness of 15,000 feet.

The Early Mississippian Madison Limestone is bluish-gray to brown and forms cliffs; the Late Mississipian Brager Limestone resembles the Madison Limestone. The Pennsylvanian and Permian age Wells formation is a sandstone with minor shale and limestone beds. Renewed subsidence in Early Permian time allowed deposition of sandstone and carbonate of the Wells Formation in a shallow marine environment.

In the Middle Permian, the seas covering Idaho were restricted by uplift to the west. The marine sedimentary rocks of Permian age in Idaho are thin and scattered except for the Phosphoria Formation in southeastern Idaho.

The Phosphoria Formation consists of a sequence of shales, phosphatic shales, limestones and cherts. In addition to covering parts of southeastern and east-central Idaho, it also extends into Montana, Nevada, Utah and Wyoming. The formation extends uniformly over approximately 175,000 square miles with an average thickness of 500 to 650 feet. Of greatest economic interest is the phosphatic shale members which are a source of rock phosphate mined in southeastern Idaho. Black shale of the Meade Peak Phosphatic Shale Member was deposited below wave base in the marine environment. The Rex Chert member of the Phosphoria was derived from accumulation of siliceous skeletal remains.

ACCRETED TERRANE IN WESTERN IDAHO

Most of the pre-Cretaceous rocks west of the Idaho Batholith in west-central Idaho and east-central Oregon are oceanic or island arc assemblages. These rocks were formed offshore in island arcs and adjacent basins (Vallier, 1967, 1977; Brook, 1979) and were accreted to the North American continent between Late-Triassic and mid-Cretaceous time. This means that before Jurassic time, the west coast of North America was situated near Riggins, Idaho.

The Suture Line

Pre-Cenozoic rocks near the western boundary of Idaho fall into one of two settings. These two settings are separated by the strontium-isotope line. All the plutonic rocks west of the dashed line have low initial ratios (<0.7043); whereas, all rocks to the east of the line have high initial ratios (>0.7055). This change in ratios is made in less than a distance of 6 miles. The strontium-isotope line therefore represents the

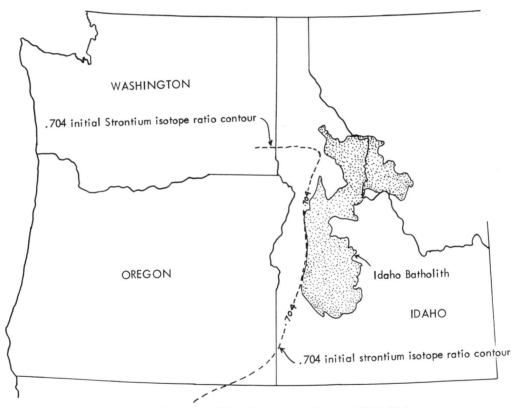

Map of northwestern United States showing the .704 initial-ratio contour. Mesozoic and Cenozoic rocks west of the dashed line have initial strontium isotope ratios less than .704; whereas, those east of the contour line have ratios greater than .704.

suture line where the accreted island arc assemblages were welded to western North America.

Paleozoic sedimentary rocks overlying Precambrian rocks of the continent make up the miogeocline on the east side of the suture line. These sedimentary rocks have been intruded by the batholith. On the west side of the line is a complex assemblage of rock derived from oceanic crust and portions of an island arc. The ages of this accreted assemblage ranges from Devonian to Early Cretaceous. Granite plutons intruded the accreted terrane; and later, Late Cretaceous marine strata covered portions of the accreted terrane which were depressed as a shallow basin.

Four Smaller Terranes

The oceanic and island arc terrane is divided into four smaller terranes: (1) the dismembered oceanic crust terrane or melange, (2) the Wallowa Mountains-Seven Devils Mountains volcanic arc terrane, (3) the Juniper Mountain-Cuddy Mountain volcanic arc terrane (may be a southern extension of the Wallowa-Seven Devils volcanic arc), and (4) Jurassic Flysh terrane of forearc basin marine sedimentary rocks. All four terranes are separated by major unconformities and faults and were intruded by plutons of Late Jurassic and Early Cretaceous age. These terranes were formed in the eastern Pacific Ocean, far from their present position, and were transported on lithospheric plates to be accreted on the edge of the continent.

Oceanic Crust Terrane

The dismembered oceanic crust terrane has undergone extreme deformation that is characteristic of tectonic melanges. This tectonic disruption probably happened in Late Triassic time. The oceanic crust terrane includes mafic rocks (ophiolite), metamorphosed chert, argillite, tuff, lava flows and limestone that ranges in age from Devonian to Middle Triassic. It includes the Canyon Mountain Complex, Elkhorn Ridge Argillite and Burnt River Schist of eastern Oregon and the lower part of the Riggins Group of western Idaho. Fossils and other evidence indicate that rocks derived from a deep ocean environment as well as from shallow water are mixed together.

Volcanic Arc Terranes

The Wallowa Mountains-Seven Devils Mountains volcanic arc terrane includes the Lower Permian and Middle and Late Triassic volcanic rocks of the Seven Devils Group and the Clover Creek Greenstone. This terrane also includes overlying Late Triassic and Early Jurassic marine sedimentary rocks of the Martin Bridge, Hural and Coon Hollow Formations and the Lucille Slate.

The Juniper Mountain-Cuddy Mountain volcanic arc terrane includes assemblages of metamorphosed basalt, andesite, dacite and rhyolite flows that are interlayered with marine sedimentary rocks.

The two volcanic arcs are separated by lavas of Cenozoic age so their relationship is not known. The volcanism that created the two arcs ended in Late Triassic. Both arcs may represent different parts of the same arc or it is possible that the two terranes represent two different arcs with different origins. Based on structural and stratigraphic similarities it is probable that the volcanic terranes are different parts of the same arc.

The volcanic arc terranes are similar to the accreted island-arc terranes termed Wrangellia that lie between Alaska and Vancouver Island. However, based on the composition of volcanic and sedimentary rocks, the accreted terrane in Idaho is not related to the Wrangellia terrane.

The Jurassic Flysch

Flysch may be defined as a widespread sedimentary formation resulting from rising land subjected to a high rate of erosion. The Jurassic Flysch of the accreted terrane includes siltstone, argillite, slates, phyllites, volcanic wacke, arkosic wacke, limestone and conglomerate. Poor sorting, angular grains and rock fragments are common to these rocks. The Squaw Creek Schist, Fiddle Creek Schist, Lightening Creek Schist and the Berg Creek Amphibolite of the Riggins group are representative of the Jurassic Flysch.

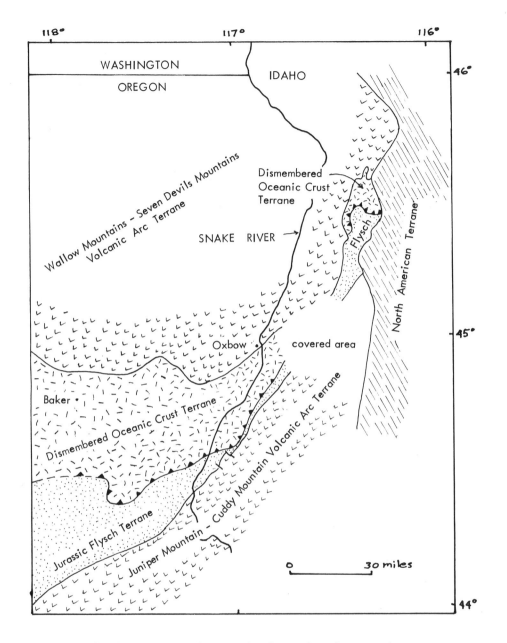

Generalized geologic map showing accreted terrane in west-central Idaho and northeastern Oregon (modified after Brooks, 1979).

The Flysch is situated between the volcanic arc and the oceanic crust terrane and is believed to have been compressed against the arc by the oceanic terrane. Deposition of the flysch probably ended in the Late Jurassic. The oceanic terrane and the volcanic arc terrane were sutured in Late Triassic and Early Jurassic time and the Flysch derived from the volcanism was deposited along the suture.

Continent-Island Arc Juncture

The continent-island arc juncture in west-central Idaho is narrow and well defined. Lund (1984) has recently described the geological character of this juncture or suture zone. On both sides of the suture, the metamorphic grade increases to amphibolite facies near the juncture. The suture zone lacks many of the features of a typical subduction zone. It is an abrupt, nearly vertical juncture between the continental metasedimentary rocks of Paleozoic to Middle Proterozoic age on the east side of the metamorphic rocks of the Permian-Triassic Seven Devils island arc and the overlying Riggins Group on the west. No transitional metasedimentary rocks with a marginal basin exists at the suture zone as is common for other known suture zones. According to Lund (1984), the suture was made by a convergent, right-lateral fault that sliced away the edge of the continent and then brought slabs of exotic oceanic (accreted) terrane in from the southwest.

Deformation and Time of Accretion

The accreted terrane was deformed in the Late Triassic and again in the Late Jurassic. The Late Triassic deformation occurred following deposition of most of the volcanic rock units. The time of the accretion is estimated to have occurred 118 million years ago (Lund, 1984; Sutter and others, 1984). Deformation and metamorphism of the Riggins Group at the contact with continental rocks occurred at that time. However, the accretion process probably occurred over a period of time ranging between Late Triassic and mid-Cretaceous. During this time and for a period afterwards, the Idaho Batholith was formed by magmas generated from subduction of the eastward-moving plate.

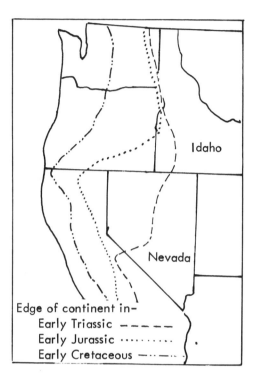

Map showing the position of the continental margin during the Mesozoic (modified after Brooks, 1979).

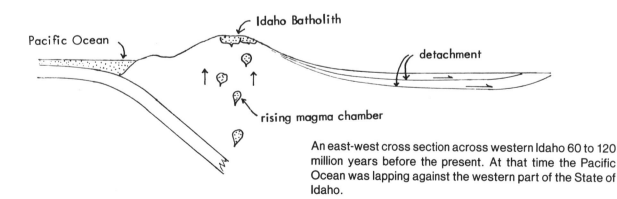

An east-west cross section across western Idaho 60 to 120 million years before the present. At that time the Pacific Ocean was lapping against the western part of the State of Idaho.

IDAHO BATHOLITH

The Idaho Batholith is a composite mass of granitic plutons covering approximately 15,400 square miles in central Idaho. The outer perimeter of the batholith is irregular and in plan view it has an hour glass shape. It is approximately 200 miles long in the north-south direction and averages about 75 miles wide in an east-west direction.

Age of Batholith

Armstrong and others (1977) called the northern part of the hourglass the "Bitterroot" lobe and the southern part the "Atlanta" lobe. He also proposed that most of the southern lobe was emplaced 75 to 100 million years ago (Late Cretaceous); whereas the northern lobe was emplaced 70 to 80 million years ago. Armstrong (1977) further noted that older plutons of Jurassic age occur on the northwest side of the Bitterroot lobe and many Eocene plutons have intruded the eastern side of the Atlanta lobe of the batholith. On the western side of the batholith, there are more mafic plutons (quartz diorites or tonalites) than to the east.

Radiometric dates and field relationships, where plutons of the batholith cut older rocks, restrict the age of the Idaho Batholith to an interval between 180 million years ago (Late Triassic) to 45 million years ago (Eocene); however, the dominant interval of emplacement was Early to Middle Cretaceous. There is a general west-to-east decrease in age for plutons of the batholith.

Rock Composition

The western margin of the Atlanta lobe is strongly folded and metamorphosed into gneissic rocks which are well exposed near McCall. The largest pluton mapped to date is a quartz monzonite in the vicinity of Warm Lake. It is about 124 miles in a north-south direction and more than 30 miles wide. However, many of the plutons of the batholith have not been delineated by geologic mapping.

Both lobes of the batholith have a different composition on the west than the east side. On the west side the rocks are tonalites or quartz diorites, whereas on the east side they range from granodiorites to granites. The boundary between the two composition types also coincides with the 0.704 Sr^{87}/Sr^{86} boundary and also the boundary between the Mesozoic and Paleozoic eugeoclinal accreted rocks on the west with the continental Precambrian rocks on the east side (Hyndman, 1985).

According to Hyndman, (1985), the tonalites on the west side originated by the melting of oceanic rocks near the subduction zone. Evidence that these tonalites were derived from oceanic rocks and have not been contaminated by melting of continental sedimentary rocks include: (1) low Sr isotope ratios, (2) low SiO_2 and K_2O, (3) high FeO-MgO-CaO, and (4) 13 to 30 percent mafic minerals.

Hyndman (1985) further proposed that the granodiorite and granites on the east side originated by melting of Belt Supergroup or pre-Belt continental crustal rocks. These continental sedimentary rocks were melted by hot mafic magmas rising from the same subduction zone that produced the tonalites. Evidence that the granodiorites and the granites on the east side contain substantial melted continental sedimentary rock include: (1) high Sr isotope ratios, (2) high SiO_2 and K_2O, (3) abundant muscovite-orthoclase-quartz minerals, and (4) rounded zircons dated at 1700 to 1800 million years derived from the continental crust of pre-Belt age.

Bitterroot Lobe

Hornblende-biotite tonalite and quartz diorite plutons were emplaced at mesozonal levels in the western and northwestern margin of the Bitterroot lobe. According to Toth (1985), plutons were small and isolated igneous-type granites and were intruded during regional compression in the Cretaceous (105 to 86 m.y. ago). Later, during Paleocene time, plu-

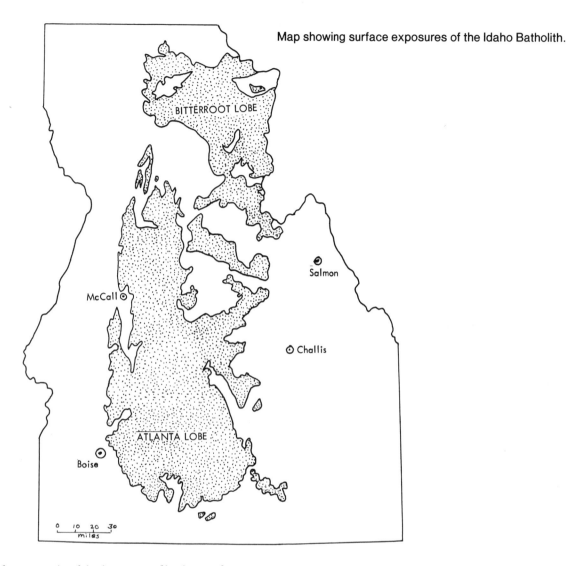

Map showing surface exposures of the Idaho Batholith.

tons of foliated muscovite-biotite granodiorite and monzogranite plutons were intruded. These plutons of sedimentary-type granites, are chemically similar and represent most of the bitterroot lobe. Toth and Stacey (1985) place the period of intrusion to be 70 m.y. ago to 50 m.y. ago, with most plutons intruded between 65 to 50 m.y. ago. Toth (1985) also observed large plutons and dikes of diorite in the southern and central parts of the Bitterroot lobe. These dikes are derived from the mantle and may have provided some of the heat necessary to cause partial melting of the crust to form the sedimentary-type granites of the Bitterroot lobe.

Atlanta Lobe

From the west side to the core there is an increase towards the east in SiO_2 and a decrease to the east in CaO, MgO and Al_2O_3. From the core to the east side there is less SiO2 and more CaO, MgO, and Al_2O_3. The western side is composed of tonalite 95 to 85 million years old. The batholith core is biotite granodiorite; and the eastern side of the lobe is muscovite-biotite granite approximately 76 to 72 million years old.

— 65 —

Initial Isotope Ratios

Rocks in western Idaho have very different initial Sr^{87}/Sr^{86} ratios. All the plutonic rocks west of the dashed line have low initial ratios (0.7043); whereas, all rocks to the east of the line have high initial ratios (0.7055). This change in ratios is abrupt and remarkable. In Idaho, the change is made in less than a distance of 6 miles. Although there is no difference in petrology of the rocks on either side of the line, there is a difference in the geologic environment in the two areas. For example, the low ratios are measured where plutons are intruded into Paleozoic or Mesozoic eugeoclinal rocks on the west side of the line. East of the line where the initial ratios are high, the plutons were intruded into Precambrian rocks. In some areas, the existence of Precambrian rocks are inferred because of cover by more recent volcanic or sedimentary rocks. Armstrong (1977) suggests that the high ratios of the plutons east of the line were caused by the assimilation of large quantities of crust by magmas ascending from the mantle. Conversely, west of the line, magmas ascending from the mantle rise through young crust which has not had sufficient time to be enriched in Sr^{87}. Therefore, plutons will form with low ratios. Armstrong (1977) speculates that the variability of the initial ratios of plutons east of the line indicates assimilation of rocks ranging in age from 500 million to as many as 2.7 billion years old. Therefore, the dashed line drawn to represent the change in initial ratios also represents the boundary between the Paleozoic and Mesozoic eugeocline and the older Precambrian crust. The dashed line also marks the suture line along which the Paleozoic and Mesozoic rocks were accreted onto the North American continent during the Mesozoic.

In the vicinity of Orofino, the isotopic boundary turns abruptly due west into eastern Washington. The trans-Idaho discontinuity (Yates, 1968) is also thought to transect the area near Orofino in a west-northwest trend. On the basis of field observations and geophysical evidence, Armstrong and others (1977) proposed that the trans-Idaho discontinuity changes direction near Orofino and follows the isotopic boundary for more than 60 miles. This portion of the trans-Idaho discontinuity may have been a transform fault active in Late Precambrian time. Stewart (1972) proposed that the onset of north-south rifting in Late Precambrian time initiated the Phanerozoic Cordilleran geosyncline.

Central Batholith

Lund (1985) proposed that in the central part of the batholith, plutons were emplaced passively after tectonism and that the intrusion of plutons did not cause orogenesis but were post orogenic. Events affecting the central part of the batholith occurred in the following order:

1. 95 to 85 m.y. ago:
   deformation at the suture zone; tectonism caused suturing of the island arc.
2. 85 to 75 m.y. ago:
   undeformed tonalite and granodiorite plutons emplaced.
3. 75 to 70 m.y. ago:
   undeformed muscovite-biotite granite passively emplaced into tonalite and metamorphic rocks.

Dike Rocks in the Batholith

Pegmatite and aplite dikes were formed during the late stages of each plutonic intrusion. The mineralogy of the dikes is similar to the enclosing intrusive. In some cases, pegmatite dikes cut aplite dikes and in other cases the reverse is true. These dikes appear to be concentrated near Eocene plutons and occur in the northeast-trending, trans-Challis fracture zone.

According to Foster (1986), the Bitterroot lobe of the Idaho Batholith contains numerous mafic dikes which make up about 20 percent of the total rock. These tabular dikes average about 8 feet thick and trend east-northeast with a vertical dip. On the basis of field evidence, Foster believes the dikes were emplaced while the batholith was still hot.

Emplacement of Plutons

Each pluton rises as a tapered cylindrical body. As a pluton is emplaced, both its outer margin and the surrounding country rock become deformed. Therefore the foliation adjacent to a pluton is generally conformable to its boundaries and to the foliation within the pluton.

Rock in and just above the zone of pluton generation are high-grade gneisses and migmatites (mixed igneous and metamorphic rock). These rocks have near-horizontal foliation. The overlying zone which is 3 to 10 miles deep, is volumetrically expanded by pluton emplacement. This expansion causes the underlying crustal zone to be extended laterally by plastic flow causing itself to be thinned and flattened.

In some Precambrian shield areas, there has been sufficient uplift and erosion to see exposures of gneisses with subhorizontal foliation. The shallow crustal level above the zone of lateral compression is subjected to horizontal tension both from the upward pressure caused by the rising pluton and the lateral movement outward of the rocks in the zone of compression. Therefore the upper crustal rocks are pulled apart into large fault blocks.

The boundary between the upper crustal roof rocks and the zone of pluton emplacement is a plane or zone of decoupling by low-angle faulting. The rocks in the lower zone of emplacement deform as a plastic whereas the upper crustal roof rocks deform as a brittle material. Upon decoupling, upper crustal roof rocks slide away in every direction (Gastil, 1979).

Field Identification of Granitic Rocks

Granitic outcrops of the Idaho Batholith are easily recognizable in the field. Under close inspection, granite has a salt and pepper appearance with the dark minerals of biotite mica and hornblende and light minerals of plagioclase and quartz. The constituent minerals are up to an inch or more in diameter and can readily be identified without a hand lens. Of course, many minor accessory minerals are too small to be identified with the unaided eye.

Weathered outcrops of granite have a distinctive appearance and can in some cases be identified at a mile or more distance. Coloration tends to be very light gray to very light tan, and in some places chalk white due to leaching by hot water. Outcrops are generally smooth and rounded due in part to surface weathering by granular disintegration and in some cases exfoliation where layer after layer is removed from the surface. Most exposures are cut by one or more sets of fractures which may give the outcrop a blocky appearance. Granite and basalt are among the easiest rocks in Idaho to identify.

MESOZOIC SEDIMENTARY ROCKS

Marine deposition continued in eastern Idaho during the Mesozoic but it was dominated by large-scale igneous activity and uplift due to emplacement of the Idaho Batholith in central Idaho.

Triassic Sedimentary Rocks

Triassic sedimentary rocks are exposed in two areas of Idaho: the marine sedimentary rocks accreted to the continent in west-central Idaho, and the sedimentary rocks of eastern Idaho, particularly in Caribou and Bonneville Counties. There was no change in deposition between the Permian and the Triassic. Although most of the Triassic formations are marine in origin, some members of the Triassic Ankareh Formation may be of continental origin. Rocks of Triassic age in southeastern Idaho also include the Dinwoody Formation and the overlying Thaynes limestone with a total maximum thickness

Subvertical beds of the resistant Nugget Sandstone Formation east of Bear Lake in southeastern Idaho.

Arrows point to tracks on bedding plane of Nugget Sandstone made about 200 million years ago by a creature of unknown identity.

of more than 5,000 feet. These are overlain by several other formations of shale and limestone with an aggregate thickness of 550 feet.

Permian and Triassic sedimentary rocks are also exposed in western Idaho between Weiser and Lewiston. These include the Seven Devils volcanics and metamorphosed conglomerates, sandstones, shales and limestones of the Lucile Group. The Lucile Group is about 6,500 feet thick and the Seven Devils volcanics and associated sediments are more than 6,000 feet thick. These typical eugeoclinal sediments were accreted to the continent during the Mesozoic.

Jurassic Sedimentary Rocks

Continental, cross-bedded sandstones were deposited in southeastern Idaho during the Early Jurassic. Then during the Middle Jurassic, portions of southeastern Idaho were occupied by marine waters.

Four major formations, having a total thickness of 6,700 feet, were deposited in southeastern Idaho. In ascending order, these include the Nugget Sandstone, Twin Creek Limestone, Preuss Sandstone and Stump Sandstone. The oldest formation, the Nugget Sandstone is, probably of continental origin because it is cross-bedded and contains ripple marks. The

Stump Sandstone and the Twin Creek Limestone contain fossils of marine invertebrates and are thus considered marine. The Pruess Sandstone was thought to be deposited in a saline lagoon. These formations are separated from each other by unconformities.

Jurassic flysch occurs in the accreted terrane of west-central Idaho. Near the end of the Jurassic all marine waters retreated from Idaho for the last time, leaving all of Idaho above sea level.

Cretaceous Sedimentary Rocks

Cretaceous sedimentary rocks are known only in southeastern Idaho. More than 14,000 feet of coarse- to fine-grained sediments were deposited in swamps, streams and fresh water lakes during the Cretaceous. Two units, the Gannett Group of Early Cretaceous age, and the Wayan Formation, deposited somewhat later in the Cretaceous, are described. The Gannett Group includes the Ephrain Conglomerate, Peterson Limestone, Bechler Conglomerate, Draney Limestone and Tygee Sandstone with a maximum thickness of 2,000 feet. Above the Gannett Group is the Wayan Formation which is known to contain petrified wood from Cretaceous palm-like trees.

TERTIARY PLUTONS OF THE BATHOLITH

Approximately 20 percent of the Idaho Batholith is composed of granitic rocks younger than the Mesozoic. The largest Tertiary-age plutons are batholith in size and are crudely aligned along a north-trending belt in the east-central part of the batholith. These plutons have long been known to be Tertiary age, if not Eocene, because they cut or intrude older rocks including the Idaho Batholith. Some of the plutons even cut Challis volcanic rocks.

More than 40 plutons of Tertiary age (42 to 46 million years old) have been identified in or near the Idaho Batholith. These intrusions range in size from dikes or small stocks to batholiths. The small stocks and dikes may be apophyses (narrow upper portion) of larger batholith-sized plutons at depth.

Pluton Characteristics

Bennett (1980) has attributed the following characteristics to most of the Tertiary granitic plutons:

1. The Tertiary granites have a pink color caused by pink potassium feldspar, whereas rocks of the Idaho batholith tend to be gray.
2. The composition range is fairly narrow — quartz monzonite to granite.
3. Miarolitic (gas) cavities are characteristic of the Tertiary plutons. These cavities indicate a shallow level (epizonal) of emplacement. The Tertiary plutons may have been emplaced within 3 to 4 miles of the surface, whereas the Idaho batholith may have been emplaced more than 6 miles from the surface.
4. Euhedral crystals (well-formed crystal faces) of smoky quartz and feldspar occur in the miarolitic cavities.
5. The Tertiary granitic rocks contain twice as much uranium and thorium than is found in the Mesozoic batholith. Because of this difference, a gamma ray spectrometer can be used to map the contacts between the Tertiary plutons and the surrounding batholith.
6. Some of the large plutons such as Bighorn Craigs, Sawtooth and Casto Batholiths have a well-developed vertical jointing. This jointing causes a very distinctive and easily recognizable ragged topography as is exemplified by the Sawtooth Mountains near the town of Stanley.
7. Other plutons show low, subdued topographic relief resulting from recent or partial removal of the roof rocks.

There is a lack of foliation or gneissic border zones in the Tertiary granitic plutons, even in the border zones. Epizonal (shallow level) plutons are emplaced in the brittle upper crust rather than the deeper mesozonal (intermediate) levels where plastic deformation causes gneissic border zones. Such foliation is fairly common in the main batholith. Also the potassium feldspar crystals are not as large in the Tertiary plutons as they tend to be in the batholith; this is probably caused by the shallow level of emplacement and quick cooling in the Tertiary rocks.

Challis Volcanism and Tertiary Plutons

The Challis volcanic field of east-central Idaho is very likely part of the same magmatic event that caused the Tertiary granitic plutons. The Challis volcanics represent the portion of the magma derived from the epizonal plutons that managed to break through the surface and be extruded as flows and tuffs. According to Bennett (1980), there is strong evidence that the Tertiary dike swarms in central Idaho also belong to the same Eocene volcanic-plutonic episode. Bennett (1980) further speculated that these Tertiary dikes, which tend to be concentrated in a northeast-trending zone, may be apophyses (narrow upper portion) of a pluton at depth. If this is true, the portion of the batholith represented by Eocene granitic rocks may be 30 to 40 percent.

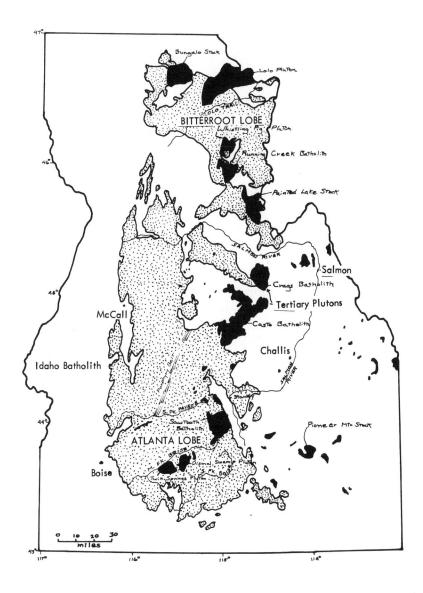

Location of Tertiary plutons (in black) in and near the Idaho Batholith (modified from Bennett, 1980).

Smoky Quartz Crystals

Bennett (1980) observed that smoky quartz crystals in miarolitic cavities are characteristic of the Tertiary granitic plutons, with perhaps the best specimens coming from the Sawtooth Batholith. Tertiary granites have twice the background radiation as the Cretaceous Idaho Batholith. This makes it possible to develop smoky quartz crystals which must be formed in a radioactive environment. Although most miarolitic cavities are only several inches in their long dimension, they may be as much as 10 feet across. These cavities tend to be preferentially confined to zones which may be caused by tension joints or fractures. During cooling of the granitic mass, these joints are caused by contraction.

Most smoky quartz crystals are less than one inch in length. Bennett (1980) noted that smoky quartz crystals left on the surface for several years will turn clear because of exposure to sunlight. Many miarolitic cavities also contain euhedral crystals of feldspar and aquamarine (beryl).

Hydrothermal Systems

The Tertiary plutons may have caused large convective hot water (hydrothermal) systems (Bennett, 1980). Meteoric waters, heated by hot rocks below, are circulated through the fracture systems.

Mineral Deposits

Mineral deposits could form along thrust faults, normal faults in the batholith and in structures caused by dike swarms in volcanic rocks and calderas. Many ore deposits in the batholith may have a tertiary pluton source at depth. Bennett (1980) has shown a close relationship between mining districts and Tertiary plutons. Deposits containing silver, lead, zinc, molybdenum, gold, copper, flourite, barite, stibnite, tungsten, beryllium and uranium have been attributed to Tertiary pluton sources. Many black sand placer deposits containing gold, monzonite, garnet, niobium, tantalum and uranium may also be derived from Tertiary plutons.

CHALLIS VOLCANISM

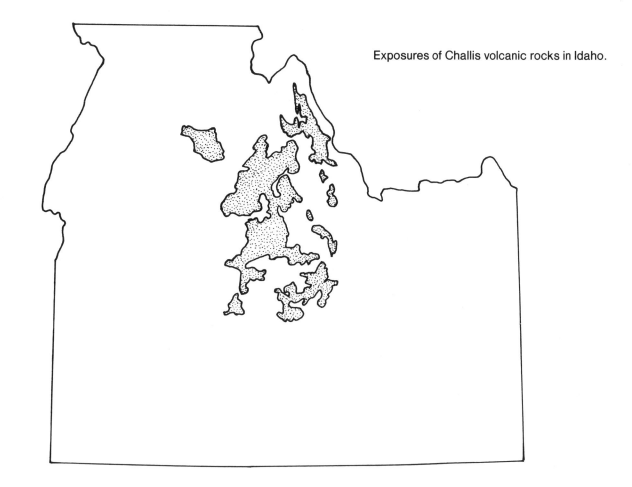

Exposures of Challis volcanic rocks in Idaho.

The Challis volcanic rocks are a thick series of volcanic flows and tuffs that cover a large part of east-central Idaho. Interbedded with rhyolitic volcanic flows and tuffs are lake bed sediments as well as fossiliferous sediments formed from other processes. Fossil plant species as well as radiometric age dating indicate an Eocene age. The volcanism started about 51 million years ago from a variety of widely-separated vents and continued until about 40 million years ago.

Extent of Volcanism

Challis volcanics now cover approximately 1,900 square miles of east-central and south-central Idaho. At the end of the eruptive period, the Challis volcanic rocks were so widespread that they covered more than half of Idaho. Hardyman and others (1985) proposed that the Eocene volcanic activity of southwestern Idaho may be related to the Challis volcanics. Thickness of the Challis volcanics is variable and in several places is known to be more than 10,000 feet.

Rock Types

There were many large-volume eruptions of intermediate lava from numerous centers. Both basaltic and rhyolitic lavas were erupted. Lavas and volcaniclastic rocks of intermediate to mafic composition were extruded from widely-scattered vents. These eruptions were nonexplosive and of small volume. Rhyolite lavas and domes and rhyolitic ash-flow tuffs were erupted from caldera complexes.

Calderas

The numerous ash-flow tuffs are generally believed to be derived from calderas. An example of one of these calderas is the Twin Peaks Caldera. It is a roughly-circular collapse structure, 12.5 miles in diameter and established about 45 million years ago.

The calderas are associated with large geothermal systems that operated throughout the Challis event. The heat in the crust from a pluton below would have caused deep circulation of water and provided an ideal environment for ore deposits to form. Because of this, calderas have important significance to exploration geologists.

Exposures Near Challis

The base upon which the Challis volcanics rest is a rugged mountainous surface of Precambrian and Paleozoic sedimentary rocks. While driving along highway 75 in the vicinity of Challis, it is possible to see many excellent exposures of the Challis volcanics as well as the irregular base on which they lie. The air-fall tuffs in this area have a soft appearance, are easily eroded and are variable in color, including lavendar, light green and several other pastel colors.

OWYHEE PLATEAU

Owyhee Mountains

The Owyhee Mountains are underlain by Cretaceous granitic rock and Tertiary volcanic rocks ranging from Eocene to Miocene age. These Cretaceous granitic rocks are bordered by Cretaceous hornblende gabbro and overlain by pre-Cretaceous metasediments and are thought to be a southward extension of the Idaho Batholith. The Eocene-age silicic volcanics correlate with the Challis volcanics. They are up to 33,000 feet thick and are dated at 44.7 million years. Olivine basalts and andesitic lavas of Oligocene age reach up to 3,800 feet thick and are dated at 30.6 million years. Miocene volcanic rocks of basalt and latite are dated at 17 million years and are 3,300 feet thick. The Miocene rocks are intruded by rhyolites. Olivine basalts and interbedded sedimentary rocks are dated at 8 to 10.5 million years.

Bruneau-Jarbidge Eruptive Center

Volcanic flows, exposed by the canyon of the Bruneau River, were erupted from the Bruneau-Jarbidge eruptive center. This eruptive center is about 59 miles long and lies southeast of the scenic Bruneau Canyon. Numerous ash flows, lava flows and basalt flows were erupted during Miocene and Pliocene time. The Banbury Basalt was erupted from shield volcanoes and filled in the low areas. The Idavada volcanics, known as the Cougar Point Tuff, consist of densely-welded, ash-flow tuffs and younger rhyolite flows about 10 to 12 million years old. Altogether there are nine or more of these welded tuff cooling units which filled a large basin. The eruptive center was named by Bonnichsen after the Bruneau and Jarbidge Rivers which have cut canyons in the area. The canyons expose both silicic and basalt flows.

Ash-Flow Tuffs (Cougar Point Tuffs)

The Cougar Point ash-flow tuffs were formed by a succession of pyroclastic eruptions that discharged hot, vesiculated magma particles into the air. The ash

Index map showing the Bruneau-Jarbidge eruptive center. Modified after Bonnichsen (1982).

was buoyed by air and transported long distances over a smooth flat surface. The hot ash consisted of shards with minor pumice and lithic fragments. The eruptive material flowed away from the source on a cushion of hot air. Once the gases were dissipated, the hot mass collapsed, compacted and cooled. The emplacement temperature is estimated to be in the vicinity of 900 to 1,000 degrees centigrade. The ash flows coalesced to a viscous liquid as indicated by flow marks and elongate vesicles and folds developed during the final stages of movement.

COLUMBIA RIVER BASALT GROUP

The Columbia River Basalt Group covers an area of approximately 77,000 square miles in Oregon, Washington and western Idaho. It forms the largest Cenozoic basalt field in North America and has an estimated total volume of approximately 90,000 cubic miles. Radiometric age determinations indicate that the group was extruded during a period from 17 to 6 million years ago. About 99 percent of the volume was erupted during a 3.5 million year period from 17 to 13.5 million years ago.

Source Fissures and Dikes

Columbia River Basalt flows were erupted from north-northwest-trending fissures in northeastern Oregon, eastern Washington and western Idaho. These fissures were fed by dikes tens of miles long. Some individual flows are thought to have exceeded 140 cubic miles in volume although most had volumes of 2 to 7 cubic miles. The duration of the eruptive period of each flow probably lasted from several days to as long as several weeks.

An average flow of Columbia River Basalt was approximately 100 feet thick, although some were more than 200 feet thick. The eruptions were not from a single vent, but from long cracks or fissures many miles long. Each individual eruption was fed by many fissures simultaneously. The basaltic magma was so fluid that it spread like water without change in thickness over tens of miles. Single flows have covered as much as 20,000 square miles. The average spreading velocity is estimated to have been 25 to 30 miles per hour.

The source of most of the Columbia River Basalt was from fissure dikes in the eastern part of the plateau. The dikes consistently trend north to north-northwest and are concentrated in three major dike swarms: the Monument dike swarm, the Grande Ronde dike swarm, and the Cornucopia dike swarm. Dikes of the same trend are also distributed across the entire plateau. Many source dikes have not been revealed because of cover or lack of erosion. However it is known that eruptions occurred periodically throughout the plateau. Distribution of the basalt is controlled by source vents, paleotopography, volume of flows, and deformation before and during eruptive episodes.

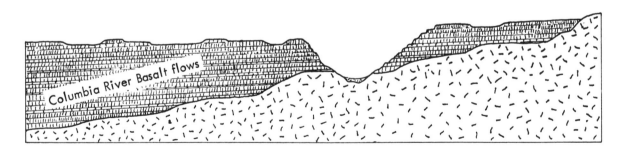

The eastern margin of the Columbia River Basalt where it laps over older rocks in western Idaho. The Columbia River Basalt covers an old erosional surface and is tilted towards the west.

Three Embayments in Idaho

The first flows of Columbia River Basalt were erupted over a landscape of rolling hills. Each successive flow filled in the low areas until a flat-surfaced plateau was formed.

Three lobes of Columbia River Basalt extended eastward into Idaho from the Columbia Plateau covering topographically low areas: the Weiser embayment, the Clearwater embayment, and the St. Maries embayment.

Flow Thickness

Individual flows and sequences of flows can be traced for many miles. They can be recognized on the basis of a variety of chemical, petrological, stratigraphic and magnetic polarity criteria. The average thickness of the flows ranges from 50 to 100 feet but some are more than 400 feet thick in basins. The maximum thickness of the group in any one place is about 5,000 feet (Waters and others, 1979). However the total thickness by adding the maximum thickness of each formation is approximately 8,200 feet (Hooper, 1980).

Saddle Mountain Basalt	6 – 13.5 m.y.
Wanapum Basalt	13.5 – 14.5 m.y.
Grande Ronde Basalt	14.5 – 16.5 m.y.
Picture Gorge Basalt	
Imnaha Basalt	16.5 – 17.5 m.y.

Sections Exposed in West-Central Idaho

The eastern plateau has been uplifted almost 6,600 feet allowing deep erosion by the Snake, Salmon, Clearwater and other rivers. Consequently the entire section is revealed in several localities of west-central Idaho.

Origin of the Columbia River Basalt

According to Hooper (1984), many of the flows were fed by fissures more than a mile wide and more than 40 miles long. This length implies that the fissures extended some 15 to 20 miles to the base of the crust where they tapped large reservoirs of homogeneous lavas. Hooper (1984) also noted that the largest flows did not change in bulk composition between the feeder dikes and the farthest extent of the flow, which in some cases, extended more than 370 miles. This could only be possible if all the magma in the flow were stored in a single, large, well-mixed reservoir. The volume of basalt in some of these flows exceeded more than 160 cubic miles.

Hooper (1984) further determined that the Columbia River Basalt Group does not consist of silicic lava indicating that it was not derived from melted crust. The crust below the basalt group appears to be of oceanic origin and to have accreted to the North American plate during the Mesozoic. All of the feeder dikes of the Columbia River Basalt Group are within the accreted oceanic terrane; none of the dikes extend into the old continental margin.

Location map of the eastern margin of Columbia Plateau in Idaho (after Camp and others, 1982).

SNAKE RIVER PLAIN

The Snake River Plain is a prominent depression across southern Idaho extending 400 miles in an east-west direction. It is arc shaped with the concave side to the north. The width ranges from 50 to 125 miles with the widest part in the east. This physiographic province was originally referred to as the Snake River Valley or the Snake River Basin. However, in 1902 T. C. Russell redesignated the province the Snake River Plains. Later the name was changed to Snake River Plain to convey a sense of uniformity throughout the province.

Although the east and west portions of the plain have little relief and are uniform topographically, there are major structural and geophysical differences between the east and west portions of the Snake River Plain.

The subsurface of the plain is known because of thousands of water wells and several deep exploration wells for geothermal resources and oil and gas. Geophysical surveys have also yielded much information on the subsurface.

Many different theories exist for the origin of the plain including a depression, downwarp, graben, and a rift. Although the plain is continuous, the surface geology and geophysical anomalies vary significantly among the western, central and eastern parts of the plain.

Western Snake River Plain

The western Snake River Plain is 30 to 43 miles wide and trends northwest. It is a fault-bounded basin with both the land surface and the rock layers dipping towards the axis of the plain. The basin is filled by interbedded volcanic rocks and lakebed sediments of Tertiary and Quaternary age.

The deep wells drilled in the western plain show interbedded basalt and sediment. One well (Anschutz Federal No. 1) about 43 miles south of Boise passed 11,150 feet of alternating sediment and volcanic rocks before it terminated in granite. This granite may be a southern extension of the Idaho batholith.

Geophysical surveys used to interpret the Snake River Plain include gravity surveys, magnetic surveys, seismic refraction profiles, thermal gradient measurements and heat-flow measurements. There is a gravity high over the plain. This gravity high coincides well with the topographic low. The gravity high anomaly over the western plain is interpreted as indicating a thin upper crust. Seismic refraction data also support this interpretation. Seismic refraction profiles indicate that the total crust under the plain is more than 25 miles thick; however, the upper crust is thin under the axis of the plain. Heat-flow measurements indicate a high heat flow anomaly along the margins of the plain and a relatively low heat flow in the central part of the plain.

Gravity and magnetic anomaly maps suggest several major strike-slip faults offsetting gravity and magnetic features in the plain. All geological and geophysical evidence indicates that the plain is bounded by normal faults. Also, there is no evidence of any pre-Cenozoic rock underlying the plain. It may not be proper to call the Snake River Plain a graben because there is no evidence that pre-Cenozoic rocks exposed north and south of the plain are downfaulted under the plain.

The western plain originated as a rift about 17 million years ago with continued development to the present. About 17 million years ago major tension in the upper crust thinned or pulled apart the upper crust along the axis of the Snake River Plain. The new elongate depression was filled with volcanic flows and sedimentary material derived from the uplands.

Middle Miocene (15 to 16 m.y. old) rhyolites and alkalic basalts are exposed in the Owyhee Mountains. These rocks are chemically and isotopically different than those of the Snake River Plain. North and northwest of Boise, Columbia River Basalt in-

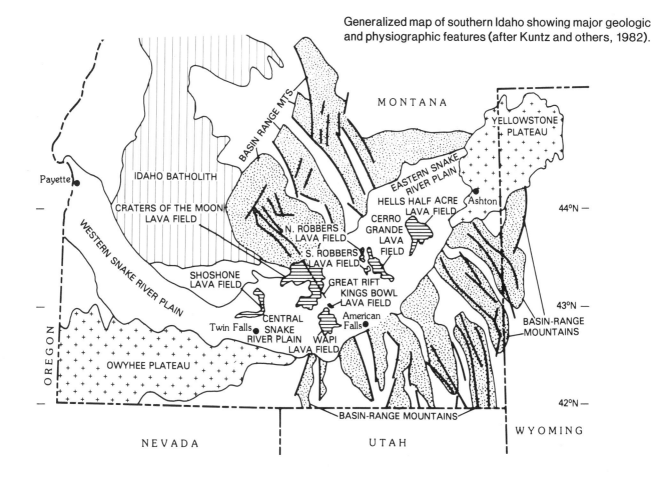

Generalized map of southern Idaho showing major geologic and physiographic features (after Kuntz and others, 1982).

tertongues with sedimentary deposits of the Payette Formation. Idavada rhyolitic tuffs and ash flows 15 to 11 million years old were discharged from now buried calderas. The Idaho Group is composed of fluvial and lacustrine sediments with interbedded basalt flows deposited in a subsiding basin. The Idaho Group includes the following formations:

Bruneau formation — 0.7 to 1.3 m.y. old
Glenns Ferry formation — 3 to 4 m.y. old
Chalk Hills formation — 7 to 8 m.y. old
Banbury Basalt — 8 to 11 m.y. old
Poison Creek formation

The Snake River Group consists primarily of basaltic lavas all less than 700,000 years old. Most of the vents of the Snake River Group are east of Twin Falls in the eastern Snake River Plain.

Central Snake River Plain

The central Snake River Plain has a prominent gravity gradient that coincides with a magnetic high; however the margin of the central plain has no well-defined topographic expression. Although much of the western plain is covered by sedimentary rocks, much of the central plain is covered by volcanics. The gravity anomaly suggests thinning. The western and central plain appear to have formed from regional tension normal to the trend of the western Snake River Plain.

Eastern Snake River Plain

The eastern Snake River Plain trends northeasterly and is underlain by mostly silicic and basaltic volcanic with very little sediments. There is no signif-

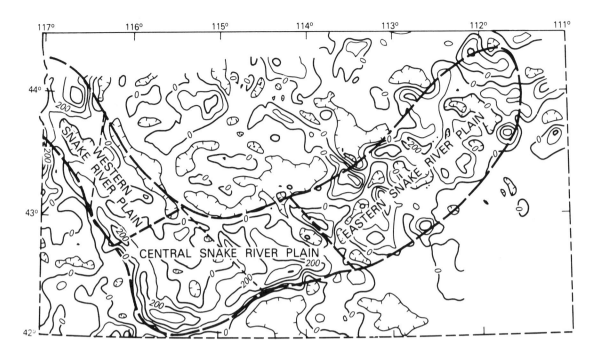

Magnetic contour map of southern Idaho. Heavy dashed lines delineate the major divisions of the Snake River Plain. Contour interval is 100 gammas. Map from Bhattacharyya and Mabey (1980).

icant fault control on the margins. The plain rises at the extreme east probably due to the proposed hot spot and associated volcanism recently moving from the Island Park Caldera to Yellowstone.

The land surface is higher at the margins than at the center, similar to the western plain. Both north and south of the eastern plain is the basin and range province with structures aligned approximately normal to the plain. The eastern plain is generally covered by Quaternary basalt flows with sources from fissures parallel to the plain, normal to the plain and along extensions of the basin and range faults.

In the eastern Snake River Plain, the gravity anomalities tend to be higher than surrounding areas. These anamalies exist as random highs and lows with no linear anomaly aligned with the axis of the plain. In fact gravity and magnetic anomalies generally trend normal to the axis of the eastern plain. These elongate anomalies trend northwest-southeast or approximately parallel to the trend of the basin and range.

The Idavada silicic volcanics in the eastern plain are similar to those in the western plain but are younger, ranging in age from 6.2 million years old to 10 million years old. At the northeast end of the plain, the last major eruption of the silicic volcanics is represented by the Yellowstone Tuffs dated at 0.6 to 2 million years old. The Yellowstone Tuffs are associated with caldera collapse followed by copious rhyolite flows erupted as recently as 700,000 years ago.

Large rhyolite domes 0.3 to 1.5 million years old rise above basalt near the axis of the plain. Rhyolite has been found in drill holes and at the margins of the plain. Abundant sediment is also found at the margins of the plain. Gravity and topographic evidence indicate a normal fault at the northwest boundary of the plain.

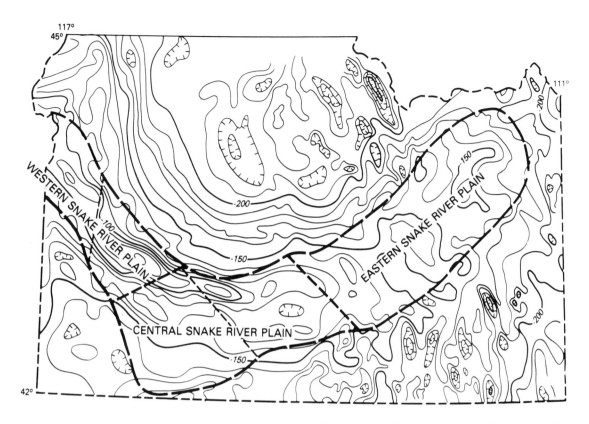

Bouguer gravity contour map of southern Idaho. Contour interval is 10 milligals (after Mabey, 1982).

Map of heat flow in the northwestern United States. Modified by Mabey (1982) from Lachenbruch and Sass (1980).

Caldera Complexes

The Island Park and Yellowstone caldera complexes are situated northeast of the eastern plain. The Rexburg caldera complex on the eastern plain has been identified and the existence of many others has been inferred. The silicic volcanic rocks in and near the Snake River Plain decrease in age from southwestern Idaho to Yellowstone National Park (Armstrong and others, 1975). This may mean that a source or center of silicic volcanics has and is progressively moving northeastward parallel to the axis of the plain. Seismic refraction profiles indicate that the eastern plain and the western plain have a thin upper crust and a thick lower crust. Silicic volcanic rocks and associated intrusive bodies apparently underlie most of the eastern plain. Rhyolite is far more

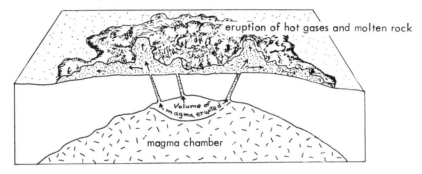

A large magma chamber forms about 6 miles below the surface of the earth. Molten rock begins to force its way to the surface. The upward pushing of the magma arches the overlying rocks into a broad dome. The arching leads to a series of concentric fractures called a ring fracture zone around the periphery of the dome.

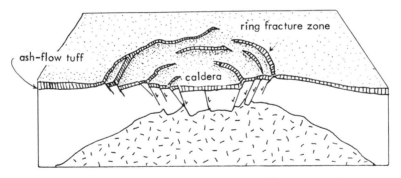

When the ring fractures tap the magma chamber, the uppermost part of which is charged with dissolved gas, tremendous amounts of hot gases and molten rock are suddenly erupted. The liquid is solidified into pumice, ash and dust as it is blown out of the vent.

The area overlying the blown-out part of the magma chamber collapses to form a caldera. The collapse takes place along normal faults that developed from fractures in the ring fracture zone. The depth of the collapse averages several thousand feet.

abundant than basalt in the eastern plain — only a thin veneer of basalt lies over a thick sequence of rhyolitic ash and flow tuffs. It is very likely that many source calderas for rhyolite are buried below the basalts.

Island Park Caldera

The Island Park Caldera may be the largest symmetrical caldera in the world. Rhyolite was erupted during the initial collapse period. Then basalt and rhyolite were alternately erupted from vents along the caldera floor. Finally basalt was erupted. The tuffs, flows and fault scarps that make up the morphology of the caldera are so young that they have been modified very little by erosion. There were three basic phases in the evolution of the caldera: growth of the volcano, extrusion of magma, and collapse.

The Island Park Caldera is an elliptical collapse structure 18 to 23 miles in diameter and is situated in the center of a rhyolite shield. The western semicircle of the scarp is exposed, and the eastern semicircle is buried under flows of rhyolite. Both basaltic and rhyolitic lava are believed to have originated from a single magma chamber below the caldera.

The rim crest of the southwestern side of the caldera stands about 1200 feet above the plain south of the caldera. The most abundant rock type composing the caldera is flow tuff, followed by ash falls and lava flows. The central portion of the caldera collapsed along a semicircular zone of faults 18 miles in diameter at the western half of the caldera.

Tension Fractures

Heat flow in the eastern plain is similar to that in the western plain — low at the center and high at the margins. Many large fractures project inward from the margins of the eastern plain; large flows of basalt have been extruded from them. The fractures must go to sufficient depth to reach molten rock. The fractures are caused by tension parallel to the plain and could be related to regional extension of the basin and range. The Great Rift is one of the most prominent fractures; it includes Craters of the Moon lava fields.

Normal faults of the basin and range are apparently related to overthrusting at depth; evidence indicates that the planes of the normal faults flatten at depth to merge with thrust faults.

Subsidence or Downwarping

The western and central plain may be a downfaulted block something like a rift or graben. The downfaulting may have been caused by regional extension or possible clockwise rotation of a block south of the plain which thinned or parted the upper crust. Gravity and magnetic surveys indicate a thick layer of dense, strongly-magnetized rock formed in the depression. The western and central plains are continuing to subside because of cooling, tension, loading of sediment and isostatic adjustment caused by the dense thick layer beneath the plain.

The central Snake River Plain has features common to the eastern and western plains. Downwarping is the most significant structural activity in the eastern Snake River Plain.

Pre-Tertiary Rocks May Not Continue Across Plain

Gravity and magnetic anomalies indicate the crust under the plain is very different than the surrounding crust. Therefore it is believed that the rocks at depth under the plain may not be pre-Tertiary rocks which are found both north and south of the plain.

Faults

Volcanic rift zones tend to be oriented along extensions of range-front faults and are caused by east-west extension. Basin and range faults are contemporaneous or younger than the Snake River Plain. These basin and range faults exist both north and south of the plain. This area has been under northeast-southwest extension during the last 17 million years.

Geophysical Characteristics

The entire Snake River Plain is underlain by a 25-mile-thick crust which is anomalously thick. The upper crust is thin relative to the average crust and the

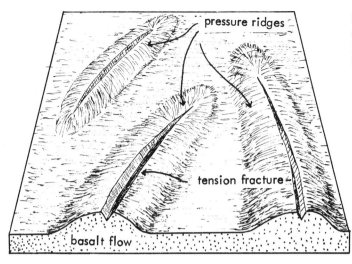

Pressure ridges with tension fractures along the crest or axis of the ridge. Thousands of these ridges, up to several hundred feet long, can be seen while driving across the Snake River Plain.

lower crust is thick relative to the average crust. Also the upper crust thickens to the east.

The near surface heat flow is relatively high throughout the Snake River Plain and particularly high at Yellowstone National Park. Cold ground water circulating throughout aquifers in the Snake River Plain reduces near surface gradients.

Basaltic Volcanism

The volcanic style of basaltic rocks in the eastern Snake River Plain is gradational between Hawaiian volcanism and flood basalt volcanism. For example, the Roza Member of basalt in the Columbia Plateau is typical of flood basalts. Approximately 350 cubic miles of lava were erupted from an 80-mile-long vent system at the rate of about 0.3 cubic mile per day. By comparison, the Hawaiian and Icelandic-type shield volcanoes are composed of thin flows 10 to 15 feet thick.

Basaltic Lava Flows

Most basalt flows in the Snake River Plains are pahoehoe basalts that were emplaced as compound flows. Compound flows are a sequence of thin individual cooling units ranging from less than 3 feet to more than 30 feet thick. The surface is hummocky with local relief, typically less than 30 feet. Common features are pressure plateaus, pressure ridges, flow ridges and collapse depressions. These features are caused by the way in which flows advance through a series of budding pahoehoe toes. Low areas and swales are filled with wind-blown sediments so that now, on the surface of older flows, only the higher ridges are visible. Aa flows are not as extensive as pahoehoe flows and can best be seen at Craters of the Moon. Basaltic lava is extruded on the Snake River Plain in three ways: flows from a central vent forming low shields, fissure flows and tube-fed flows.

Low Shields

Low shields are characterized by a small size and low profile. They have slope angles of 0.5 degrees and average 10 miles across and less than 1.6 cubic miles of lava. An excellent example is the Wapi lava field. This field covers 116 square miles with compound lava flows of pahoehoe. It is characterized by features such as lava toes, collapse depressions, flow ridges and pressure ridges, but lacks lava tubes. The Wapi lavas have a carbon 14 date of 2,270 years. Many of the low shields have pit craters at the summit and many craters show evidence of collapse. Shields tend to be aligned along rifts or fissures.

Fissure Flows

Fissure vents are associated with rift zones. The youngest fissure flows on the Snake River Plain are

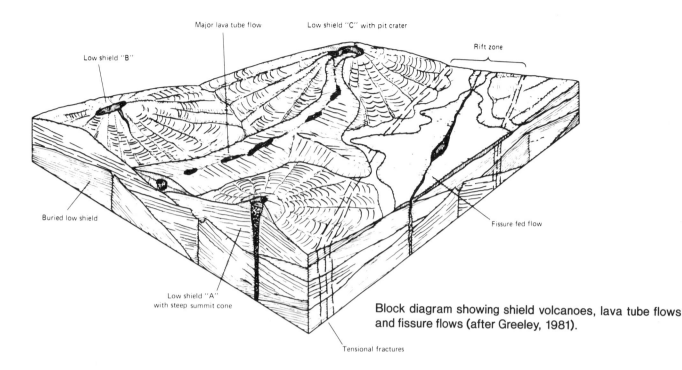

Low shield "B"

Major lava tube flow

Low shield "C" with pit crater

Rift zone

Buried low shield

Low shield "A"
with steep summit cone

Fissure fed flow

Tensional fractures

Block diagram showing shield volcanoes, lava tube flows and fissure flows (after Greeley, 1981).

located at Kings Bowl and the Craters of the Moon National Monument. Craters of the Moon covers 580 square miles whereas Kings Bowl covers about 1 square mile. Flow thickness is generally less than 5 feet although ponding or lava lakes may cause thicker layers. Point source eruptions along a fissure are common. For example, spatter cones and cinder cones at Craters of the Moon are examples of point source eruptions.

Lava Tube Flows

Lava tubes and channels originating from fissures and low shields are a very major conveyance for the emplacement of lava. These tubes are commonly more than 12 miles long and range from 2 to 30 feet across.

Shoshone Ice Cave is a segment of a complex lava tube — lava channel system, i.e. a system that had both roofed and unroofed segments. Many of the roofed parts later collapsed. The Shoshone lava tube system covers approximately 80 square miles. Smaller subsidiary tubes removed lava from the main tube.

Snake River Group

The Snake River Group includes most of the basalt flows in the Snake River Plains that were extruded during the Pliocene to Holocene epochs. The youngest flows are no more than a few thousand years old and the oldest are about four million years old. Approximately 8,000 square miles of southern Idaho are covered by basalt flows and interbedded sediments of the Snake River Group.

Geophysical studies and drill holes indicate that the plain may be underlain by basalts as much as five miles thick. However 5,000 feet may be an average thickness. Because only the upper 1500 feet were sampled by drill hole, it is possible that some of the basalts not reached by the drill hole are flows of the Columbia River Group.

The Snake River Basalts tend to be extruded from central vents rather than fissures. In the Snake River Plain there are numerous small shield volcanoes 200 to 400 feet high. On a clear day, from almost any place on the Snake River Plain, one can see low hills on the horizon that are either cinder cones or shield

Balanced rock formed by differential weathering of silicic ash-flow tuffs.

volcanoes of basalt. Menan Buttes in western Madison County is an example of a recent cinder cone. At Craters of the Moon National Monument, very recent flows and volcanic structures can be examined.

Idavada Volcanics

The name Idavada volcanics is applied to a variety of silicic volcanic rocks that crop out in the vicinity of the western Snake River Plain. These silicic rocks include primarily welded ash-flow tuffs; however, also included are vitric tuffs and lava flows. The type locality is Idavada, a place near the intersection of U.S. highway 93 and the Idaho-Nevada State line. Along Goose Creek, a section of silicic tuffs more than 3000 feet thick is exposed. On the north side of the Snake River, a thick section of the Idavada volcanics lies unconformably on granite and makes up most of the Mount Bennett Hills. For example, the scenic Gooding City of Rocks, located in the Bennett Hills, is made up of Idavada silicic volcanic rocks. Pinnacles,

bizarre forms and hoodoos are typically formed by differential weathering and erosional processes on the Idavada volcanics. Balanced Rock, south of Twin Falls, is also composed of these volcanics and is a good example of the same weathering phenomenon. The Idavada volcanics also border the southern edge of the Snake River Plain in Cassia, Twin Falls and Owhyee Counties.

The Idavada volcanics are of Miocene age, ranging from 9 to 14 million years old. The flows are oldest in the western Snake River Plain and are consistently younger to the east.

Origin of the Snake River Plain

The central and eastern plain is apparently a structural downwarp because strata along the flanks dip towards the center; also there is little evidence for boundary faults. By contrast, the area in the vicinity of Yellowstone appears to be experiencing uplift. This eastward propagation of vulcanism may be

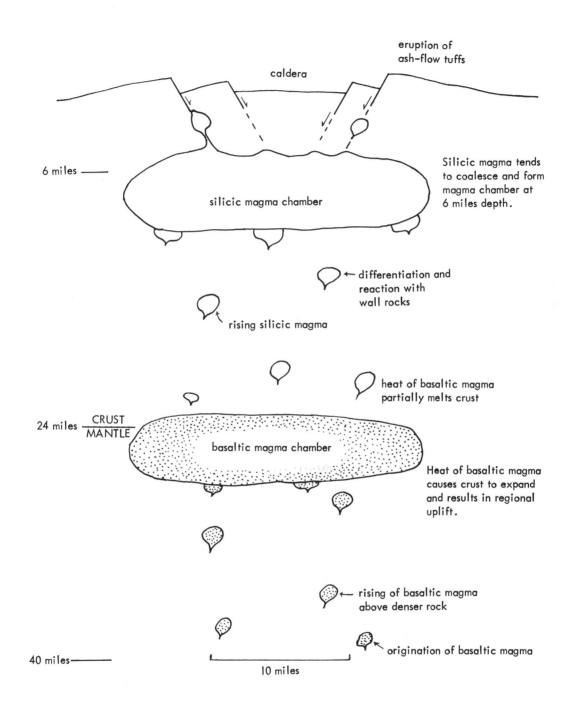

eruption of
ash-flow tuffs

caldera

6 miles ———

silicic magma chamber

Silicic magma tends
to coalesce and form
magma chamber at
6 miles depth.

← differentiation and
reaction with
wall rocks

↖ rising silicic magma

heat of basaltic magma
partially melts crust

24 miles $\dfrac{\text{CRUST}}{\text{MANTLE}}$

basaltic magma chamber

Heat of basaltic magma
causes crust to expand
and results in regional
uplift.

← rising of basaltic magma
above denser rock

← origination of basaltic magma

40 miles———

10 miles

Generalized vertical cross section of Snake River Plain
shows possible origin of basaltic and silicic rock and the
manner in which volcanic rocks reach the earth's surface
(modified after Leeman, 1982).

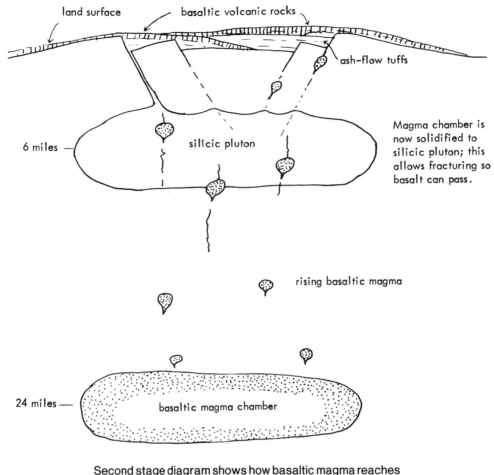

Second stage diagram shows how basaltic magma reaches the surface once the shallow silicic magma chamber solidifies (modified after Leeman, 1982).

caused by the migration westward of the continent at a steady rate over a deep mantle plume or hot spot rooted more than 100 miles below the surface. Several hypotheses exist to explain the origin of the Snake River Plain:

1. Extension to the north coupled with crustal thinning.
2. Migration of the continent or the North American plate over a stationary hot spot which now exists at Yellowstone National Park. The hot spot has a northeastward migration of silicic volcanic centers moving at the rate of 1 to 2 inches per year. Uplift is associated with volcanism and silicic volcanism is followed by basal-

tic volcanism. The lower crust is thickened and made more dense by injection of basaltic magma. After passing over the hotspot, the crust settles due to contraction from cooling and the density of the basalt. This hypothesis is favored.
3. Propagation of crustal fracture from west to east.
4. Passive deformation.

Geologic Model for Snake River Plain Volcanism

Basalt magma formed in the mantle moves upwards because it is less dense than surrounding mafic mantle rocks. However basaltic rock is denser than crustal rock so the basaltic magma column must extend deep enough into the mantle to allow hydrostatic pressure to force it up through the lighter crust. The basaltic magmas probably originated at a depth of approximately 40 miles. The initial basaltic magmas probably stagnated in the deep crust; however, repeated injection of more magma led to a large magma chamber and a thicker lower crust. During the accumulation of basaltic layers, heat transfer to the crustal wall rocks would cause partial melting (anatexis) of the more silicic crust.

The zone of partially-fused wall rocks continues to enlarge as basalt is added. Because partial melts of silicic magmas are less dense than the basaltic magmas, they would tend to coalesce and move higher in the crust to form magma chambers at about 6 miles deep. Intermediate to silicic magmas would continue to differentiate and interact with wall rocks as well as hydrothermal fluids. These magmas would raise the temperature of the crust and the heat would cause the crust to expand and result in regional uplift.

Numerous eruptions of ash-flow tuffs occur during caldera collapse; after collapse, resurgent doming takes place and the cycle is repeated many times. Small rhyolite domes extruded after the main rhyolitic phase represent the residual components of the original silicic bodies. As long as the silicic magma bodies existed as fluids, fissures could not propagate to allow the basaltic magmas to pass. Rhyolitic volcanism ceases with solidification of the silicic magma.

Three Time Transgressive Facies

Throughout the Snake River Plain there are three time transgressive facies of volcanic rocks. This means that a similar rock such as the Idavada volcanics is found throughout most of the Snake River Plain but is younger from west to east. These three facies include:

1. Silicic volcanic facies composed of volcanic sediments, air-fall and ash-flow rhyolite tuffs, rhyolite flows and subordinate basaltic flows.
2. Basaltic lava facies with interbedded sediments; a few rhyolite flows and domes overlap.
3. An uppermost facies of continental sediments, basaltic lavas, rhyolitic ash-flow and air-fall tuffs.

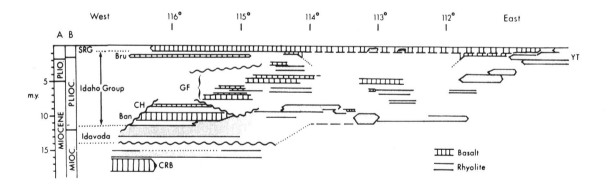

Stratigraphic relations and time-transgressive history of volcanic events. Stratigraphic units are as follows: Snake River Group (SRG), Bruneau (Bru), Glenns Ferry (GF), Chalk Hills (CH), Banbury Formation (Ban), Yellowstone Tuff (YT), and Columbia River Basalt age-equivalent rocks (CRB). After Leeman (1982).

YELLOWSTONE PLATEAU VOLCANIC FIELD

The Island Park area occupies the western part of the Yellowstone Plateau volcanic field. It is transitional between the eastern Snake River Plain and the active part of the field in Yellowstone National Park.

Three Cycles of Rhyolitic Volcanism

Most of the field has originated in three cycles of rhyolitic volcanism during the past 2.2 million years. Each cycle began with the eruption of small volumes of rhyolite followed by rhyolites erupting every several hundred years from a growing system of arcuate fractures above a large and growing magma chamber. Each cycle climaxed with an explosive eruption of a large volume of fragmented rhyolitic magma. Emptying part of the magma chamber as a result of the eruption caused the chamber roof to collapse and form a large caldera. After each cycle, rhyolite again erupted for several hundred thousand years and partly filled the caldera by the end of each cycle.

Each Successive Caldera Moves Eastward

The magma within the magma chambers of the first two cycles has now solidified. The rhyolitic source areas and associated calderas of each cycle covered different but overlapping areas. Each successive caldera is positioned east of the previously formed caldera.

Basalt Eruptions

Basalt eruptions were limited to the margins of the rhyolitic source area; however, when the silicic magma chamber solidified in the first two cycles, basaltic magma could penetrate through fractures in the caldera.

Yellowstone Group of Ash-Flow Sheets

The three ash-flow sheets that erupted at the climax of each cycle were key units to work out the geologic history of the plateau. They are collectively named the Yellowstone Group and include the Huckleberry Ridge Tuff (2.0 million years old), the Mesa Falls Tuff (1.3 million years old) and Lava Creek Tuff (0.6 million years old). The first volcanic cycle in the Yellowstone Plateau began 2.2 million years ago with the eruption of the Huckleberry Ridge Tuff. During the second cycle, the Mesa Falls Tuff was erupted; it is generally pinkish in color and forms large, rounded, boulderlike outcrops.

Volcanism Shifts from Island Park to Yellowstone

After the first two cycles, the rhyolitic activity shifted away from the Island Park area to the Yellowstone Plateau. During the past million years, rhyolitic magmas beneath Island Park have solidified and the Island Park has subsided 300 to 600 feet relative to Yellowstone. During the past 200,000 years, the silicic pluton beneath Island Park has solidified and basalt has erupted through the caldera floor.

Magma Chamber Collapse and Ring Fractures

The third cycle began 1.2 million years ago. Approximately 600,000 years ago rhyolitic lavas erupted from gradually-forming arcuate fractures. During this time, rhyolitic magma chambers formed at shallow crustal levels. Before the intermittent eruptions, the roof would stretch and dome and then sag to form arcuate fractures.

The climactic eruption vented through the ring fracture 630,000 years ago. After the eruption, the magma chamber collapsed along two ring fractures to form the Yellowstone caldera. Calderas form by collapse of large magma-chamber roofs. Subsequent rhyolitic volcanism filled the caldera with more than 1,000 feet of silicic volcanics. These flows form the Madison, Pitchstone and Central Plateaus of Yellowstone National Park. Each cyle lasted about a million years and began with emplacement of a rhyolitic magma chamber, followed by major

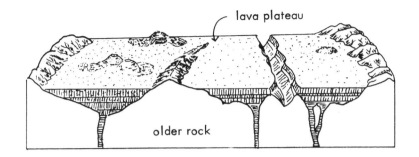

A lava plateau shown covering irregular topography of older rock.

pyroclastic eruptions and finally cooling and solidification of magma at depth.

Hot Spot above Mantle Plume

The Yellowstone system, like the Hawaiian system, is stationary relative to the deep mantle. It migrates relative to the North American plate in the direction opposite to plate motion. This system is a stationary hot spot above a mantle convection plume.

Hydrothermal System

The seismic swarm in the Yellowstone Plateau is related to prominent, high-temperature hydrothermal systems which are believed to lie above an active magmatic heat source. The lack of swarm seismicity in the Island Park Caldera indicates no major hydrothermal convection system is circulating actively above a shallow heat source.

CENOZOIC SEDIMENTARY ROCKS

The entire state of Idaho has been above sea level throughout the Cenozoic Era. During the Early Cenozoic, emplacement of the plutons caused continued uplift in central Idaho. However, as the east-west compression ceased, block faulting formed the Beaverhead Range, Lost River Range, Pioneer Range and Sawtooth Mountains. By 25 million years ago, Idaho began to look similar to the way it looks today.

The Beaverhead Formation

The Beaverhead Formation may be the oldest Cenozoic formation in Idaho, ranging in age from Late Cretaceous to the Lower Eocene. This formation occurs over a broad area east of the Batholith and extends into of western Montana. The Beaverhead Formation is a continental deposit of conglomerate and sandstone which was derived from the rapid uplift caused by emplacement of the Idaho Batholith.

The Wasatch Group

The Wasatch Group is widely exposed in Utah, Wyoming and the southeast corner of Idaho. It consists of a coarse conglomerate with a few limestone beds and reaches a total thickness of about 1,500 feet in Idaho. Eocene fossils have been found in the Utah part of the Group.

Kenney, Geertson and Kirtley Formations

The Kenney, Geertson and Kirtley Formations are mapped as the uppermost sedimentary units of the Challis volcanics in the area of Salmon. They are separated from each other by unconformaties but have a similar lithology including conglomerates, sands, shales and tuffaceous material. All three were deposited in lake and stream environments.

The 500-foot-thick Kenney Formation is Late Oligocene in age and the oldest formation. Also 500 feet thick is the Geertson Formation. It is the middle formation and is presumed to be Late Oligocene or Early Miocene age. The youngest formation, the Kirtley, has been dated as Middle Miocene from fossil leaves. Beds of almost pure fossil plant material have been transformed to lignite. The Kirtley formation was originally named the Carmen Formation.

Latah and Payette Formation

The Latah Formation in northern Idaho and the Payette Formation of southwestern Idaho were both formed as separate lenses of river and lake sediments separated by lava flows of Columbia River Basalt. The Latah Formation of Miocene age is composed of clays, silts and sands. The Payette Formation is approximately 1,200 feet thick and has been dated as Miocene to Early Pliocene on the basis of fossil leaves. It includes clay, silt, sand, fine gravel and volcanic ash deposits primarily in lakes with only minor stream deposits.

Idaho Group

The sediments of the Idaho Group are confined to the Western Snake River Plain. They were deposited on the Idavada Volcanics which were extruded during the formation of the western plain. Malde and Powers (1962) elevated the Idaho Formation to group status and divided it into seven overlapping formations ranging in age from Middle Miocene to Middle Pleistocene. The seven formations of the Idaho Group are composed of clastic beds and intercalated basalt flows. The clastic sedimentary beds are poorly consolidated and range in texture from sand to clay. However, beds of gravel, volcanic ash and diatomite are also prevalent. The beds form massive light-colored layers hundreds of feet thick which typically erode into badland topography. In no single place are all seven formations exposed in a continuous sequence. Exposures of the Idaho Group crop out continuously along the Snake River from Homedale to Hagerman. A composite section assembled from all exposed sections would have a total thickness of about 5,000 feet.

The seven formations recognized in the Idaho Group are, in ascending order: the Poison Creek Formation, the Banbury Basalt, the Chalk Hills Formation, the Glenns Ferry Formation, the Tuana Gravel, the Bruneau Formation and the Black Mesa Gravel. Fossils from these formations range in age from Early Pliocene to Middle Pleistocene. Many mammal fossils have been found throughout the Group.

Most of the lake bed (lacustrine) sediments in the western Snake River Plain can be placed in the Late Miocene Chalk Hills Formation and the Pliocene Glenns Ferry Formation (Kimmel, 1982). The Glenns Ferry and Chalk Hills sediments were each deposited in large lakes. These lakes occupied approximately the same basin which covered much of the western Snake River Plain. The Chalk Hills Formation was deposited several million years before deposition of the Glenns Ferry Formation.

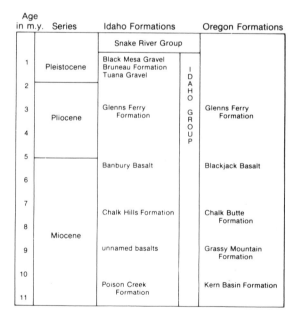

Stratigraphy of the western Snake River Plain. Modified from Malde and Powers (1962) and Armstrong and others (1975) by Kimmel (1982).

Hagerman Horse Quarry

Abundant fossil remains of mammals and other vertebrates have been collected from deposits of the Glenns Ferry Formation. The best known fossil assemblage has come from the "Hagerman Lake Beds" on the west side to the Snake River opposite the town of Hagerman. This quarry was extensively worked by field parties of the U.S. National Museum and much of the recovered material is on display in Washington, D.C. The fauna, mostly of horse-like animals, has been dated as Late Pliocene to Middle Pleistocene. The principal collections are from the "Hagerman horse quarry." The vertebrate remains found at the horse quarry include those of shrew, gopher, mole, weasel, otter, rabbit, peccary, camel, antelope, horse, and mastodon, as well as those of fish, reptiles and birds.

Salt Lake Formation

The Salt Lake Formation is exposed mainly in the eastern part of the Snake River Plain. It includes most of the Tertiary-age (Pliocene) sedimentary rock in the region that is not mapped as the Wasatch Formation. The Salt Lake Formation consists chiefly of poorly-consolidated sand, silt and gravel deposited by rivers and lakes. Also included with the Salt Lake Formation are beds of freshwater limestone, and volcanics such as welded tuffs and basalts intercalated at several horizons.

Lake Sediments

During the Tertiary, large shallow lakes covered many basins in Idaho. Some of these lakes originated from damming by glacial debris and lava flows. Lakes were also formed by abundant water occupying low areas of the topography. Sedimentary material was carried into the lakes by tributary streams and deposited on the lake beds. These sediments include clay, silt and sand volcanic ash and organic material from plants and animals. The lake beds are covered by volcanic rocks in many places and also are exposed at the surface. Many lake bed deposits are richly fossiliferous. For example, by parting the beds

Bruneau Canyon formed by the Bruneau River cutting down through volcanic and sedimentary rock layers.

of Miocene and Pliocene time one might find leaves of laurels, ginkos, pines, sequoias, ferns, scouring rushes, beeches, oaks, willows, aspens, maples, plums and magnolias. These floral specimens indicate that the climate during the Miocene and Pliocene epochs was more mild and humid than it is today.

Valley and Basin Sedimentary Fill

The valleys and basins of Idaho are filled with lake and stream sediments, much of which were deposited during the interglacial stages of the Pleistocene. The remains of giant bison, mastodons, mammoths and other Ice Age animals have been collected from Pleistocene interglacial deposits in southeastern Idaho. These deposits may be several miles thick in the

down-faulted valleys of the basin and range.

Recent Alluvium and Loess Deposits

Alluvium of gravel, sand, silt, and clay is being deposited along streams. These thin, narrow strips of sedimentary material generally cover the bedrock in stream valleys. Loess is wind-deposited silt and clay. It is derived by glaciers grinding rock into fine particles or by the sorting action of streams. Loess deposits blanket the Palouse Hills in the vicinity of Moscow where they form low rounded hills. Deposits of loess attained their massive thickness just west of Moscow where locally they are as much as 200 feet thick. The fine-grained silts are picked up, transported and deposited by the wind. In eastern Washington, the loess is called the Palouse Formation.

Part 3

LARGE-SCALE
FAULTING

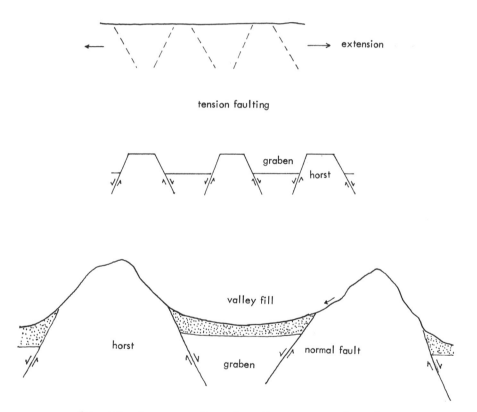

Generalized cross sections show the sequence of events
through which crustal extension may lead to normal faulting
and Basin and Range topography.

IDAHO-WYOMING THRUST BELT

The Idaho-Wyoming Thrust Belt is located in southeastern Idaho, western Wyoming and north-central Utah. This thrust belt is a small part of a much larger, geologically-complex Overthrust Belt that extends 2200 miles from Alaska into Central America. The belt is a part of the extensive north-south-trending North American Cordillera Mountain Range which originated by intense east-west compressional deformation spanning more than 200 million years. Many different thrust sheets comprise the belt. These sheets were typically transported eastward for distances of 10 to 20 miles; however, total displacements generally exceed 100 miles.

Oil and Gas Exploration

Since a major discovery of oil in the Pineview field of Utah in 1975, the western Overthrust Belt has become well known as one of the most promising exploration frontiers for oil and gas in North America. Between 1975 and 1983, 26 new oil and gas fields were found in the Wyoming-Utah-Idaho thrust belt; however, no commercial quantities of oil or gas have as yet been discovered within the state of Idaho.

Accreted Terrane

Throughout most of Paleozoic time, more than 60,000 feet of sediments consisting of lime, mud, silt and sand were deposited in an ocean basin at the western edge of the North American continent. These thick sequences of sediments were deposited on the continental shelf and slope just to the west of the present position of the Overthrust Belt and formed a miogeocline. From Late Devonian through Mesozoic time, exotic terranes from Asia and volcanic island arcs in the Pacific Ocean were carried eastward on the Pacific Plate and accreted on the western margin of the North American Continent. Plate margin accretion activity was most pronounced from mid-Mesozoic through Early Tertiary time when the eugeoclinal oceanic rocks were brought against the miogeoclinal rocks of the continental slope.

Cause of Thrusting

During the accretion process, the eastward-moving Pacific Plate was subducting or decending along a deep oceanic trench beneath the western continental margin of North America. This subducting plate caused the formation of numerous magma bodies to move upwards into the continental crust and form the great Sierra Nevada and Idaho Batholiths. Possibly in response to the upward intrusion of these large granitic masses, the Overthrust Belt formed to the east. The thrusting was driven by gravity and resulted from crustal thickening caused by emplacement of the batholith. This uplift of the Idaho Batholith was accompanied by the development of folds and thrust faults as well as possible gravitational gliding off the highlands. Most of the thrust faults were directed to the east and cut the Beaverhead Comglomerate. The Beaverhead Conglomerate is believed to have formed as a result of rapid uplift caused by the batholith.

Date of Thrusting

The Paleozoic and Mesozoic sediments were strongly folded and thrusted eastward beginning during Late Jurassic (about 140 million years ago) in the west and ending as late as Eocene time (55 m.y. ago) in the east. This 85 million year period of compressive tectonics was followed by normal or extensional faulting of the Basin and Range within the Overthrust Belt. Therefore, the ages of foreland thrusting are determined to be youngest in the east and oldest in the west. The earlier thrust was the Jurassic Paris thrust of the Bear River Range; the last thrust is the Eocene Labarge thrust east of the Wyoming Range. Dating of the thrust is extremely difficult and is accomplished by (1) determining age of strata cut by thrusting, (2) determining the age of

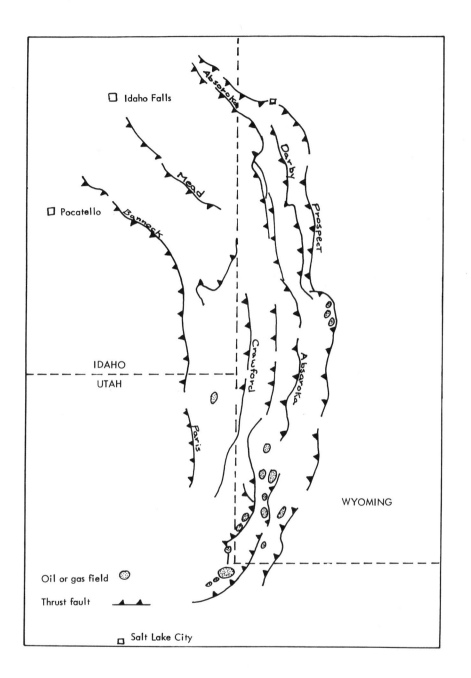

Index map of the Wyoming-Utah-Idaho thrust belt showing
major thrust faults and oil and gas fields.

strata deposited during and immediately following thrusting such as conglomerates, and (3) determining the age of strata which overlap and postdate the thrusts.

Sevier Orogeny

The period of intensive Late Jurassic to Eocene compressive thrust faulting and folding in the Cordilleran Overthrust Belt has been designated the Sevier Orogeny. During this period, huge masses of rock were ruptured into thrust sheets 20 to 50 miles wide, several miles thick and hundreds of miles long. Eastward horizontal movement on the individual thrust sheets is measured in tens of miles.

The Sevier Orogenic Belt is a narrow north-south zone of structural disturbance that runs through western Montana, eastern Idaho, Wyoming, Utah and Nevada. This belt consists of large-scale thrust faults and folds with vergence to the east. These thrust faults and folds have resulted in significant shortening that was initiated in Late Jurassic time and continued through the beginning of the Tertiary.

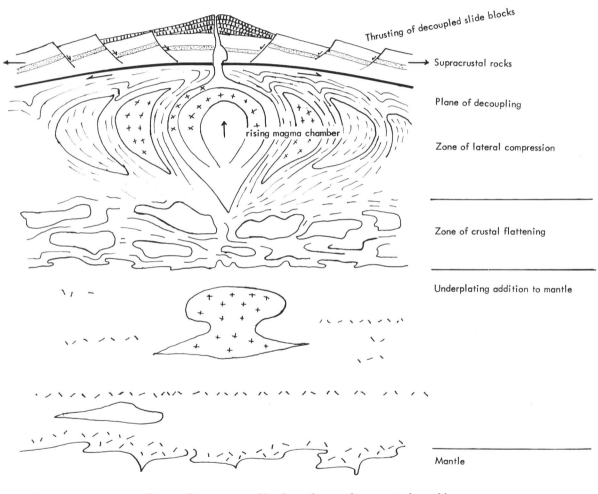

Decoupling zone resulting from the emplacement of granitic magma chambers. Continued uplift causes the surface layer to detach and slide away from the area of uplift (modified after Gastil, 1979).

On the basis of fossil distribution found in the earliest conglomerate deposited during the orogeny within the thrust belt, Heller and others (1986) suggest that the initial thrust movement may not be older than 119 million years. This age of initial thrusting is also supported by subsidence analysis of sedimentary sequences within and to the east of the thrust belt. The rapid increase in subsidence is believed to have been caused by the initiation of faulting in the thrust belt.

Four Major Thrust Fault Systems

Four major thrust-fault systems have been identified in the region. From west to east and oldest to youngest: Willard-Paris-Bannock, Mead-Crawford, Absaroka and Darby-Prospect-Hogsback. Each major thrust fault has many overlapping thrust slices. Before horizontal compression, the Overthrust Belt was approximately 130 miles wide; however, total stratal shortening of 50 percent or about 65 miles was accomplished by thrust faulting and folding. The thrust sheets ruptured along flat faults more or less parallel to bedding in weak or incompetent rock layers such as shales and cut steeply across bedding in strong or competent layers.

Younger Rocks Thrust over Older Rocks

Only the sedimentary rock section is shortened by folding and faulting. The Paleozoic and Mesozoic rocks are structurally detached from the Precambrian granitic basement rocks below by a regional decollement (detachment surface) and shifted eastward over the Precambrian basement rocks along the decollement or thrust surface. Despite the compressive deformation to the overlying Paleozoic and Mesozoic rocks, the Precambrian basement rocks are little affected. As a result of the thrusting and imbrication of strata, older rocks are thrust over younger rocks. In some cases, rocks as old as Cambrian in the hanging wall are thrust over rocks as young as Cretaceous.

Folds

Like thrust faults, folds for the most part affect only strata above the decollement surfaces. Folds are generally concentric in form and are vergent to the east.

Extension Through Snake River Plain

The Cenozoic Snake River Plain effectively divides the thrust belt. Correlation of geology north and south or the plain is difficult. However, evidence indicates that at one time the thrust belt was continuous before the plain existed. There is no evidence that overthrust structures underlie the Snake River Plain.

Thrust Belt in East-Central Idaho

The thrust belt in east-central Idaho has a width of more than 120 miles where it is positioned between the Idaho Batholith and southwestern Montana. This belt includes the Medicine Lodge and the Grasshopper thrust plates and an unknown number of other thrust plates.

Thrust plates are characterized by open to tight folds and imbricate thrust faults. The basal decollemont (detachment) zones of the plates are composed of intensely-sheared, crushed and brecciated rocks. The decollemont at the base of the Medicine Lodge plate is up to 1,000 feet thick.

The thrust faults have caused abrupt changes in the stratigraphic sequence of sedimentary rocks from place to place throughout the region. Sedimentary strata which were at one time far removed are now overlapped.

Gravitational gliding from a high area in central Idaho was the mechanism that caused the regional thrusting. Of the two major thrust faults in east-central Idaho, the Medicine Lodge plate is structurally higher, larger, and more dominant than the Grasshopper plate. The rocks of the Lost River Range, Lemhi Range and Beaverhead Mountains are dominated by these two thrust systems with their basal decollement zones and associated imbricate thrust faults. The leading edge of the thrust system, primarily in southwest Montana, is characterized by tight folds and imbricate thrust faults.

The basal decollement zones consist of brecciated and lightly-sheared rocks. In such areas the character of the original rock is difficult to identify. Rocks above the basal decollement zone in the Medicine Lodge thrust plate are deformed into isoclinal folds overturned to the east. The overturned limbs tend to be broken by small imbricate thrust faults that dip 10 to 20 degrees to the west.

The leading edge of the Medicine Lodge thrust plate is just east of the Beaverhead and Bitterroot Mountains along the Idaho-Montana line. Sections of the plate are also exposed in the Lemhi and Lost River Range for a total exposed width of 80 miles.

The basal zone of the Medicine Lodge decollement in the Lemhi Range and Beaverhead Mountains is a brecciated zone 300 to 1,000 feet thick. Rocks in the plate above the basal zone are deformed by overturned folds verging to the east with lower limbs broken by closely-spaced imbricate thrusts.

The Precambrian Yellowjacket Formation lies below the Medicine Lodge decollement almost everywhere in east-central Idaho. The Yellowjacket is believed to be in place because it lacks the deformation one would expect of tectonically transported rocks.

The Medicine Lodge plate rocks include sedimentary rocks older than 800 million years overlain by Ordovician and younger Paleozoic quartzite, dolomite, limestone and shale. Based on stratigraphic and radiometric evidence, Ruppel (1982) proposed that thrust faulting began about 100 million years ago and was completed about 70 to 75 million years ago.

The Grasshopper plate consists of a thick sequence of Proterozoic sedimentary rocks deposited in the Belt seaway. These rocks are, in places, overlain by Paleozoic rocks. Thrust plates appear to be developed in succession by new plates developed beneath older ones. The Medicine Lodge plate lies structurally above the Grasshopper and is probably older than the Grasshopper. The Medicine Lodge plate contains rocks from farther west than does the Grasshopper.

The Medicine Lodge plate may have been transported as much as 100 miles from the miogeoclinal area of central Idaho. Miogeoclinal rocks deposited in central Idaho are transported eastward into tectonic contact with rocks deposited in the Belt seaway. Folding and faulting in the Medicine Lodge plate may have been caused by crumpling of the eastward-moving plate against the continent.

Oil and Gas Potential of the Overthrust Belt

The oil and gas potential for the overthrust belt as well as the rest of Idaho depends on the presence of a geologic environment that would allow the generation, migration and trapping of petroleum. The most critical factors include: (1) source rocks of organic-rich, fine-grained rocks such as shales; (2) opportunity for maturation so that hydrocarbons can be generated and expelled from the source rocks; (3) accessibility to porous reservoir rocks; (4) stratigraphic or structural traps such as faults, folds or pinching out of reservoir rocks; and (5) impermeable rocks over the trap that seal the reservoir and prevent the escape of hydrocarbons. The overthrust belt has all of these critical factors.

Although nine formations in the thrust belt contain possible source rocks, all existing oil discoveries probably were derived from Cretaceous marine shales. Overriding of these shales by the Absaroka thrust plate about 75 m.y. ago probably caused expulsion and entrapment of the hydrocarbons. Almost all of the oil and gas in the thrust belt has been trapped in overturned folds in the hanging wall of the Absaroka thrust plate.

Reservoir rocks in the thrust belt consist of limestone, dolomite or sandstone. Six reservoir formations in Mesozoic rocks include the Jurassic Nugget Sandstone and Twin Creek Limestone, Cretaceous Kelvin Limestone Formation, the Triassic Thaynes Limestone, Dinwoody and Woodside Formations. Paleozoic rocks contain five productive reservoirs including the Permian Phosphoria Limestone, the Pennsylvanian Weber Sandstone, Mississippian Madison Limestone and the Ordovician Big Horn Dolomite.

Most of the oil and gas produced from the thrust belt to date is attributed to (1) a large volume of organic-rich Cretaceous shales; (2) shales cut by the Absaroka thrust, leaving shales on footwall; (3) oil and gas generated and expelled from shales after overthrusting by the Absaroka plate; (4) migration upward of hydrocarbons into reservoir rocks in the hanging wall; and (5) the sealing of reservoir rocks by traps of impermeable shale, anhydrite or salt.

The main problem in locating reservoir rocks in the thrust belt is the complex geology caused by multiple thrusts and folds at depth. As a result it is generally impossible to ascertain the structure at depth on the basis of surface mapping alone. Exploration geologists and geophysicists are now able to look thousands of feet below the surface and map the subsurface by using advanced seismic reflection instruments equipped with computer-aided processing techniques.

North American Cordillera

The North American Cordillera is a major mountain belt that extends from the Aleutian Island Arc in southwestern Alaska into Mexico. The entire state of Idaho is encompassed by this huge belt. In mountain belts, the cover of sedimentary rocks is much thicker than over the central continental areas. Most of the central U.S. has a sedimentary cover 3,000 to 7,000 feet or less, whereas, in the mountain belts the layered sedimentary rock is generally 5 to 10 times as thick. Also in the mountain belts the sedimentary rock tends to be strongly folded and faulted; whereas, in the central continental areas it shows little deformation. The mountain belt is characterized by recumbent folds, isoclinal folds, reverse faults and large overthrust faults, all structures indicating strong compressional deformation.

The Cordilleran Mountain Belt was created by a series of orogenies. An orogeny is an episode of intense deformation that generally affects an area measured in hundreds of miles. During these orogenies, belt-shaped areas were strongly folded and faulted by reverse and thrust faults. The deeper rocks were subjected to high-grade regional metamorphism and converted to quartzites, schists and gneisses. These orogenies were also generally accompanied by the emplacement of batholiths and with associated volcanic activity.

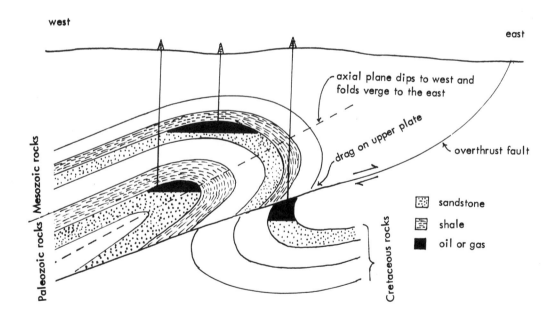

Generalized cross section of oil and gas traps in the overthrust belt.

MAJOR FAULT ZONES

Two major fracture zones are thought to cut across all or most of Idaho as well as extend into surrounding states. Yates (1968) proposed a large pre-Cretaceous northwest-trending transcurrent fault zone. Savage (1967), Kiilsgaard and Bennett (1984) and Oneill and Lopez (1985) proposed a major northeast-trending fault with movement from Middle Proterozoic to Holocene time.

Trans-Challis Northeast-Trending Fault System

Carl Savage was one of the first to point out the character and magnetitude of the northeast-trending fracture zone and describe how it nearly cuts across the entire state. Savage (1967) stated:

"One of the principal zones of disturbance affecting the Challis volcanics extends from eastern Gem County through the vicinity of the Middle Fork of the Salmon River and across Lemhi County, a distance of more than 150 miles. Near the Middle Fork, this zone is marked by a broken arch in the volcanic rocks. The granitic mass near the axis of the fold was intruded during the arching of the rocks. Beyond the limits of the Challis volcanics the zone is marked by fractures, many of which are filled by igneous rock."

The trans-Challis fault system was mapped by the U.S. Geological Survey from 1979 to 1983. This fault system was created by extension in Idaho north of the eastern Snake River Plain during the Eocene (Bennett, 1986). In Idaho the fault system is 170 miles long and 15 miles wide. Several eruptive centers of the Challis volcanics are situated on the fault system. Most Eocene volcanic rocks are believed to be related to extension (Bennett, 1986). Many major mineral deposits, particularly gold, occur along the fault system. These include deposits near Shoup, Leesburg, Custer and the Boise Basin. The Beaverhead, Lemhi and Lost River Ranges, which make up the Basin and Range mountains in east-central Idaho, are bounded on the south by the Snake River Plain and

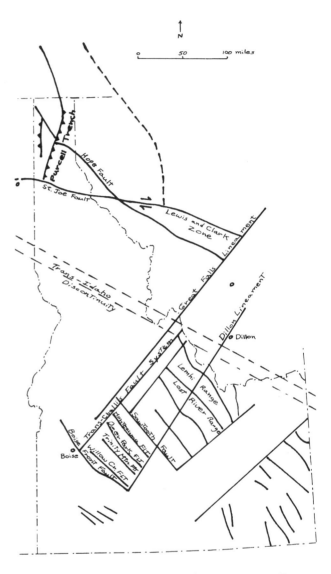

Major selected faults in Idaho (modified after Bennett, 1986).

terminate on the north at the trans-Challis fault system.

Many of the mineral deposits in the batholith along the zone are related to Tertiary intrusive rocks, particularly those in the Atlanta lobe. Many of the

A parallel fracture set near Lowman, possibly part of the trans-Challis fault system.

veins follow Tertiary dikes. Tertiary plutonic rocks have intruded along the faults leaving swarms of large dikes. The dikes give dates of approximately 29 million years. Mineralization in the form of veinlets in the Tertiary rocks is slightly younger than the dike rocks.

Highway 21 between Idaho City and Lowman follows this northeast-trending fault. Numerous roadcuts reveal excellent exposures of the deformation caused by this fault zone. Not only are rocks of the Cretaceous Idaho Batholith highly sheared, but the much more recent basaltic dikes that are commonly intruded along the shears are also fractured and sheared by recurrent movement along the faults. Even where shearing is not apparent, the granitic rock is granulated and bleached white, possibly by hot water moving through the fractured rock. As you follow highway 21 back and forth through the mountains, it becomes obvious that the width of this enormous fracture zone is more than 10 miles in certain places. The fracture system is characterized by other evidence such as stream valleys, ridges, dikes, mineralized veins and linear magnetic and gravity anomalies aligned parallel to it.

The Great Falls Lineament

The trans-Challis fault system is a southern extension of the Great Falls lineament. O'Neill and Lopez (1985) proposed the name "Great Falls Tectonic Zone" for this regional tectonic feature. They trace the zone from the Idaho Batholith northeastward, across east-central Idaho, through cratonic rocks of central Montana and southwestern Saskatchewan. They indicate that the zone is 937 miles long. They also suggest that fault movement was initiated along the zone as early as Middle Proterozoic time with recurrent movement to Quaternary time.

Dillon Lineament

Another major northeast-trending lineament parallels the trans-Challis fault system, but is located about 65 miles to the southeast. This lineament is also related to extension and was named the Dillon lineament (Bennett, 1986). The Dillon lineament passes through Chilley Buttes, the epicenter for the Borah Peak Earthquake on October 28, 1983, and passes northeasterly through the Lost River Range, the Lemhi Range and then the Beaverhead Range.

Trans-Idaho Discontinuity

Yates (1968) proposed that a major transverse zone, named the Trans-Idaho Discontinuity, trends south 50 degrees east from southeastern Washington through south-central Idaho to western Wyoming. This discontinuity serves as a boundary between contrasting geologic provinces of the Canadian Cordillera and the Cordillera to the south. A major change in the width of the Cordillera also occurs at the discontinuity. Yates plotted four different stratigraphic and petrologic elements on a map of the western United States to show how bends or separations in the elements define the zone of discontinuity.

The Trans-Idaho Discontinuity is buried beneath Tertiary basalts of the Columbia Plateau and is obscured by later intrusion of the Idaho Batholith. Yates (1968) determined the discontinuity was initiated before the Permian because Cambrian features are deformed more than those of the Permian.

Yates (1968) noted that although the four elements enter and leave the covered area of this discontinuity along northeast trends, all four can only be connected by a sharp bend in course or by a northwesterly-trending fault. He further indicated that the isopachs representing thicknesses of the Middle and Late Cambrian miogeosynclinal sedimentary rocks are the best evidence of the discontinuity.

Yates (1968) interprets the discontinuity as a strikeslip fault or zone of faults with a left-lateral

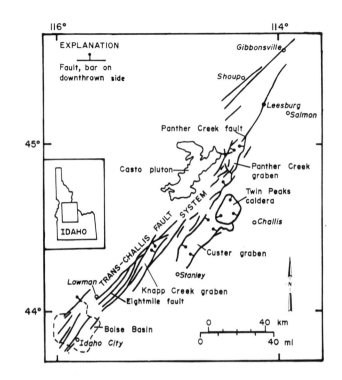

Major geologic features of the trans-Challis fault system in central Idaho. Modified by Bennett (1986) from Kiilsgaard et al. (1986).

movement between 200 and 400 miles long. The movement was progressive, beginning before the Permian and ending by Late Cretaceous. Because the discontinuity would be covered by basalts west of the batholith and engulfed by the batholith, it could only be physically observed east of the batholith. At this date, field work in this area has not revealed evidence of such a large structure.

BASIN AND RANGE PROVINCE

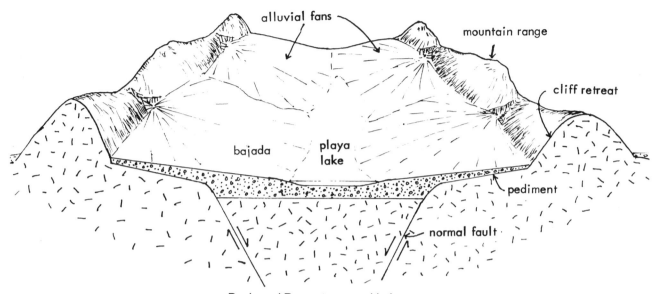

Basin and Range topographic features.

Basin and range structure is caused by uplifted block-faulted mountain ranges separated by valleys. The physiography of the States of Arizona, New Mexico, California, Utah, Nevada, Oregon and Idaho is dominated by these long, linear mountain ranges and intervening valleys. The valleys and mountains are separated by high-angle extension faults. The valley elevations range from 4,200 to 5,200 feet, whereas the mountain crests range from 6,500 to 11,800 feet.

The Basin and Range Province is characterized by mountain ranges separated by flat valley floors. Each range is bounded by large faults along which the range has moved upwards relative to the adjoining basins or valleys. In other words the topography is strongly controlled by faulting.

Bajada

Heavy rains promote rapid erosion along the steep mountain fronts. Loose rock and sediment are washed down narrow stream channels and are de-

An alluvial fan is shown where a mountain range adjoins a large valley or basin.

posited as alluvial fans at the base of the ranges. The water from the stream may flow to the valley bottom and form a playa lake. Playa lakes are shallow and temporary, lasting only several days after a storm. Continued deposition of alluvial fans at the base of a mountain may form a bajada. A bajada is a broad, gently-sloping depositional surface formed by the coalescing of alluvial fans. A bajada may have a gently-rolling surface caused by the merged cone-shaped fans.

Pediment

A gently-sloping, flat erosional surface at the foot of the mountain is called a pediment. This surface is generally covered with a veneer of gravel. The pediment surface develops uphill from a bajada as the mountain front retreats. As you might suspect, it is difficult to distinguish a pediment surface from a bajada surface because both have the same slope and gravel cover. However, the pediment is an erosional surface, whereas the bajada is a depositional surface and may be hundreds of feet thick.

Regional Geology

During the first half of Cenozoic time, the structure of the western United States was dominated by events connected to the subduction along the western side of the continent. Widespread silicic volcanic rocks were extruded from 65 to 17 million years ago.

During Late Cenozoic time, extension of the crust in what is now the basin and range province was associated with the extrusion of numerous flows of basaltic and rhyolitic lavas. Andesitic rocks were emplaced in the Cascade magmatic arc and tremendous volumes of basaltic lava were erupted in the Columbia Plateau area.

High Heat Flow and Thin Crust

Basalt flows are concentrated near the margins of the Basin and Range Province; however such flows are sparse within the province. A high heat flow and thin crust also characterize the Basin and Range Province. The crust in the province ranges from 12 to 22 miles thick, whereas the crust in the rest of the Rocky Mountains ranges from 22 to 31 miles thick.

Normal Faults

There is a complex system of normal faults in the Basin and Range that controls the topography. The mountains are 9 to 12 miles across and they alternate with alluviated valleys of approximately the same width. The ranges or linear mountain blocks are formed by vertical movements along faults on one or both sides of the block. Faults are also distributed throughout the ranges and valleys.

The mountains (horsts) and valleys (grabens) are bounded on both sides by normal faults. The mountain ranges tilt from a few degrees to more than 30 degrees. On the east side of the province, tilting tends to be towards the east; whereas on the west side, tilting tends to be towards the west.

Valley fill ranges from about 500 feet to more than 9,800 feet thick. The structural relief between bedrock in the valleys to the crest of the adjacent mountains ranges from 6,500 to 16,000 feet. Therefore, the faults have up to three miles of vertical displacement.

The ranges may be tilted by assymetric grabens, rotation of blocks along downward flattening faults (listric faults), and rotation of buoyant blocks.

Crustal Extension

The normal faults of the Basin and Range are indicative of extension normal to the fault lines. The amount of extension depends on whether the faults flatten at depth or continue at the dip of 60 degrees. If the faults do not flatten and continue down to where brittle rupture is replaced by laminar flow, the extension would only be about 10 percent. But if the faults flatten downward, extension might be as much as 50 percent of the present width. Tilting of Tertiary welded tuffs and lake bed sediments that were horizontal to subhorizontal before faulting require rotation tilting by the faulting. This can only be explained by flattening downward of major faults.

The crust of the southern Basin and Range terrane is about 15 miles thick; whereas, the crust of the Colorado Plateau is about 25 to 28 miles thick. This thin crust may be a function of the amount of extension in the Basin and Range region. Therefore, on this basis, approximately 40 percent of the present southern Basin and Range may represent extension. Using the same approach, 30 percent of the present width of the northern Basin and Range may represent extension.

Mesozoic and Cenozoic igneous activity has increased the crust of both the northern and southern Basin and Range. Mesozoic thrusting has also increased the thickness in the northern Basin and Range. So perhaps the extension should be higher.

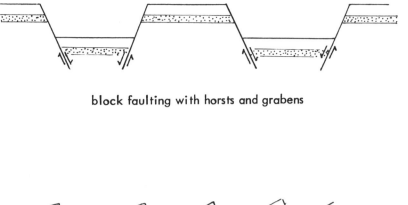

block faulting with horsts and grabens

listric fault

Blocks tilted along downward flattening listrict faults.

Two possible methods by which faults may cause the mountains and valleys of the Basin and Range province.

Further evidence of crustal extension includes high surface heat flow, voluminous magmatism, low velocity of seismic waves in the upper mantle, and high attenuation of seismic waves in the upper mantle. In the northern Basin and Range, the structures continue across the Snake River Plain but not the Idaho Batholith.

Age of the Basin and Range

The late Cenozoic structure that formed the Basin and Range Province began about 17 million years ago. About 10 million years ago the present topography was formed.

Origin of the Basin and Range

Many theories have been proposed to account for the origin of the Basin and Range structure. Some geologists have proposed that the extension of the province is caused by subduction of the East Pacific Rise beneath North America, whereas others have suggested that the Basin and Range structure results from a mantle plume. Neither one of these two theories is highly regarded. Another more accepted theory holds that extension is related to spreading caused by upwelling from the mantle behind an active subduction zone; this is also called back-arc spreading. Back-arc spreading seems to best explain the anomalous upper mantle, the high heat flow, the regional uplift and the extension. Also the volcanism of the Basin and Range and the extensive extrusion of the basalts of the Columbia River Basalt Group are further evidence of back-arc spreading.

As basins grow older, they grow larger and the deformational style becomes less complex because fewer faults control the deformation. And as the basins widen, there is also a broadening of the spacing between the faults that are effective in basement development. There appears to be an optimum spacing between large, steep, normal faults of 6 to 10 miles. Typical widths of major range or basin blocks average 19 miles.

East-Central Idaho Basin and Range

The Lost River, Lemhi and Beaverhead Mountain ranges in east-central Idaho make up the northern portion of the Basin and Range Province. These three northwest-trending ranges are separated by equally long intermontane valleys. These ranges have long been considered to be bounded on one or both sides by normal faults. However, Ruppel (1982) has proposed that these three ranges are flat-topped block uplifts. A thick veneer of sedimentary rock above these blocks was drape folded. These drape folds, consisting of sedimentary layers, were passively folded over the edges of rising blocks of crystalline basement rocks. The sedimentary layers were deformed by thrust folds before the upward movement of the blocks.

Vertical Uplift of Ranges Along Reverse Faults

The normal faults at the boundaries of the ranges are minor secondary faults caused by gravitational collapse of rock sliding down the flanks of ranges into the adjacent intermontane basins. Therefore the basin and range structural relief is caused by vertical uplift of the mountain blocks relative to the adjacent valleys. These uplifted blocks, which are cored by crystalline metamorphic rocks, were moved up along steeply-dipping reverse faults of Precambrian age. The material that slid off the blocks probably represents a large part of the valley fill.

Age of Block Faulting

Although the steep reverse faults that control the blocks of basement rock were first found in the Precambrian, the major uplift took place in Miocene time. The uplift was probably vertical because the blocks have flat tops. Gravitational sliding of rock off the ranges was contemporaneous with the uplift.

Relative Vertical Displacement

Gravity studies in the Lemhi Birch Creek Trench indicate a structural relief of about 13,100 feet from the crest of the Lemhi Range to the base of the Tertiary fill in the valley bottoms. Therefore, the relative vertical displacement along the steep reverse faults is about 13,100 feet.

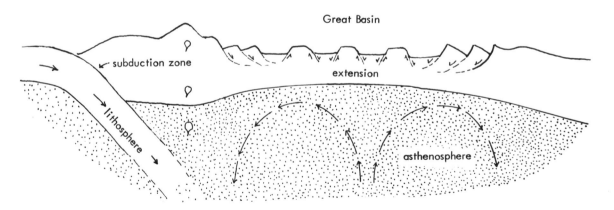

East-west cross section through the western United States including the Basin and Range. Back-arc spreading on the continental side of the arc occurs at the same time as the arc is underthrust by the Pacific Plate. Spreading or extension is caused by heat generated from friction along the subduction zone and upwelling of the mantle.

Part 4

GEOLOGIC
ATTRACTIONS

Natural arch formed by collapse of lava tube. Photo taken
on Cerro Grande flow near Atomic City.

THE GREAT RIFT SYSTEM

The Great Rift system consists of a series of north-northwest-trending fractures, which extend 50 miles from the northern margin of the eastern Snake River Plain, southward to the Snake River. In 1968, the Great Rift was designated as a national landmark. The system has been divided into four separate sets of fractures. These four sets from north to south include: (1) the Great Rift set which trends N. 35° W. and cuts across the Craters of the Moon National Monument; (2) the Open Crack rift set which trends N. 30° W. and apparently has not experienced extrusive activity; (3) the King's Bowl rift set which trends N. 10° W; and (4) the Wapi rift set which is believed to trend north-south, but is covered by the Wapi flow. The total rift system is 62 miles long and may be the longest known rift zone in the conterminous United States.

Recent Volcanism of the Eastern Snake River Plain

Very fresh basalt can be found at five different locations: the Cerro Grande and other flows near Big Southern Butte; Hells Half Acre lava field near Blackfoot; Wapi lava field; Craters of the Moon lava field; and King's Bowl lava field. The last three originate from the great rift system. The younger flows lack vegetation so that they clearly stand out on aerial photographs.

King's Bowl Rift Set

The King's Bowl Rift set includes a central fissure with sets of symmetrical tension cracks on both sides. It is about 6.5 miles long, 0.75 mile wide and trends N. 10° W. The main fissure is about 6 to 8 feet wide and is mostly filled with breccia and feeder dikes. In certain areas it is possible to descend into the rift several hundred feet. King's Bowl, which was created by one or more phreatic eruptions, is the most prominent feature on the rift. The ash blocks and rubble around the crater are evidence for an explosive erup-

tion. Well developed pipe-shaped vesicles are exposed in a massive flow on the east wall of King's Bowl. These vertically-aligned vesicles indicate the path of gas escaping from the base of the flow. The direction of the flow is indicated by the bend in the vesicles. These vesicles average about one-half inch in diameter.

Crystal Ice Cave

Crystal Ice Cave consists of natural and man-made passages through the King's Bowl Rift set. In this cave one can observe dikes, breccia zones and soil horizons between flows. The cave is named for the ice formation that developed from the freezing of surface water that seeped into the fissure. The King's Bowl lava field represents the last activity in the area and has been dated at 2,130 years.

Inferno Chasm Rift Zone

The Inferno Chasm Rift Zone consists of a number of volcanic features all aligned along a rift trending N. 4° W. These features from north to south include Wildhorse Corral, Cottrell's Blowout, Inferno Chasm, Grand View Crater and possibly Papadakis Perched Lava Pond. All of these features are summit vents for coalescing lava shields.

Wild Horse Corral

Wild Horse Corral is an irregular-shaped depression about 3,070 feet long and 1,850 feet wide. The long axis is subparallel to the rift set. A flat terrace, approximately 165 feet wide, encircles the canyon walls and the crater floor. Wild Horse Corral may have started as two eruptions and coalesced into a single large fissure vent.

Bear Trap lava tube is situated west of Wild Horse Corral. This tube trends west-northwest for a distance of 3 miles. The Bear Trap lava flow probably came from the Wild Horse Coral vent.

A lava lake may have filled Wild Horse Crater pe-

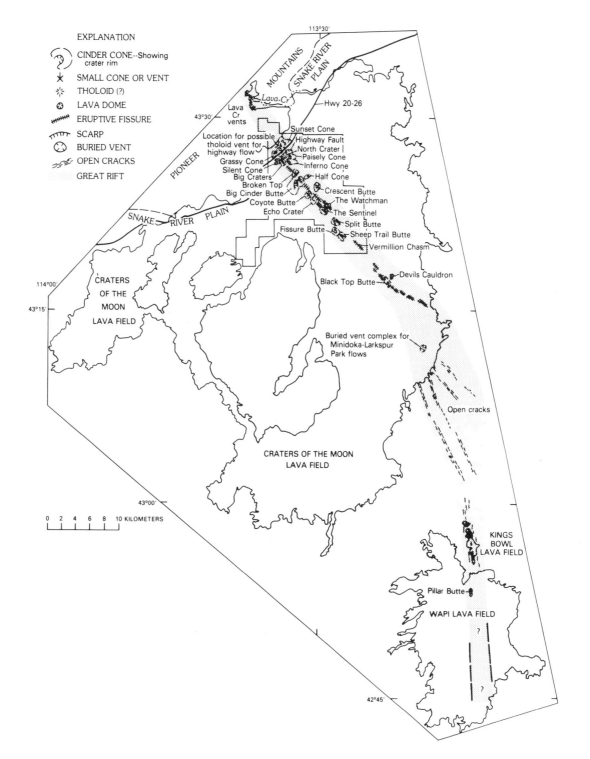

Map of the Great Rift showing geographic, volcanic and
structural features (after Kuntz and others, 1982).

— 111 —

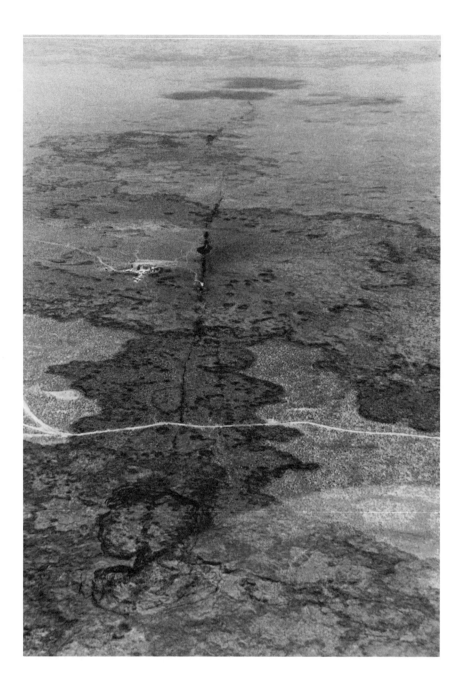

Looking northwest along the Great Rift. Note the dark lava
flows on both sides of the rift which were extruded through
this large crack in the earth's surface. *Courtesy of Lawrence L. Dee.*

riodically. After the lake was drained, the vent collapsed creating the present crater. The lava lake again filled and partially drained leaving a 165-foot-wide terrace around the crater walls.

Cottrell's Blowout

Cottrell's Blowout was started from a fissure vent along the Inferno Chasm Rift set. It is 1,950 feet long and 525 feet wide with a maximum depth of 140 feet. This feature was built by a succession of thin, gas-charged flows. Cottrell's Blowout formed as a result of a collapse to form a crater. The collapse was caused by the withdrawal of magma down the vent.

Inferno Chasm

This feature is an irregular circular vent 575 feet in diameter and 70 feet deep. It has a meandering lava channel that extends about 4,700 feet to the west.

Grandview Crater

Grandview Crater is a shallow depression that served as a vent for a lava shield near the southern end of the Inferno Chasm Rift Zone.

Papadakis Perched Lava Pond

Papadakis Perched Lava Pond is the remnant of a former lava lake on the west side of the Inferno Chasm Rift Zone. It is a fan-shaped, shallow depression, approximately 3,800 feet long and 2,600 feet wide. The lava lake was fed by a spatter cone 2,000 feet west of the rift zone.

Split Butte

Split Butte, situated about 6 miles southwest of King's Bowl, is believed to be a maar crater. The name refers to a split or gap in the upper tephra layers at the east side of the butte. Prevailing west winds have caused the tephra ring to be asymmetrical. The winds caused more pyroclastic debris to be piled on the east side. The split, which is located on the east side is believed to be caused by wind erosion.

The tephra ring had an explosive pyroclastic phase. When the first flow erupted, it passed through ground water. This caused glassy ash to form due to the cold water coming in contact with the hot lava. After the water saturated sediments were sealed, pyroclastic activity ceased and a lava lake formed. The lava lake partly overflowed and then crusted over. After withdrawal of liquid lava below the crust, the central portions of the crust collapsed.

King's Bowl

King's Bowl is a crater 280 feet long, 100 feet across and 100 feet deep. It stands directly over the main fracture of the Great Rift. Kings Bowl crater is the source of the 2,222 year old King's Bowl lava flow. Immediately west of the crater is an ejecta field where large blocks of rubble blown from the vent are strewn all over the ground. The size of blocks decreases with distance from the crater. A field of squeeze-up structures nearby was caused by lava being squeezed up through fractures. Some are hollow indicating that lava was drained out shortly after formation. The ash and ejecta fields were caused by ground water coming in contact with lava upwelling from the vent.

Wapi Lava Field

The Wapi Lava Field is located at the southern end of the Great Rift System. The Wapi lava field is a broad shield volcano covering approximately 260 square miles. The cone consists of many aa and pahoehoe flows which are replete with lava tubes and channels. The Wapi lava field formed about 2,270 years ago, almost simultaneously with the King's Bowl lava field.

Sand Butte

Sand Butte is located 23 miles southwest of Craters of the Moon National Monument. Sand Butte first formed as a tuff cone and was later filled by a lava lake. It is situated on a 3-mile-long, north-south-trending fissure. The fissure ranges from 200 to 410 feet wide. Sand Butte, like Split Butte, was formed by the phreatomagmatic interaction of ground water and basaltic magma. Pyroclastic flow was the primary method of deposition.

Spatter cones aligned along rift.

The basalt was erupted after the phreatic phase ended. This is demonstrated by tongues of spatter which overlie the tephra deposits. The final event was the partial filling of the crater by a lava lake. Finally the lava lake subsided to form a shallow crater.

Big Southern Butte

Big Southern Butte, Middle Butte and East Butte are three large buttes which can be seen rising above the eastern Snake River Plain while driving between Arco and Idaho Falls on Highway 20. All three buttes are situated east of the highway. Middle Butte appears to be an uplifted block of basalt. Although no rhyolite is exposed at the surface, the butte was probably formed by a silicic intrusion forcing the basalt upwards into the form of a butte. Big Southern Butte and East Butte are rhyolite domes. East Butte has been dated at 600,000 years, whereas Big Southern Butte has been dated at 300,000 years.

Big Southern Butte, because of its prominence and size, was an important landmark for the early settlers. It rises 2,500 feet above the plain and is approximately 2,500 feet across the base. Access to the top of the butte is available by a Bureau of Land Management service road. The butte was formed by two coalesced cumulo domes of rhyolite that uplifted a 350-foot section of basalt. The basalt section now covers most of the northern side of the butte. The dome on the southeastern side was developed by internal expansion (endogenous growth). Rupture of the crust at the surface caused breccia to form. Obsidian, pumice and flow-banded rhyolite are important components.

Once part of a continuous flow on the surface of the Snake River Plain, the large basalt block was pushed up and tilted by intrusion of the rhyolite. The basalt block now dips about 45 degrees to the northeast. This block consists of 15 to 20 individual flow units.

Lava Tubes

Lava tubes are important for the emplacement of lava on the Snake River Plain. Lava tubes are the subsurface passage ways that transport lava from a vent to the site of emplacement. They form only in the fluid pahoehoe flows. Tubes originate from open flow channels that become roofed over with crusted or congealed lava. However a tube may also form in a massive flow. Lava tubes exist as a single tunnel or as complex networks of horizontally-anastomosing tubes and may occupy up to five levels. Most tubes tend to be 6 to 13 feet across. Access to some tubes may be gained through collapsed sections. Features in tubes include glazed lava, lava stalactites and ice.

Great Rift Unrelated to Basin and Range

Although many of the volcanic rift zones in the central and eastern Snake River Plain may be extensions of northwest-trending, range-front faults, the Great Rift does not appear to be a continuation of such a fault.

CRATERS OF THE MOON NATIONAL MONUMENT

Craters of the Moon is one of several exceptional geological wonders in Idaho. It is a veritable outdoor museum of volcanic features. While traveling through the area between Carey and Arco, the land darkened by basalt flows may, at first glance, appear to be a monotonous landscape. However, once you enter Craters of the Moon National Monument and inspect the area at close range, you will find a great variety of facinating features. The Loop Road and the network of trails are designed to give you a self-guided tour of one of the great geological museums of the world. Features such as crater wall fragments, cinder cones, mini-shield volcanoes, lava bombs, spatter cones, lava tubes, tree molds and rifts are among the best examples, both in variety and accessibility you can observe anywhere in North America.

In 1962 the monument was enlarged to approximately 80 square miles covering a significant portion of the 575-square-mile Craters of the Moon lava field. The total field consists of 7 cubic miles of lava flows and pyroclastic deposits, including more than 60 lava flows and 25 cinder cones.

The triple twist tree which grew out of a fracture in the North Crater Flow has 1,350 growth rings.

Cast of tree limb in recent flow at Craters of the Moon
National Monument.

The Great Rift is a 53-mile-long and 1 to 5-mile-wide belt of shield volcanoes, cinder cones, lava flows and fissures. Three lava fields are aligned along the rift: Craters of the Moon, Wapi and Kings Bowl. Craters of the Moon lava field covers an area of 640 square miles and is the largest Holocene (less than 10,000 years old) lava field in the conterminous United States.

In the area of the Great Rift, the Snake River Plain is broad and flat. It has lava flows at the surface with thin lens-shaped beds of eolian sand and alluvial sand deposits about 3,300 to 6,800 feet thick. The rift zone is aligned at right angles to the long axis of the eastern Snake River Plain.

Ages of the Lava Fields

The lava flows in the Great Rift area were dated by charcoal from tree molds and beneath lava flows. This charcoal gave radio-carbon ages of 2,222 years old, plus or minus 60 years, for the King's Bowl lava

field. Palemagnetic measurements have also been used to correlate lava flows and determine the volcanic history in the area.

The flows were extruded during eight eruptive periods beginning about 15,000 years ago until the last eruption about 2100 years ago. Each eruptive period lasted several hundred years with a separation between eruptions of several hundred to several thousand years. Another eruptive period is likely within the next 1,000 years because the last eruption occurred about 2,100 years ago.

As more and more flows are dated in the Snake River Plain, it is possible to relate the radiometric date to the surface character of a flow. For example, as a flow ages, the surface becomes lighter, more deeply weathered, more oxidized, more dust covered and more vegetated.

Eruptions Along the Great Rift

The Great Rift is the source of volcanism that formed the Craters of the Moon, King's Bowl and Wapi lava fields. Along the 1 to 5-mile-wide rift you

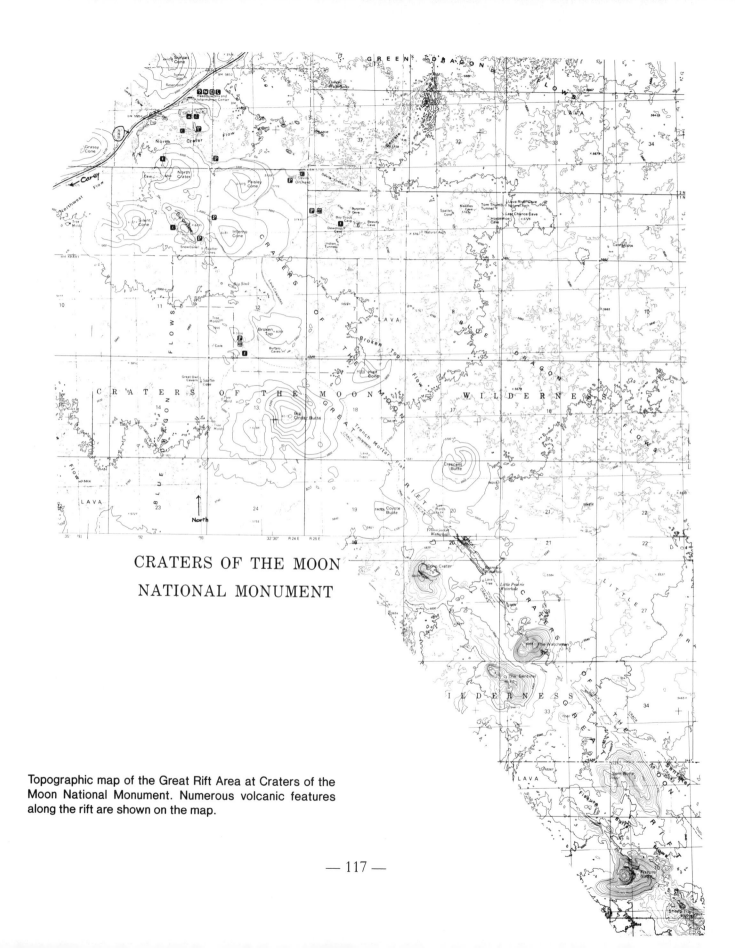

CRATERS OF THE MOON
NATIONAL MONUMENT

Topographic map of the Great Rift Area at Craters of the
Moon National Monument. Numerous volcanic features
along the rift are shown on the map.

Looking at crestal fracture in pressure ridge. Note small
lava "squeeze up" that was extruded through the crack.

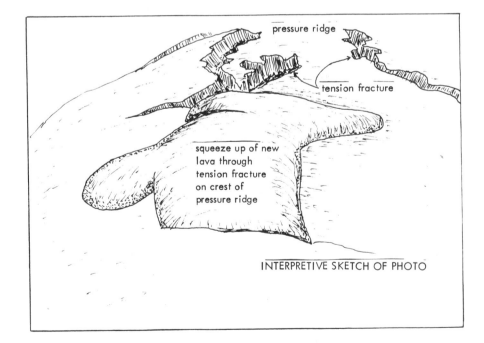

pressure ridge

tension fracture

squeeze up of new
lava through
tension fracture
on crest of
pressure ridge

INTERPRETIVE SKETCH OF PHOTO

will find a belt of cinder cones and eruptive fissures. The magma, which formed the flows and other features you now see at the surface, originated from chambers of magma at depths of 40 to 90 miles. This magma, being less dense than the surrounding rock, rose along the deep fracture system of the Great Rift.

Excellent examples of eruptive fissures exist in craters such as the Trench Mortar Flat area between Big Cinder Butte and the Watchman cinder cones. The first eruptions along the fissures were characterized by fountains of lava, commonly referred to as "curtains of fire." These curtains of fire were active along a fissure for a distance of up to two miles. In addition to the large flows that were extruded from the fissures, ridges and spatter ramparts were built along the fissure. In the final stage of activity along the fissure, spatter and cinder cones were formed.

Lava Flows

As each new lava flow was extruded at Craters of the Moon, it followed the lowest elevation, just as water would. Consequently, a number of high areas or knolls called "kipukas" are completely surrounded by lava flows. Several kipukas can be observed at Craters of the Moon. Geologists classify the fine-grained, black rock at the monument as basalt. Basalt, the most abundant igneous rock, consists of microscopic mineral grains (mostly plagioclase feldspar), volcanic glass and gas vesicles (air bubbles). Basaltic lava is erupted at temperatures of about 1800 degrees fahrenheit and flows over the ground surface as large tongues of molten rock.

At Craters of the Moon, you can see excellent examples of the three types of basaltic lavas: blocky, aa and pahoehoe. Blocky flows consist of a surface of smooth-faced blocks. Aa flows are blocky or platy but the fragments are covered with spines and have a very jagged surface. Pahoehoe flows are characterized by thin sheets with low flow fronts. At the surface they are ropy, smooth or filamented. The upper surface of the fresh pahoehoe is made of a dense to vesicular glass. This surface is commonly a greenish blue or an irridescent blue. The Blue Dragon flows, which make up most of the surface east of the Great

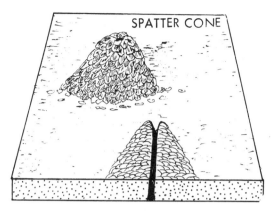

Block diagram of a spatter cone.

Rift, have an unusual irridescent-blue color. In a single flow, one lava type can change to another; for example, pahoehoe lava can change into aa lava when it cools, becomes more viscous and loses gas.

Most of the flows in the Craters of the Moon consist of pahoehoe-type lava and were fed through a system of lava tubes. In many locations, the roofs of lava tubes have collapsed, leaving a mass of broken lava and rubble on the floor of the tube. Many such collapsed areas in the Broken Top and Blue Dragon flows provide "skylights" and entrances to lava tunnels for the numerous visitors to the monument.

The older flows in Craters of the Moon lava field can be determined by the nature of the surface. Younger flows have unweathered glassy crusts and a surface that is typically blue. Older lavas tend to be covered by wind-blown deposits and their surface is light colored from weathering and is strongly oxidized. A few of the flows in the craters area have an aa type surface. Aa flows have a rough, jagged surface.

Cinder Cones

Numerous cinder cones exist throughout the Snake River Plain. However there are more than 25 exceptionally well developed cinder cones aligned along a 17-mile-long, northwest-southeast-trending segment of the Great Rift. Cinders are very vesicular

Spatter cones (in foreground) and cinder cone (in background).

clots of lava blown out of a vent in the earth's surface. Cinder cones are developed by the accumulation of cinder and ash in cone-shaped hills. Many cinder cones at the monument are a composite of two or more cones with overlapping craters and flanks. These cones consist of agglutinated and nonagglutinated ash layers typically interlayered with a few thin lava flows. Some cones, such as the Inferno Cone and the Paisley Cone are assymmetric or elongate reflecting the wind direction at the time of the eruption. As a general rule, winds from the west caused more downwind accumulation of cinders on the east sides of cones. Many cinder cones have been breached on one or more flanks as a result of erosion by lava.

Volcanic Bombs and Spatter Cones

Volcanic bombs are blown from volcanic vents as clots of fluid lava. As they move through the air while still hot and plastic, they deform into aerodynamically-shaped projectiles of lava. Spatter cones are relatively small cones formed by blobs of molten rock hurled out of volcanic vents. The hot, plastic blobs weld to the outer surface of the cone and quickly harden into rock.

SAWTOOTH PRIMITIVE AREA

The Sawtooth Primitive Area covers about 314 square miles and includes parts of the Challis, Sawtooth and Boise National Forests. The area is accessible by many roads and trails. The trails are normally usable by foot from July to October, enabling hikers to reach the high country. Although the trail system is excellent, travel on foot away from trails is extremely difficult because of the rugged terrain.

The Sawtooth Range was named because of its jagged sawtooth profile along the skyline. Relief in the area ranges from an elevation of 5,000 feet where the South Fork of the Payette River leaves the area to 10,830 feet at Thompson Peak — the highest peak in the range.

In addition to the magnificent scenic beauty of the area, a large number of geologic features can be observed. The present land forms have been produced primarily by a combination of faulting, jointing and glacial ice. Most of the area making up the Sawtooth Mountains is underlain by rocks of the granitic Idaho Batholith and the younger Sawtooth Batholith.

Major Rock Types

The Thompson Creek Formation is the oldest rock in the area and may be of Precambrian age. It consists of well-foliated mica schist interlayered with metamorphosed carbonate rocks. Where the carbonate rocks have intrusive contracts with the granitic rocks, skarn minerals may be well developed. For example, exposures of garnet-epidote skarn may be observed south of Goat Creek.

Light gray granitic rocks of the Idaho Batholith underlie about one-half of the Sawtooth Mountains. The batholith is undoubtedly the single most abundant rock in Idaho, covering approximately 20,000 square miles. The batholith contains varying amounts of quartz, orthoclase, plagioclase and biotite, and has been dated at 108 million years.

The Sawtooth Batholith is a distinctive pink granite which contrasts sharply with the gray granitic rocks of the Idaho Batholith. The color is caused by the presence of perthitic orthoclase. The Sawtooth Batholith is younger than the Idaho Batholith. Dikes of the pink granite intrude the gray granite and also xenoliths of the older gray granite are found in the younger pink granite.

Dark Tertiary dikes, generally northeast-trending, penetrate the older granitic rocks. They tend to occur in large swarms several miles long and a mile wide.

Faults

The Sawtooth Range is an uplifted fault block bounded by two subparallel to parallel normal faults. On the west side of the range is the Montezuma Fault. On the eastern front of the Sawtooth Range, a major fault is indicated by evidence such as linearity of the eastern front of the range, truncated spurs and the aeromagnetic pattern. However there is little physical evidence of the fault, such as broken or brecciated rock, because of the alluvial cover.

Joints

The granitic rock of the Sawtooth Range is thoroughly jointed. The joints dip steeply and are closely spaced. The two most common sets strike northeast and northwest. The jagged ridges of the range were developed because the joints made the rock susceptible to erosion by frost wedging.

Beryl (Aquamarine Deposits)

Beryl deposits have been known in the Sawtooth Mountains for many years. Beryl mineralization is generally confined to the Sawtooth Batholith or near its periphery. Areas of good beryl mineralization include the valleys of upper Pinchot Creek, upper Fall Creek, Benedict Creek, Spangle Lakes, Ardeth Lakes, Edna Lake and Toxaway Lake. Aquamarine occurs as scattered single grains, as northeast-trending zones of clustered grains and as sunbursts on joint

Looking west at Stanley Basin, Red Fish Lake and the Sawtooth Mountains in the background. The tree-covered lower hills surrounding the lake are underlain by glacial debris.

surfaces. High-angle pegmatite dikes contain crystals of aquamarine in vugs or cavities. Aquamarine in pegmatites is associated only with quartz and orthoclase and is clear of inclusions. Aquamarine also occurs as spherical concretions of aquamarine, albite and quartz.

Geomorphology

The Sawtooth Range is a high, uplifted fault block, commonly called a horst. This range is bounded on the east by the Stanley Basin which is a down-dropped block or graben. The basin is covered by a thin veneer of alluvium. The Montezuma Fault bounds at least part of the western boundary of this northwest-trending range.

The Sawtooth Range is comprised of a spectacular variety of features produced by mountain glaciation. Included are the sharp sawtooth-shaped peaks, arêtes and matterhorns and the intervening cirques and glacial valleys. Many of the cirques are occupied by cirque lakes. Most of the present land forms were caused by glacial ice rather than running water or some other erosional agent. So much bare rock is exposed that geologic mapping is easily accomplished.

The Stanley Basin is covered by a variety of glacial moraines. Many lakes were impounded by lateral and terminal moraines. Two major advances of glaciation are thought to have occurred during the Late Pleistocene. The topography is continuously modified by such processes as frost wedging, rock falls, talus and soil creep, rock-glacier flow and stream erosion.

Glaciation

The spectacular mountain forms were created by glaciation during Pleistocene time. Almost all features of mountain glaciation, both erosional and depositional, can readily be observed in the area. Many large, glaciated valleys with their characteristic U-shaped profile dominate the area. Along these valleys, many hanging valleys or hanging tributaries may be observed. Cirque basins, matterhorn peaks, arêtes and cols are examples of well-developed glacial features caused by ice at the heads of valleys. Other evidence of moving ice includes polished and striated rock outcrops.

Origin of Lakes

Most of the 500 plus lakes in the area were caused by glacial ice. In the high country, the lakes occupy shallow basins carved in the rocks; whereas, at lower elevations lakes tend to be contained by lateral and terminal moraines. Examples of such impounded lakes include Alturas, Pettit, Yellow Belly, Stanley and Redfish Lakes.

Glacial Deposits

Glacial Deposits consist of unsorted clay, sand, cobbles and boulders left by melting glaciers. This material was removed from the mountains and transported to the site of deposition by glaciers.

Along the eastern front of the Sawtooth Mountains is a series of elongated ridges standing approximately 1,500 feet above the Stanley Basin. These ridges may be distinguished from the bare, jagged Sawtooth Mountains in several ways. They are rounded and covered by a thick stand of lodgepole pine. Redfish Lake is contained by lateral moraines on the sides and a terminal moraine at the end near the lodge.

CANYON FILLING LAVAS

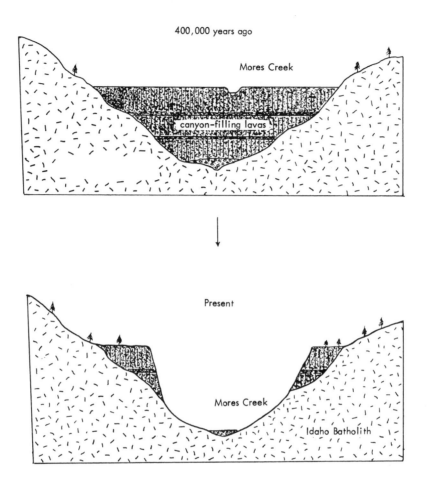

Cross section across Mores Creek showing canyon-filling lavas. Upper diagram shows how the canyon looked 400,000 years ago. The lower diagram shows the same canyon at the present time. The erosion caused by the creek left only remnant wedges of basalt on some of the canyon walls.

Erosional remnants of basalt on canyon walls northeast of Boise. The bench formed by the upper surface of the basalt wedge represents the highest level reached by basalt in the canyon.

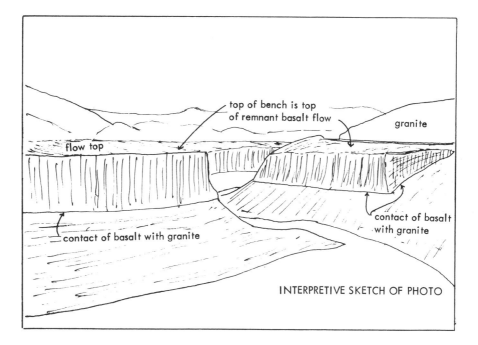

Canyon Filling Lavas Near Boise

Basalt terraces may be seen along Mores Creek and the South Fork of the Boise River. These basalt terraces are found along the canyon walls carved into the granitic Idaho Batholith. At least five successive flows have periodically filled the Boise River drainage and cut more deeply into the canyon than did the previous flows. Therefore terraces of the older flows are higher on the canyon walls than the younger flows.

The basalt of Mores Creek forms terraces along the canyon wall of Mores Creek which is a tributary to the Boise River. The basalt of Mores Creek has been dated to be 400,000 years old.

The Boise River drainage was established in the granitic batholith rocks more than four million years ago. River gravels, developed on the stream bed before the volcanic activity, were later covered by the basalt of Mores Creek. These early gravels can now be seen in several outcrops along highway 21 approximately midway between Boise and Idaho City. Although Mores Creek was temporarily raised to the surface of the canyon filling lavas, the creek has not only cut back down through the lavas, but now occupies a level some 15 to 20 feet below the original level just before the emplacement of lava.

BRUNEAU SAND DUNES

When wind looses its velocity and its ability to transport the sand it has carried from the surface, it deposits it on the ground. Sand deposits tend to assume recognizable shapes. Wind forms sand grains into mounds and ridges called dunes, ranging from a few feet to hundreds of feet in height. Some dunes migrate slowly in the direction of the wind. A sand dune acts as a barrier to the wind by creating a wind shadow. This disruption of the flow of air may cause the continued deposition of sànd. A cross section or profile of a dune in the direction of blowing wind shows a gentle slope facing the wind and a steep slope to the leeward. A wind shadow exists in front of the leeward slope which causes the wind velocity to decrease. The wind blows the sand grains up the gentle slope and deposits them on the steep leeward slope.

Bruneau Sand Dunes

The Bruneau Sand Dunes State Park, established in 1970, is located about 8 miles east-northeast of Bruneau and about 18 miles south of Mountain Home. Camping facilities are available and a lake on the north side of the large sand dune may be used for boating and fishing.

Although there are many small dunes in the area, two large, light-gray overlapping sand dunes cover approximately 600 acres. These two imposing dunes are striking, particularly because they dwarf most of the nearby land features. The westernmost dune is reported to be the largest single sand dune in North America, standing about 470 feet above the level of the lake.

The existence of these dunes is attributed to the constant wind blowing sand in from the southwest. As the wind loses velocity over the basin, sand is deposited on the dunes. Sand has been collecting in the basin for more than 30,000 years.

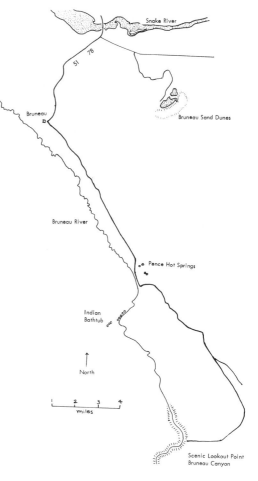

Location map showing access routes to the Bruneau Sand Dunes and the lookout point to the scenic Bruneau Canyon.

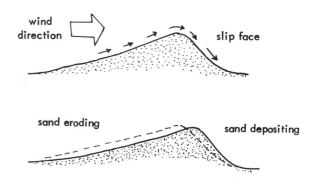

Looking at Bruneau Sand Dunes.

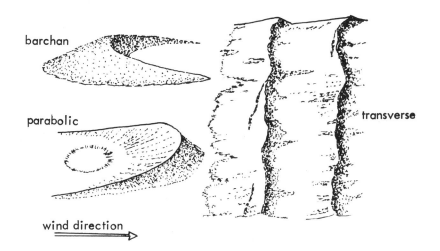

barchan

parabolic

transverse

wind direction

Different types of sand dunes are shown in the above illustrations. Sand dunes form with a gentle upwind slope and
a steeper slip face downwind. Movement of sand causes
the dunes to move slowly downwind.

HOT SPRINGS IN IDAHO

Robert E. DeTar, Geologist

Hot water bubbling out of the ground has been known about and used in Idaho for hundreds, probably thousands of years. Concentrations of artifacts at and petroglyphs on rocks near hot springs are evidence that the areas were known about and used by Indians. More than 200 hot or warm (thermal) springs occur in Idaho and are distributed throughout several geologic provinces. In order for a spring to be classified as thermal it must be at least 68°F (20°C). Some of Idaho's hot springs reach temperatures as high as 200°F (94°C). Even higher temperatures have been encountered in deep wells.

Origin of Hot Springs

Hot springs develop when rain and melted snow waters infiltrate into the ground. This ground water then sinks deep into the earth and is warmed by the heat contained in the earth's interior. Because hot water is less dense it is pushed back to the surface by the continued sinking of heavier, cold water. Annual replenishment to the system by cold meteoric water creates a continuous system which is called hydrothermal convection. Hot springs develop when the upwelling hot water rises along faults or other fractures in the earth's crust and flows out onto the surface.

Sources of Heat

Why do some areas of the earth have hot springs and others do not? For example, there are few if any hot springs identified in Idaho north of Idaho County. While there is heat in the earth beneath any spot on the surface, this heat is concentrated closer to the surface in some areas. One means of near surface concentration is a shallow magma chamber within the earth's crust such as would exist beneath a volcano. Yellowstone National Park is centered on such a volcano. We know from measuring the way in which the vibrations of distant earthquakes pass through the Yellowstone area that there is a body of molten rock (magma chamber) at a depth of about 3 to 6 miles. The resulting hydrothermal systems are world famous.

Another area where the heat of the earth can be concentrated near enough to the surface to generate hydrothermal systems is where the crust of the earth is stretched and thinner than normal. Such a condition exists over southern Idaho in the Snake River Plain and Great Basin areas. A number of large warm water systems occur in this region of Idaho including the Boise, Twin Falls, Bruneau-Grandview, Raft River and Mountain Home systems.

Hot to warm springs also occur within the rocks of the Idaho Batholith. The heat in the batholith is believed to result from the decay of radioactive elements contained in many of the minerals which commonly occur in the granitic rocks.

Relationship of Faults to Hot Springs

Now that we have our sources of heat, we need a path for getting the hot water to the surface. In an active volcanic area such as Yellowstone, faulting is created by upward pressure exerted by rising magma, by explosive eruptions, and by deflation of a depleted magma chamber after an eruption. The latter mechanism is the most common and forms what is called a ring fracture system which approximates the outline of the magma chamber. Yellowstone has the added advantage of being astride a zone of active north-south to northwest-trending faults known as the Intermountain Seismic Belt. The broken rocks within the fault zones in Yellowstone act as an excellent conduit for circulating ground-water.

The Snake River Plain and Great Basin area of southern Idaho are being stretched. This is a very advantageous geologic situation for the formation of hydrothermal systems because this not only creates a thin crust to bring heat closer to the surface but it also

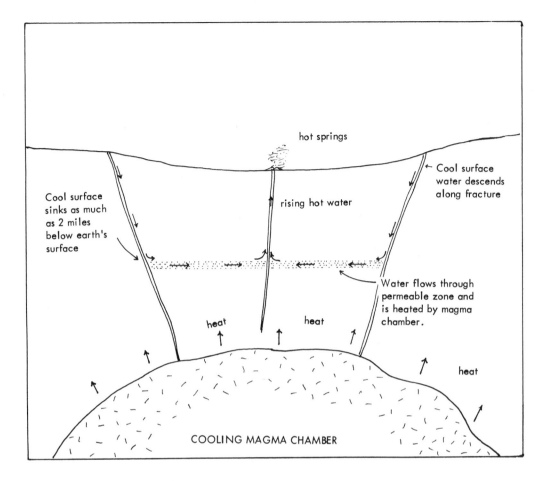

Illustration shows thermal system in which surface water circulates to great depth where it is heated then returned to the surface as hot springs.

develops numerous normal faults and keeps them relatively open so that water can easily circulate through them.

Hot springs in the batholith are also the result of deep circulation of ground water in fault zones. It appears from recent geologic mapping that some of the normal faults of the Great Basin continue into the batholith. The batholith has also been subjected to other episodes of faulting.

Mineral Deposits

An interesting feature of hot springs is their associated mineral deposits. Yellowstone, for example, contains several types of hot springs deposits, some of which have resulted in spectacular rock formations.

Minerals are more readily dissolved in hot water. The type of minerals deposited depends on the temperature of the water and the type of rocks it passes through on its way to the surface. Mammoth Hot Springs in Yellowstone is a large hot spring deposit of calcium carbonate (calcite). Table Rock near Boise is a hot spring deposit composed of silica, mostly in the form of chalcedony. At Mammoth Hot Springs the hot water is rising along faults in Paleozoic-age limestone which is composed almost entirely of calcium carbonate. The relationship here is evident. Hot water dissolves the calcium carbonate at depth, transports it to the surface and then redeposits it at the surface as the water cools and loses its ability to keep the minerals in solution. At Table Rock, near Boise, the hot water passes through mostly volcanic rocks and some sedimentary rocks that have been derived from the granitic rocks of the Idaho Batholith. These types of rocks generally contain about 60 to 70% silica. Once again the relationship is evident. Hot water dissolves the silica out of the rocks and redeposits it near the surface as the water cools and the silica drops out of solution.

Boise Geothermal System

To put our concepts to work and reinforce them let's take a look at an individual system. The Boise system is one of the most studied within Idaho and is generally representative of systems in the southern part of the state. This system is located on the northern margin of the western Snake River Plain graben. The heat source for this area of Idaho is the stretched and relatively thin crust. For reasons that are not well understood the heat in the western Snake River Plain is concentrated along the margins of the Plain. This is fortunate because the faults along which the plain is downdropped also occur along the margin. The main Boise Front fault can be readily seen as a distinct topographic break between the plain and mountains along the north edge of Boise. Comparison of rocks in the foothills of the Boise Front with those encountered in wells drilled in the plain has further confirmed the existence of offset along this fault and in fact has made possible the identification of a series of faults. The water of the Boise system circulates to depth along this series of faults, is heated, and is driven back to the surface by hydrothermal convection. In Boise, springs no longer flow at the surface because wells drilled into the fault zone to tap the hot water have intercepted and withdrawn the hot water rapidly enough that it no longer reaches the surface.

There is an interesting feature of the Boise system that may explain why it and other systems along the margin of the plain are located where they are. Recent geologic mapping has identified a major northeast-trending fracture system within the Idaho Batholith which appears to extend through the Boise geothermal area. This fracture system provides an excellent channel for the ample meteoric water which falls as rain and snow on the Boise Front to infiltrate into the ground and finally into the high temperature zones along the margin of the Snake River Plain. Further work may make it possible to correlate other fracture systems in the batholith to hot springs along the northern margin of the Snake River Plain and thus explain why hot springs do not occur at regularly-spaced intervals.

Geothermal Energy

In recent years hot spring systems, also known as geothermal systems, have become an important source of alternative energy. In a few rare locations in the world, water in the ground is hot enough to exist as steam. In these instances, wells have been drilled into the heart of the steam zone and the steam is used to operate a steam turbine to generate electricity. Such systems exist at Yellowstone but will not be developed because they are within a National Park. The more common type of geothermal system is the hot water type such as occurs in southern Idaho. Electricity has been experimentally generated in the Raft River area south of Malta but further research and development are needed before commercial operations can begin. Boise boasts the oldest geothermal heating system in the United States. In operation since 1890, the system now serves about 400 homes and is tied in to eight major downtown buildings. Other applications in southern Idaho include the use of warm water for fish farming and greenhouse heating.

BORAH PEAK EARTHQUAKE

Steven W. Moore, Geologist
and R. David Hovland, Geologist

East-central Idaho awoke to a crisp autumn morning on Friday, October 28, 1983. Suddenly, the peaceful mountain morning was shattered as powerful forces within the earth's crust were unleashed. Normal morning activities were interrupted as window panes vibrated and alarmed people ran out of their houses. These were the first-hand effects of a major earthquake.

The authors were in the Salmon area returning from a geologic project when the earthquake struck. After the initial radio reports of the location of the earthquake, we traveled to the Mackay-Challis area and were among the first geologists to witness firsthand the effects of the earthquake.

The earthquake occurred at 8:06 a.m. (MDT) with an epicenter located in a sparsely populated mountainous area between the small rural communities of Challis and Mackay. Challis and Mackay, Idaho lie in the northwest-trending valley on the west side of the of Lost River Range. Updated calculations indicate that the Borah Peak earthquake registered a Richter magnitude of 7.3. The epicenter was located about 19 miles northwest of Mackay, at the south margin of the Thousand Springs Valley just west of 12,662-foot Borah Peak, at latitude 44.05 degrees N., longitude 113.88 degrees W. The hypocenter, or depth in the crust at which the fault rupture began, was about 9 miles. The earthquake caused two deaths in Challis and an estimated $15 million damage in the affected region.

Geologic Setting

The earthquake occurred along a fault zone on the southwestern flank of the Lost River Range. The core of the Lost River Range is composed mostly of folded and thrust-faulted Ordovician through Pennsylvanian sedimentary rocks including limestone, dolomite, quartzite, siltstone, and sandstone. The northern end and east-central parts of the Lost River Range and the Salmon River, Boulder, and White Knob Mountains are dominated by the Eocene Challis Volcanics. The Challis Volcanics include lavas, pyroclastic rocks, and volcaniclastic sedimentary rocks. The composition of the Challis Volcanics ranges from rhyodacite to magnesium-rich basalt.

The Lost River Range is one of several northwest-trending mountain ranges in east-central Idaho. The topography is typical of the Basin and Range Province. Ranges are separated by broad sediment-filled valleys, and have range-front faults on their southwest flanks. This earthquake was the largest in the western United States since the 7.1-magnitude Hebgen Lake, Montana earthquake of 1959, and the largest in Idaho since the 6.1-magnitude Pocatello Valley earthquake on March 27, 1975.

East-central Idaho is within the Intermountain seismic belt, a zone of concentrated seismic activity that extends northward from Arizona through northwestern Montana. The October 28, 1983 earthquake is associated with a seismic zone that extends westward from the Yellowstone-Hebgen Lake area into central Idaho north of the Snake River Plain.

Ground Shaking

Primary effects of the Borah Peak earthquake included ground shaking and surface rupture directly related to fault movement along the western flank of the Lost River Range. Ground shaking was most intense near the epicenter between Challis and Mackay, but the earthquake was also felt over most of the northwestern United States and in parts of Canada. The initial shock was followed by numerous aftershocks. In the 10 months following the main earthquake, there were at least 20 aftershocks with a magnitude of 4.0 or greater.

Aerial view looking north at fault scarps along western edge of the Lost River Range, south of Dickey Peak.

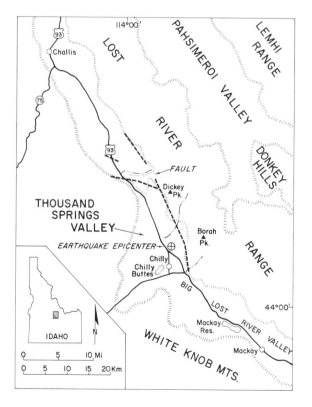

Secondary effects produced as a consequence of the earthquake included seismically induced landslides, ground cracking, and modification of the hydrologic system. Damage to roads, buildings, and other structures occurred in the area between Mackay and Challis.

Ground Rupture Produced by Fault Displacement

Fault displacement that produced this intense earthquake was expressed in spectacular surface ground rupture along a northwest-trending, 22-mile-long zone on the western flank of the Lost River Range. A west-northwest-trending section of faulting that branches off of the main surface fault trace

Location map of area affected by Borah Peak earthquake. Dashed line is new surface faulting produced by earthquake.

Looking east at gravel road disrupted by the Borah Peak earthquake. Several subvertical faults offset the road.

west of Dickey Peak gives the surface faulting pattern a Y-shape. Much of the zone of surface rupture follows the Holocene and upper Pleistocene fault scarps of the Lost River fault. Fault scarps, the most common features along the zone of surface faulting, look like small steps or cliffs. Fault scarps are produced when adjacent blocks of the earth's crust move relative to each other and are displaced along a fault plane.

Detailed study of the surface faulting and focal mechanisms reveals that the dominant fault movement associated with the Borah Peak earthquake was dip slip, or vertical. That is, the Lost River Range was uplifted vertically along the fault relative to the adjacent valley. Maximum throw (vertical displacement) measured along the west flank of Borah Peak is about 9 feet. A more minor component of left-slip is also evident, indicating that that the Lost River Range block also moved laterally northward, relative to the valley to the west, as well as upward. The high

relief and linear northward-trending mountain ranges in this region and elsewhere in the Basin and Range Province have been produced by similar repeated fault movements over geologic time.

The surface fault trace is complex and comprised of multiple, gently curved, subparallel fault scarps extending along a trend of approximately N15°W to N25°W. The zone of extensive ground rupture is more than 300 feet wide in some locations. The complex nature the fault rupture can be clearly observed in the area immediately north of Birch Springs. Along this section of the mountain front, two to four en echelon (subparallel) scarps are visible. The maximum scarp height north of Birch Springs is as much as 16 feet. The newly created fault scarps dip from 70 degrees to near vertical and face westward toward the valley. However, within a few days after the earthquake, many fault scarps, particularly those in well-sorted stream sand and gravel deposits, were rapidly degraded to angle of repose dips of about 30 degrees. At the base of the mountain-front slope, a small down-dropped block or graben approximately 75 to 100 feet also formed.

Although most of the fault scarps face west representing the actual fault movement, other minor faults referred to as antithetic faults, faults whose scarps face the opposite direction of the main scarp, also occur as a result of the tensional stresses in the crust. In the case of minor grabens along the fault zone, antithetic faults form the western edges of the grabens and their scarps face the east, opposing the main fault scarps.

Displacement along the multiple scarps generally occurred in poorly sorted, unconsolidated, Quaternary gravels and other alluvial materials. Closely spaced, parallel tensional cracks are abundant over much of the 200-to 300-foot fault zone north of Birch Springs and other areas. The complexity of the fault zone and the variability of fault-scarp morphology is to a great degree a function of the material and the amount of water saturation.

Landslides Induced by Seismic Shaking

Landslides, rock falls, rock slides, and other ground failures were induced in a area of approximately 1600 square miles surrounding the epicenter as an immediate result of the intense seismic shaking. The steep and rugged terrain of the Lost River Range, and of the adjacent Salmon River, Boulder, and White Knob Mountains significantly contributed to the susceptibility to landsliding as a result of earthquake shaking in the region. Earthquake-triggered slope failures occurred in a variety of materials including colluvium, glacial deposits, talus slopes, and in fractured bedrock areas.

The majority of the landslides were rock falls or rock slides. Particularly susceptible to rock falls and rock slides were steep and rocky slopes composed of Challis Volcanics. Open joints and fractures, typical of weathered Challis Volcanics, produced inherent slope instability in this unit allowing large blocks to be easily loosened with seismic shaking.

Seventy-five miles north of the epicenter along steep roadcuts and cliffs on Highway 93 near Salm-

on, the road was severely obstructed by rock falls and rock slides originating in outcrops of Challis Volcanics. Dozens of boulders of Challis Volcanics, some as large as 10 feet in diameter, tumbled down steep slopes of Challis damaging several houses. Some boulders rolled as much as 200 feet out into the valley.

Debris flows and Liquefaction in Water-Saturated Sediment

Other types of ground failures were related to the level of water saturation of sediment. At Birch Springs, seismic shaking produced ground failure and downslope movement of water-saturated colluvium that resulted in a large rotational slump-debris flow. Some of the most spectacular effects occurred at the southern end of Thousand Springs Valley near Chilly Buttes where severe liquefaction occurred in Holocene valley fill sediment. Liquefaction occurs when intense seismic shaking causes complete loss of cohesion of sediment by the transferral of load from the sediment particles to the pore fluid. More than 40 sediment boils (turbid upflows of water, silt, and sand) were produced adjacent to Chilly Buttes when seismic shaking released large quantities of ground water into alluvium. After "boiling" of the sediment ceased, a series of large craters with sediment aprons were left. There is evidence that old craters formed by an earlier liquefaction event were also reactivated into sediment boils during the seismic shaking. New craters produced by the liquefaction were as much as 75 feet in diameter and 16 feet deep.

Dramatic Changes in the Hydrology

Soon after the earthquake, dramatic changes occurred to the hydrologic systems in the Thousand Springs Valley and adjacent areas along the fault zone. Significant hydrologic changes also took place as far away as Yellowstone National Park where the eruptive cycles of many geysers, including Old Faithful, were modified. Early reports of hydrologic effects included increases, decreases, or stoppage of well and spring flows. In the epicentral area, ground water levels rose as much as 13 feet in a water well, then declined for several months before leveling off at

Earthquake damage to the Custer Hotel, Main Street, in Mackay.

about 5 feet above pre-earthquake levels. Reports also mentioned well water becoming murky or silty soon after the earthquake. The earthquake produced a tremendous outflow of water that amounted to as much as 0.25 cubic miles in excess of normal hydrologic output for the region.

At Chilly Buttes on the day of the earthquake, seismic shaking produced a new northwest-trending fissure about 200 feet long and a new cold spring formed on the east side of the northern butte. From the new spring, a tremendous flow of groundwater burst from newly opened fractures in the limestone buttes producing extensive flooding in the valley to the east around the site of Chilly. In the valley floor a few hundred feet to the north and east of Chilly Buttes, more than 40 sediment boils issued huge volumes of water that added to the flooding.

Also, immediately after the earthquake, water levels began to rise at the underground Clayton Silver Mine located 32 miles northwest of the epicentral area and about 15 miles west of the nearest known surface rupture. This flooding of underground levels in the mine necessitated the stoppage of mining oper-

ations and the subsequent use of high-capacity pumps to handle this increased flow.

Ingram's Warm Spring Creek, located south of Challis, experienced an interesting change in flow. After the earthquake, the warm spring ceased to flow and dried up leaving hundreds of fish on the dry creek bed. Eight days later, the spring began flowing at an increased flow rate and peaked 46 days later with a flow rate of 51 cubic feet per second, nine times the pre-earthquake flow. The major river and streams draining the earthquake-affected area flowed at above normal rates for a period of several months following the earthquake.

Largest Earthquake in 24 Years

The Borah Peak earthquake was the largest earthquake to hit the western United States in 24 years and was one of the only six historic earthquakes of magnitude 7.0 or greater in the Basin and Range recorded since 1872. The earthquake had significant immediate effects on the land surface, hydrologic system, and man-made structures. The Borah Peak earthquake remains as a reminder of the dynamic nature of the earth's processes.

OAKLEY QUARTZITE

Cross section of quartzite quarry on Middle Mountain south of Oakley.

In south-central Idaho a very unusual rock is mined from a group of quarries situated on the west flank of Middle Mountain. This mountain, which terminates several miles south of the town of Oakley, has the appearance of a tilted fault block with a gentle slope on the west side and a steep slope on the east side. In the vicinity of the stone quarries, the crest of Middle Mountain reaches an elevation of 8457 feet. The quarries are situated about half way up the west flank of Middle Mountain at an elevation ranging from 6000 to 7500 feet. This rock is unusual because it splits into large flat plates up to 8 feet in diameter and less than one-half inch thick. Geologists call this stone a micaceous quartzite because it is composed primarily of quartzite and muscovite mica.

Marketing History

The micaceous quartzite, sold under the trade name of "rocky mountain quartzite" or "Oakley stone," has been mined and sold in significant quantities since 1948. By the middle 1950's, this quartzite was well known by the stone industry throughout the United States. A national market was quickly established because it was much thinner than competing stone veneers. A ton of quartzite from Middle Mountain could cover 150 to 300 square feet; most competing stone veneers would generally cover less than 60 square feet per ton. This superiority in coverage as well as durability and color played a significant role in the stone's penetration of Canadian and European markets by the early 1970's. In Idaho, the quartzite veneer is commonly used to pave entryways, to cover fireplaces and to cover the exterior of homes.

Origin of the Quartzite

As the name implies, the micaceous quartzite is a metamorphic rock. The foliation or planes of parting in the micaceous quartzite were created by deformation and metamorphism of an original quartz-rich sandstone. The original sedimentary rock was composed of thin clay-rich beds alternating with quartz-rich beds. When pressure was applied normal to the bedding by the emplacement of the granitic pluton, the sedimentary layers thinned and flowed away from the directed pressure. The pressure caused the clay layers to flatten into mica-rich layers. The alternating quartz-rich layers were also flattened so that porosity was removed and the quartz grains formed an interlocking mosaic.

Spacing between the foliation or planes of parting is very consistent, averaging about 0.75 inch, but

— 137 —

Quartzite veneer building stone in pallets ready for shipping.
Note the large flat plates less than one-inch thick.

ranging from 0.25 to 4 inches. The foliation planes also tend to be flat, except at small localized areas.

Extraction from the Quarry

Large plates are removed from the outcrop using only small hand tools such as pry bars, hammers and chisels. Typically the plates are removed from the underlying rock by driving a chisel in along the thin mica-rich layers (foliation). Once broken free from its source, an individual plate may be shaped on the edges. The workers sort each plate by color and size and then place it in one of the several pallets kept within several feet of the working face of the quarry. The largest plates are packed vertically to prevent breakage during handling and transportation; all other sizes are packed horizontally. When the pallet is completed, it weighs almost 2 tons.

THE QUIET CITY OF ROCKS

Overview of the strange rock forms in the Quiet City of Rocks.

The "Quiet City of Rocks" covers a 10-square-mile area in Cassia County, approximately 4 miles from the Idaho-Utah border. It is situated 15 miles southeast of Oakley and about 4 miles west of Almo. You can reach the City of Rocks by traveling through Oakley on the west or through Almo on the east; both routes involve travel on graded gravel roads.

The City of Rocks has been designated as a natural and historic national landmark and is under study by the Bureau of Land Management and the National Park Service for inclusion in the park system. The major obstacle to establishing better protection and management of the area is the mixed ownership. The Forest Service administers 1,120 acres; the Bureau of Land Management administers 1,040 acres; 640 acres is owned by the State of Idaho; and the remaining 4,000 acres is in private ownership.

Visitors go there to hike, camp and rock climb. Al-

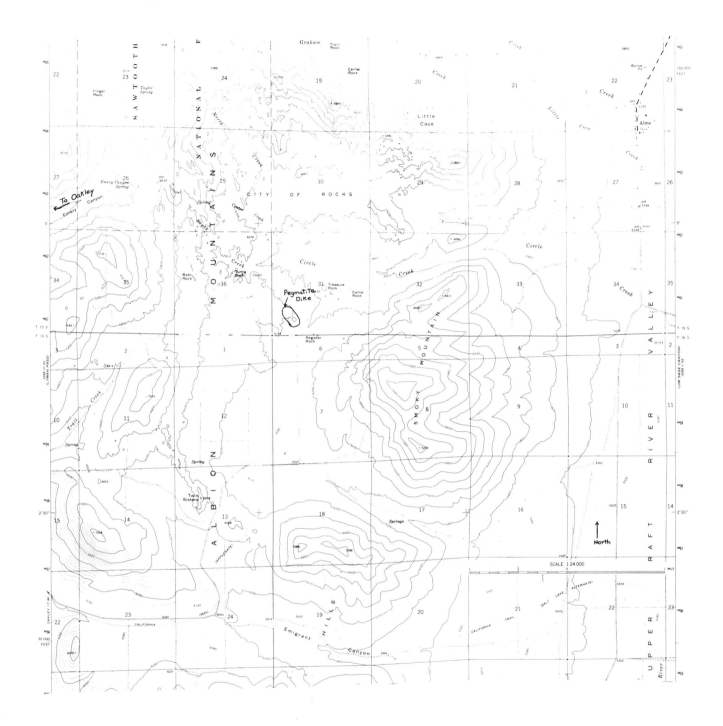

Topographic map of the Quiet City of Rocks showing major
roads and physical features.

though the camp areas are unimproved, picnic facilities are available near Twin Sisters and are maintained by the BLM.

Historical Background

The junction of the California and Salt Lake-California connection trails is located 1.5 miles south of Twin Sisters. The California Trail, which passes through the City of Rocks, was established in 1843. Joseph Walker led a wagon train off of the Oregon Trail at Raft River 50 miles to the northeast, through Almo, then through the City of Rocks and on to California. Immigrants were fascinated by the City of Rocks and those who maintained diaries recorded their impressions. Typical is the following description given by a Mr. Lord on August 17, 1849: ". . . numerous artificial hydrants forming irregular pointed cones. Nearby they display all manner of fantastic shapes. Some of them are several hundred feet high and split from pinnacle to base by numerous perpendicular cracks or fissures. Some are domelike and the cracks run at different angles breaking up the large masses into huge blocks many of which hang tottering on their lofty, pointed beds . . . I have not time to write the hundredth part of the marvels of the valley or rocks . . ."

Geologic Setting

The City of Rocks near Almo, also known as the "Quiet City of Rocks," is situated in the Cassia Batholith. This small batholith covers more than 60-square miles in the southern part of the Albion Range. The batholith was at one time covered by a thin shell of Precambrian quartzite. Once the upper shell of protective quartzite was eroded away, the granite below eroded down at a more rapid rate. Consequently the City of Rocks is situated in a basin. Within the City of Rocks, more than 5,000 feet of granitic rock are exposed from the top of Cache Peak to the bottom of the basin.

Jointing

Jointing is well developed in some parts of the batholith and is an important structural control in es-

tablishing the basic forms in the City of Rocks. Spacing of the joints varies widely. There are three intersecting joint sets: a northwest trend, a northeast trend, and a horizontal trend.

Jointing controls the arrangement of outcrops. Joints facilitate the weathering processes by providing a plumbing system for solutions to migrate into the outcrops to cause the alteration and disintegration of surface layers of granite. These large fracture channels for fluids make it possible for blocks to separate and form tall, isolated monoliths such as spires and turrets.

Rock Types

The Cassia Batholith contains rock ranging from granite to granodiorite. The inner core occupied by the City of Rocks tends to be granodiorite; whereas granite is more common for the outer area. A gneissic texture is characteristic of the outer zone.

The Almo Pluton

The granite in the City of Rocks is part of the Almo pluton. Armstrong (1976) has determined that this epizonal (shallow) pluton is 28.3 million years old, much younger than most of the granitic rock in Idaho. The shallow emplacement of the pluton is indicated by its lack of foliation at the margins and the discordant contacts it makes with the surrounding older quartzite.

Pegmatites

Scattered pegmatite dikes, which have the composition and texture of coarse-grained granite, may be observed throughout the Cassia Batholith. Pegmatites range from thin seams to lenticular bodies up to 50 feet across and several hundred feet long. One exceptionally large pegmatite crops out in the City of Rocks. This pegmatite may be one of the largest to be found in Idaho with exposed dimensions of 200 to 300 feet wide and 400 to 500 feet long. Large masses of orthoclase feldspar, quartz and muscovite are well exposed over two rounded knolls that make up the pegmatite. Some of the masses of quartz and feldspar are tens of feet in diameter. Masses of muscovite dis-

Case-hardened surface of granite results in resistant exterior shell of rock to remain after core is removed by weathering and erosion.

play radiating crystals. Smoky quartz and miarolitic cavities are common. Numerous small workings over this large pegmatite show evidence of past interest and activity.

Weathering

Although jointing controls the general form of outcrops in the City of Rocks, weathering is the agent responsible for creating the bizarre and fantastic shapes that characterize the area. On the surface of the outcrops the weathering occurs by granular disintegration. In other words one layer of crystals after another is successively removed from the surface. This leaves the newly exposed surface in a smooth rounded condition with no sharp or ragged edges or corners. The detrital material weathers from the granite and is carried by wind and water to low areas among the prominent forms. The grains of quartz, feldspar and mica at the surface of outcrops are friable and easily disintegrated with hand tools.

Natural arch composed of granite in the Quiet City of Rocks.

Chemical weathering occurs by solutions which penetrate the cleavage cracks in crystals and between mineral grains. Once the solutions are in these narrow boundaries, they cause new minerals to form which have a larger volume than the space available. This process of hydration and other chemical changes cause the disintegration and exfoliation.

Case Hardening

In addition to granular disintegration, case-hardening is important in developing the unusual erosional forms. In some areas an outer layer has been hardened by the deposition of other minerals such as iron oxides. Once a form has a case-hardened protective shell, the granular surface material is removed much more quickly underneath the shell. In some cases only the protective upper shell is left. In this way, caves, niches, arches, bath tubs or sinks, toadstools and hollow boulders are formed. The case-hardened crust is generally darker in color than the lighter under sides.

THE GOODING CITY OF ROCKS

Lawrence L. Dee
Geologist

Overview of the strange rock forms at the Gooding City of Rocks.

The Gooding City of Rocks is situated in the Mt. Bennett Hills about ten miles northwest of the city of Gooding, Idaho. The Bennett Hills form an east-west-trending range of rounded hills which rise some 1600 feet above the surrounding Snake River Plain. Elevations in the area range from 4400 feet at the south edge to 6200 feet on the north. Drainages in the area include Fourmile Creek on the east, and to the west, Coyote, Dry, Cottonwood, and Clover Creeks.

Structural Setting

The Mt. Bennett Hills are located on the northern edge of the Snake River Plain in an area where the Cenozoic volcanic rocks overlap the Idaho Batholith. The hills consist of a horst (an uplifted block of the earth's crust) bounded by the Camas Prairie graben (a depression) on the north and the Snake River Plain downwarp to the south. They are made up of a sequence of volcanic rocks of Miocene age which have been intruded by rhyolites of Pliocene age. The hills rise abruptly out of the Snake River Plain along east-west-trending faults and then dip gently south to plunge beneath the Snake River Plain basalts.

Landforms Made of Tuff

The major landforms making up the City of Rocks are highly-dissected plateaus with deeply eroded and deeply cut stream channels. The many streams and their tributaries, even though many flow only in the spring of the year, have helped dissect the volcanic rocks into weird and exotic forms. These spectacular landforms occur primarily in a geologic formation known as the City of Rocks Tuff, a member of the larger Idavada Group. A tuff is a fine grained rock formed mainly of glass particles in which crystals of feldspar, quartz and other minerals are imbedded. The deposits are believed to have been produced by the eruption of dense clouds of glowing volcanic glass in a semi-molten state. As the material fell to the ground the glass particles were welded and fused together. Many layers are solely composed of glass and obsidian (volcanic glass) formed within the welded tuff formation.

Obsidian Used by Early Man

Early man prized obsidian for the making of arrow and spear points as well as tools and ceremonial devices. Obsidian chips resulting from the manufacture of these items can be found scattered throughout the Bennett Hills, and especially at sites where early man found obsidian weathering out of the tuffs.

Joints Control Landforms and Features

The many pillars and arches in this tuff are a result of two forces; structural deformation and mechanical erosion. Weathering processes such as freezing and thawing have sculpted the rocks along multi-directional joint patterns (natural fractures in the rocks) to create a myriad of exotic features. For instance, closely-spaced horizontal joints make some columns appear like stacks of coins, whereas converging horizontal and vertical joints create weak points which are typically weathered to form concave

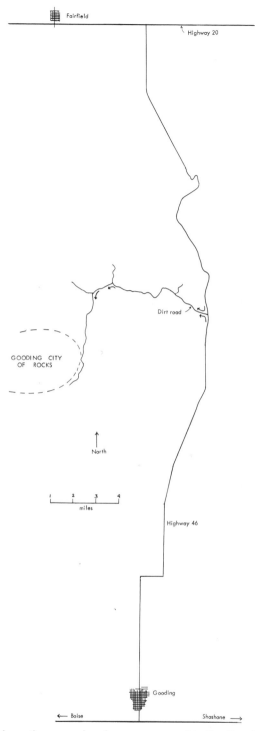

Location map showing access road to the Gooding City of Rocks. Access is available by traveling south on highway 46 from highway 20 or going north from Gooding on Highway 46.

Closeup view of the pinnacles and hoodoos of the Gooding City of Rocks.

features. Creation of the concave features such as undercut pillars, mushroom caps, and arches are also products of the weathering process. Alternating hard and soft layers in the rocks allow differential weathering and erosion to further shape the surface.

In some locations within the City of Rocks, major northwest-southeast-trending joints can be seen to form "fins" of rock oriented in the direction of those joints. The fins and other geologic features in the City of Rocks are quite similar to those found in the Arches National Monument in Utah.

Hoodoos

Some of the more unusual landforms found within the area are columns, arches, monoliths, and especially hoodoos. A hoodoo is a rock formation that originates in the following way: rocks are fractured during periods of faulting; water then penetrates the cracks and causes them to widen. This leaves a pillar of rock separated from the parent rock. The alternating hard and soft layers of the tuff give an undulating or wavy appearance to the hoodoo. These features are common in volcanic areas and are usually concentrated in regions where most of the rain fall occurs during a short period of the year.

Diatomite

An interesting mineral called diatomite is found on the western edge of the City of Rocks. The mineral, which resembles chalk, is made up of the skeletons of millions of single cell plants called diatoms. These planktonic drifters lived in great shallow inland lakes which covered portions of the Snake River Plain during the Pleistocene Epoch. As they died, their skeletons accumulated by the billions until deposits were formed which contained thousands of tons of mineable diatomite. The City of Rocks diatomite deposits are among the largest in the world.

Development of the Camas Prairie

Recent studies on the origin of the Camas Prairie indicate that it is a downwarped block or graben which occupied a structurally weak geologic transition zone between the Snake River Plain volcanics and the Idaho Batholith. It is thought that the surface of the present day Camas Prairie was originally at the same level as the top of the present day Bennett Hills. Faulting along the northern margin of the Bennett Hills and the southern margin of the Soldier Mountain foothills caused the block to drop, creating the present day Camas Prairie. It was subsequently filled with sediments and volcanic rocks probably to depths of several thousand feet. Evidence of the faulting on the northern margin of the prairie can be seen in the many hot springs that surface along the fault zone. Additional evidence of major faulting is found in the north face of the Bennett Hills which appears to be a large escarpment (steep face which abruptly terminates the hills) with a number of major faults running parallel to it.

Before the faulting and the downdrop of the Camas Prairie block, drainage off the Soldier Mountains ran across the block and down the south face of the Bennett Hills. These drainages brought in rocks which are not naturally found in the Bennett Hills and could only have been derived from the mountains to the north. A large deposit of these gravels has been mined near the junction of the City of Rocks road with Highway 46. It is interesting to examine the rocks in this deposit and compare them with those occurring in the Bennett Hills today.

When the Bennett Hills were connected to the High Soldier Mountains a large drainage field was created whose outlet would have been the south face of the Bennett Hills. This would explain the deeply eroded and incised drainages in the south face of Bennett Hills, especially considering how difficult it would have been to create these features without the addition of a tremendous amount of runoff.

SNAKE RIVER GOLD

Lawrence L. Dee, Geologist

Introduction

The Snake River begins at the continental divide in the Teton Range of Western Wyoming. Flowing southward, it follows an arc across southern Idaho until it eventually heads north and forms the western border of the state, and finally joins the Columbia River in south-central Washington. Gold has been found throughout most of the 800 mile length of the Snake River from the headwaters near Yellowstone National Park to Lewiston, Idaho.

The source of the Snake River gold was the subject of considerable speculation around the turn of the century. Some researchers felt that the gold was supplied by streams entering the Snake and by lavas lying close to the river. Many theories were advanced to explain how such a large river could have the huge number of fine gold deposits that were being found.

We now recognize that the gold was derived from the deposits in the Rocky Mountains near Yellowstone National Park and that it originated as fine particles. An interesting fact concerning Snake River gold is that the Green River of Utah contains similar fine gold, also derived from the same source.

Snake River Gold

Snake River gold is unlike most of the gold that was mined during the gold rush days in Idaho. It is found in very fine particles called "flour" or "float" gold. There are good reasons for these names. While not as fine as flour, they probably seemed like it to the hard working miner. The particles do float if contaminated with oil or if the recovery water is too turbulent. This was one of the many problems faced by the miner attempting to recover the Snake River gold from the sand and gravel. The main consideration was and still is today, that the gold is so fine and light that the particles have little value. Thus it took a tremendous amount of work to obtain enough gold from the gravels to return a profit. It is estimated that at least 1000 colors or particles were necessary to equal one cent in value using the old gold value of $20 per ounce. At a gold value of $300 per ounce, 67 colors would be needed to equal one cent.

Millions of dollars in gold remain in the Snake River sands and gravels. Modern prospectors and miners still attempt to recover the bright colors which, unlike most placer gold, are almost pure. So far no one has shown that it can be done at a profit except for a handful of gravel operators with processing plants along the river. They are able to sell the tremendous amounts of gravel which must be mined in order to produce enough gold to realize a profit.

Mining History

The earliest recorded mining on the river was by soldiers from Fort Boise who mined near where the Boise River joins the Snake. Rich gold discoveries in the Boise Basin in 1863 encouraged two thousand miners to rush to the upper Snake River believing there was gold in abundance. The newspapers later reported their disappointment when they could either not find gold or it was so fine that they could not recover it. Later in the century, the burlap sluice was devised and then it became feasible to mine some of the better deposits along the river.

By the 1870s, most of the miners on the river were Chinese. As was generally the case in western placer camps, the Chinese were relegated to the low grade deposits which the Snake generally contained.

The deposits said to provide the best returns on the entire river were located on Bonanza Bar west of American Falls. This site, as well as the area from Raft River to Buhl, was extensively worked during the late 1800s and into the 1900s. Many old mining sites were reopened during the Depression when a man could make two or three dollars a day working the gold bearing gravels and enjoy himself while doing it.

Several sizeable mining camps sprang up along the Snake during the late 1800s. Dry Town, near the present town of Murtaugh, had four stores, a restaurant, and about six residential tents. A local newspaper stated that "Shoshone City, the largest hamlet on the river, consists of four canvas shanties, and a tent, all used as trading posts." A town called Springtown was built on the north and south sides of the river near the Hansen Bridge, and a camp called Mudbarville existed near Buhl.

Gold Dredges On The Snake

Several large dredges were built and operated on the Snake in attempts to economically recover the fine gold. The first, the Burroughs Dredge, was reportedly built about 1892 and operated from the mouth of the Raft River down to the Starrhs Ferry Canyon. The dredge consisted of a boiler, engine, and six-inch sand pump. The richest gravel it found was at the mouth of the Raft River which ran 37 cents a cubic yard (gold at $20/ounce). The Burroughs dredge was very modern for its time and was capable of washing about 200 cubic yards of gravel per day. However, it suffered greatly from downtime because of the large boulders that were caught up in its suction pipe.

The second dredge was built by the Sweetser-Burroughs Mining Company and operated in the river in the area from where the Raft River joins the Snake to near Burley. This suction-type dredge operated for about ten years and, because of its low operating costs, did return profits. The mining company also built large water wheels in the river just below the present site of Minidoka Dam, and raised water for sluicing the sand on 216 acres of mining claims. This did not prove very successful and the wheels were later used for irrigation.

Gold Deposits

Early mining and geological reports on Snake River gold mining indicate that some deposits produced thousands of ounces of gold but were generally exhausted within a year or two. In 1890, one writer stated that a mining claim could be opened for about $5000 and return from $10-$50 per day (gold at $20/ounce); it was stated that $5000-$10,000 in gold could be recovered from an acre of ground by special blanket sluices designed to save the fine gold. The writer did not say how many men would be needed for the returns, but he stated it must have been a large crew.

As in most placer mining districts, the deposits that were easiest to work and most productive were quickly claimed and worked out. In later years, as well as today, what remained were bar and bedded gravel deposits containing very fine gold in quantities which today probably do not exceed $5 per cubic yard at the very most. The values reported by credible miners and prospectors today range from a few cents to a high average of $3 per cubic yard.

In the early days of Snake River mining, the gold was recovered by use of a device called a "burlap table." Recovery was reported to be 90 percent or more if properly operated. It would be difficult to utilize this labor intensive device today unless gold prices were to rise considerably.

The era of Snake River gold mining remains an exciting part of Idaho's history. The Snake River deposits are certainly one of the most interesting and unique gold deposits in North America.

Distribution of the Gold

Snake River gold is generally distributed throughout the length of the river and can be panned just about anywhere. The gold deposits occur wherever sediments are present in the river itself, adjacent to the river, and above the river. The early miners apparently found large deposits of the fine gold in the river, called river bar deposits. They also discovered gold above the river in deposits known as "skim bars" and "bench gravels."

The large bar deposits in the river were worked by the early dredges — some quite successfully. The small to medium sized mining operations on land worked the skim bar and bench deposits. The skim bar was an ancient river bar in which the gold was

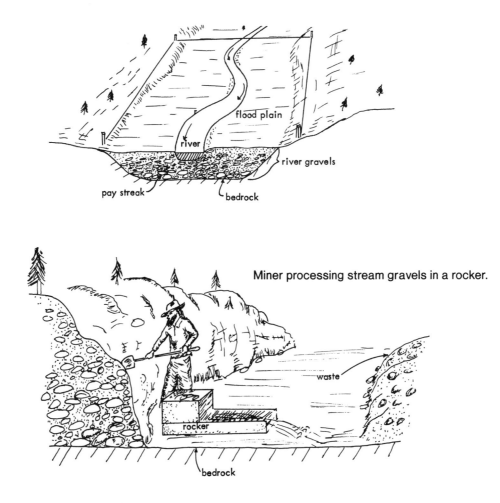

flood plain

river

river gravels

pay streak

bedrock

Miner processing stream gravels in a rocker.

waste

rocker

bedrock

concentrated in the top few inches or feet of sand and gravel. These were usually worked by one or two men using rockers.

Bench gravels were elevated bars in which the gold was concentrated in "paystreaks" at the surface or somewhere in between the surface and bedrock. These paystreaks varied in thickness from a few inches to several feet and could occur almost anywhere within the deposit. An unusual mining situation existed at Drytown, near the present town of Murtaugh, where the gold was mined by digging the sand and gravel from between huge boulders deposited by the Bonneville Flood.

Unlike most coarse gold placers where the weight of the gold particles allows them to settle on or near bedrock, the Snake River flour gold is not concentrated on or close to bedrock. The reason for its erratic distribution is that the gold particles are so light that the action of the water moves them along rather than allowing them to concentrate at every point where the current slows as it would in a coarse gold deposit. The concentration of Snake River gold was largely based on the speed of the river current at the time the gold was deposited. Thus the term "flood gold" refers to fine gold deposited during spring floods.

Often the deposit was covered with barren sand and gravel which could be tens of feet thick. This was removed by hydraulicing or ground sluicing until the paystreak was reached. The paystreak was then mined by washing the gravel through the special burlap sluices used to recover the gold.

PHOSPHATE RESOURCES IN SOUTHEASTERN IDAHO

R. David Hovland, Geologist
and Steven W. Moore, Geologist

Southeastern Idaho contains both the thickest and richest phosphate deposits in the western United States. Idaho phosphate accounts for as much as 14 percent of the total phosphate produced in the United States, and is second only to phosphate production in Florida and North Carolina. Phosphate is of economic interest primarily for production of fertilizer and a myriad of products from detergents to soft drinks.

The geology of southeastern Idaho was first studied by members of the 1877 Hayden Survey. They recognized some of the broad structural features and the Carboniferous and Triassic rocks in the area; however, the Permian phosphate deposits were not discovered until 1889 by Albert Richter. Since that time geologic efforts have focused on the area's vast phosphate resources and secondarily as a possible source of vanadium and uranium.

Phosphoria Formation

The Idaho phosphate deposits are sedimentary rocks that occur in the Permian Phosphoria Formation. The Phosphoria Formation is centered in Idaho, but extends regionally into northeastern Nevada, northern Utah, western Wyoming, and southwestern Montana. In southeastern Idaho, the Phosphoria is subdivided into three members, in ascending order: the Meade Peak Phosphatic Shale Member, the Rex Chert Member, and the cherty shale member. The rich phosphate beds occur in the Meade Peak Phosphatic Shale which reaches a maximum thickness of about 230 feet in southeastern Idaho. Since the Meade Peak is a relatively soft lithologic unit, it is rarely exposed, but is recognized at the surface by the presence of adjacent erosion-re-

sistant units. The region is structurally complex and strongly folded so the bedding of the Meade Peak is commonly tilted to steep angles. Because of differential erosion and the tilting, the Meade Peak is characterized by a dominant surface swale that occurs parallel to the strike of the bedding.

Phosphate occurs in the Meade Peak in sedimentary rocks called phosphorite and phosphatic mudstone. Phosphorites are composed dominantly of phosphate minerals, varieties of the mineral apatite, that occur in tiny spherical particles called ooliths and peloids (less than 2 mm in diameter) and in larger nodules and fossil fragments. Ooliths, the most abundant of the smaller particles, are accretionary particles composed of concentric bands around a nucleus. Individual phosphatic particles are hard and nearly black. Weathering of phosphate-rich rocks produces a bluish-white coating referred to as "phosphate bloom" which aids in recognition of phosphate in surface samples.

Deposition in a Shallow Sea

The Phosphoria Formation was deposited in a shallow sea during the Permian Period. While phosphate-rich water may have originated and upwelled from deeper ocean waters, phosphate-rich sediment accumulated, was reworked and deposited as sediment in the relatively shallow waters of an epicontinental seaway or embayment. Some phosphate deposition is also thought to have occurred as a result of diagenetic processes, that is, formed by precipitation of apatite within intergranular spaces and pore water after initial deposition of sediments. The formation and concentration of spherical peloids and oolites, as described above, required agitation by

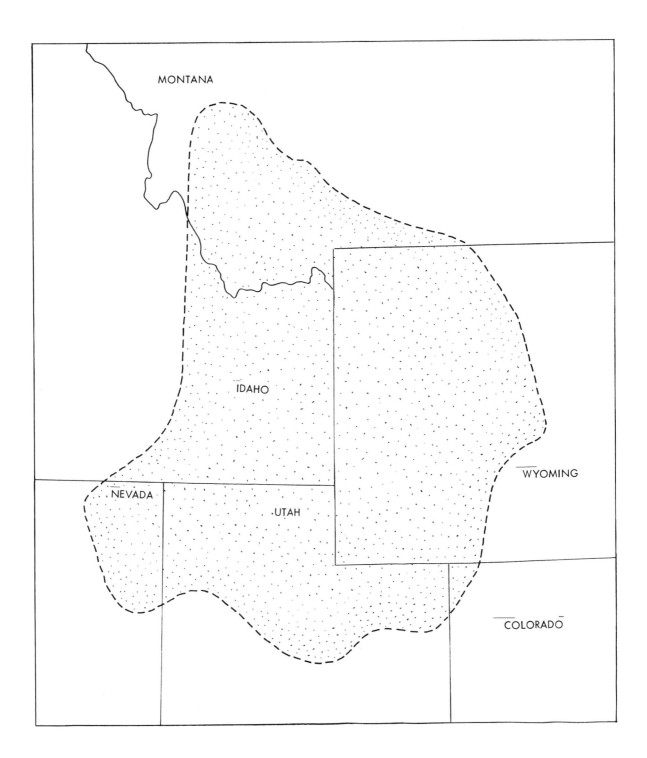

Shaded part of map shows regional extent of phosphate
units of the Phosphoria Formation in the western states.

Looking south at the Maybe Canyon Mine.

wave action and winnowing of sediment that would occur in a shallow-ocean environment in times of maximum regression of the sea.

Structural Setting

The geometry of the southeastern Idaho phosphate deposits is attributable to the complex structural geologic setting of the region. Most of the structural deformation of the region is the result of major episodes of tectonic activity occurring in the Mesozoic and Cenozoic eras. Southeastern Idaho is part of the Idaho-Wyoming thrust belt where regional compression from Late Jurassic to Cretaceous time resulted in substantial crustal shortening. This crustal shortening, achieved by thrust faulting and folding, is responsible for the effective doubling of the overall stratigraphic thickness. In Tertiary time, regional extension of the Basin-and-Range Province produced north- to northwest-trending normal faulting in southeastern Idaho. Recent seismic activity indicates that Basin-and-Range-type deformation continues to the present. As a result of the overprinting of these structural events, the Phosphoria Formation and associated stratigraphic units are folded, faulted, and tilted.

Mining of Phosphate

In southeastern Idaho, phosphate is mined in large open-pit mines. Because the phosphate beds are tilted and oriented along large folds, open-pit mines in southeastern Idaho are long, linear trenches excavated along strike of the bedding. Phosphate rock is mined downward along the dip of bedding to an economic depth (currently as much as 300 feet or more). The economic viability of a particular phosphate deposit is related to many factors including the thickness and grade (P_2O_5 content) of the rock, the amount of overburden that needs to be stripped off to reach the phosphate beds, location, market considerations, and structural geologic complications. The depth to which the phosphate is weathered is also a critical factor. The more weathered the phos-

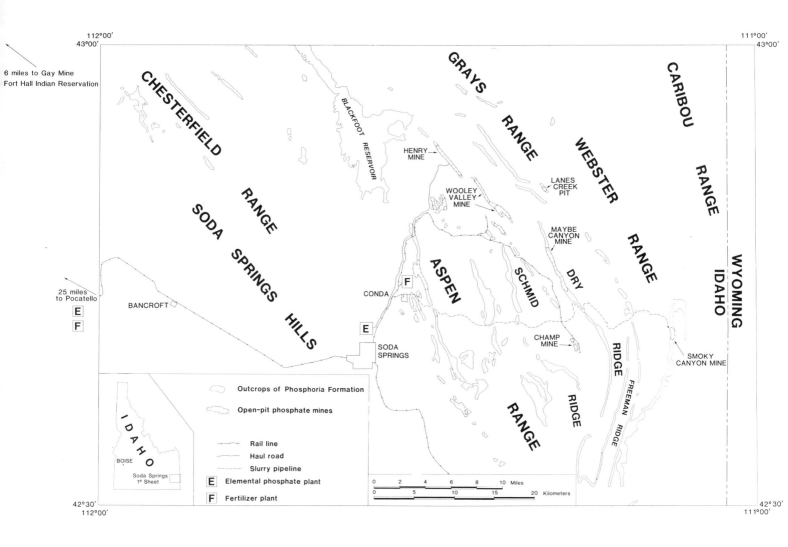

Outcrops of Phosphoria Formation, open-pit phosphate
mines, transportation and phosphate-processing facilities
in the Soda Springs area, southeastern Idaho as of 1985.
Active phosphate mines are labeled.

phate is generally the richer the ore and the more easily mined. Phosphate ore is mined using large mine shovels and scrapers and is transported by ore truck, rail line, or slurry pipeline to processing plants in Soda Springs, Pocatello, and other locations in the region.

Processing of Phosphate Ore

Phosphate rock in southeastern Idaho is either: 1) processed into chemical fertilizer products by a wet process that dissolves phosphate rock with sulfuric acid to produce phosphoric acid; or 2) processed into elemental phosphorus by smelting a mixture of agglomerated phosphate rock, silica, and fine-free coke in a submerged-arc electric furnace. Phosphate rock in the western phosphate field is generally classified as followed:

High grade (or acid grade) is plus 31% P_2O_5
Medium grade (or furnace grade) is 24 to 31% P_2O_5
Low grade (or beneficiation grade) is between 16 and 24% P_2O_5.

High-grade rock is used directly in fertilizer plants; medium-grade rock can be used directly in the elemental plants; and low-grade rock needs to be upgraded (beneficiated) to furnace or acid grade.

Potential Byproducts of Phosphate Production

Phosphatic units of the Phosphoria Formation are enriched in many rare elements; however, only vanadium is currently being recovered as a byproduct of elemental phosphate production in the western phosphate field. Vanadium is used as an alloying element in steel to improve its strength, toughness, and ductility. Other elements with potential as byproducts are uranium, fluorine, rare earth elements, silver, cadmium, chromium, molybdenum, arsenic, selenium, strontium, tellurium, and zinc. Some elements such as fluorine, uranium and its decay products, cadmium, thallium, and mercury should be recovered to avoid environmental risks from phosphate products or waste materials from phosphate processing.

Reclamation of Mined Lands

While open-pit mining of phosphate has definite impacts on the natural environment, substantial progress has been made in southeastern Idaho to mitigate impacts and reclaim surface disturbance through the cooperative efforts of phosphate companies with Federal and state agencies. Land reclamation is the process of returning land disturbed by mining to productive uses. Specifics of the mine operation dictate the type and timing of the reclamation done. Reclamation of the surface disturbed by mining includes the regrading of waste dumps and mine cuts to stable gradients and the establishment of vegetation. The establishment of the suitable vegetative cover aids in improving the soil, protecting the land surface from erosion, improving aesthetic values, and in restoring the land to productive uses such as grazing and production of crops.

Future of Idaho Phosphate

As in the past, the future of the Idaho phosphate industry will depend on the market demands for phosphate fertilizer and chemical products which is strongly influenced by fluctuations in the agriculture and consumer industries.

ORBICULAR ROCKS IN IDAHO

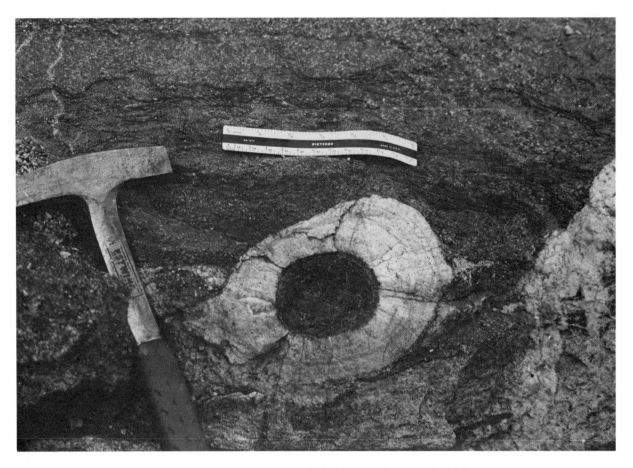

Large orbicule more than 8 inches in diameter found in roadcut near Shoup.

Orbicular rocks are ellipsoidal- to spheroidal-shaped masses of rock consisting of successive shells of dark minerals (biotite) and light minerals (feldspar). The occurrence of orbicular rocks is a rare phenomenon. There are slightly more than one hundred known localities throughout the world. The State of Idaho happens to have two of these localities: one in the Buffalo Hump area and one near Shoup. The orbicular rocks near Shoup crop out approximately two miles west of Shoup along the roadcut on the south side of the Salmon River. These orbicules tend to occur in clusters and have an average size of a tennis ball.

The light-gray, granitic intrusion that carries the orbicules also contains many angular blocks of dark schist, gneiss and quartzite brought up from great depths. The orbicules were formed by crystallization of alternate layers of plagioclase and biotite around preexisting rock fragments. One large orbicule measured 8 inches in diameter and contained approximately 15 shells of biotite and plagioclase.

MENAN BUTTES

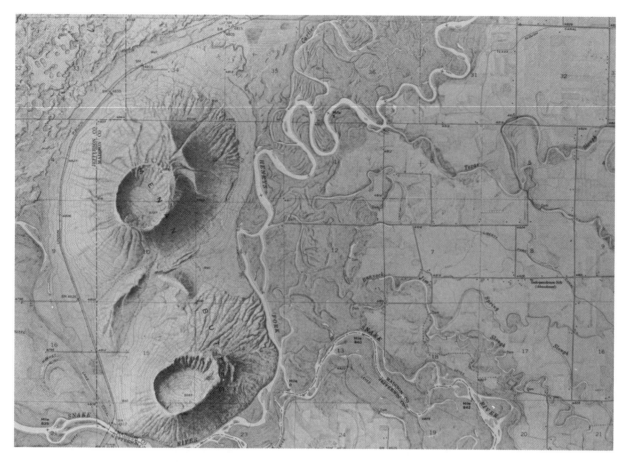

U.S. Geological Survey map showing the physiography in the vicinity of Menan Buttes. Note how the buttes formed in the flood plain of the Henrys Fork River and caused the river to be diverted. Also note the assymmetry of the cones caused by wind blowing pyroclastic material towards the northeast.

The Menan Buttes are located on the Snake River Plain about 20 miles north of Idaho Falls in southeastern Idaho. Five cones were erupted along a north-northwest-trending fissure. Both of the two large cones are approximately two miles long in a northeast direction and about two-thirds as wide. Each cone has a large summit crater several hundred feet deep and about one-half mile long. The northern cone stands about 800 feet above the surrounding plain and the southern cone about 550 feet.

Eruption Diverted the River

The two cones consist of glassy olivine-basalt tuff. They were erupted through the water-saturated

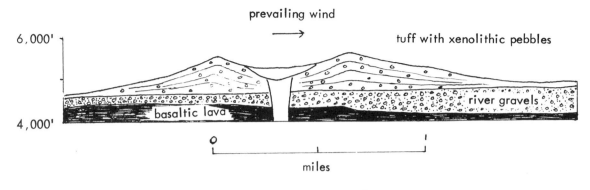

prevailing wind

6,000'

tuff with xenolithic pebbles

basaltic lava

river gravels

4,000'

0   1

miles

Cross section of North Menan Butte.

flood plain of the Snake River. As a result of the buildup of the tuff during the eruption, Henry's Fork of the Snake River was diverted to the south so that it now joins the Main Fork of the Snake River at the east edge of the south cone.

Shape of the Cone

Most of the volcanic vent eruptions in this part of the Snake River Plain are basaltic shield volcanoes. Steep-sided cones built of tuff are rare. The asymetric shape of the cones was caused by prevailing wind blowing towards the northeast. This wind carried most of the pyrclastic fragments blown out of the crater towards the northeast. Therefore the southwest slopes are steeper than the northeast slopes.

Composition of the Cones

The cones were built of glass fragments blown explosively from the crater vent. The successive tuff beds from each eruption are conformable so that the beds inside the crater dip towards the center, whereas those beds on the outer slopes of the cones dip outwards at angles of 20 to 30 degrees. The layers range in thickness from less than an inch to several feet thick. The tuff is dark olive gray in color and consists almost entirely of glass.

Cone Contains River Gravels.

Because the cones were erupted through the riverbed, they contain many xenolithic (foreign rock)

cobbles, pebbles and sand grains from the river bed. The largest xenolithic pebbles and cobbles are most prevalent near the crater's edge. Some rounded cobbles are as large as one foot across. This rounded river-derived material consists of aplite, granite, quartzite, basalt and rhyolite. Approximately 1 to 2 percent of the material in the cone was derived from the river gravels.

Steam-Charged Eruptions

The unique character of the tuff was caused by fluid lava making contact with the water in the river alluvium. Upon contact with water, the lava chilled and was erupted explosively by steam. Small fragments of lava were probably solidified to glass while driven explosively by steam from the crater.

Below the cones, the river gravels are interbedded with basalt flows. Blocks of this basalt, up to 5 feet in diameter are numerous near the crater rims and give one a good idea of the power of the steam-charged eruptions.

Age of the Buttes

Both buttes are approximately the same age which is believed to be very Late Pleistocene to Early Recent. Eruption of the cones caused a southwest diversion of the Henry's Fork. Before the eruption, the Henry's Fork flowed where North Butte now is situated.

BONNEVILLE FLOOD

Lake Bonneville was the precursor of the Great Salt Lake. The shorelines of this ancient lake can be seen on the higher slopes of the Wasatch Mountains, more than 984 feet above the present level of the Great Salt Lake. Before the catastrophic Bonneville flood, Lake Bonneville covered an area of more than 19,691 square miles.

Approximately 15,000 years ago Lake Bonneville, a late Pleistocene lake, suddenly discharged an immense volume of water to the north. This flood is thought to be caused by capture of the Bear River which greatly increased the supply of water to the Bonneville Basin. These flood waters flowed over Red Rock Pass in southeastern Idaho and continued westward across the Snake River Plain generally following the path of the present Snake River. Although this enormous flood was first described in the literature by Gilbert in 1878, Harold Malde (1968) of the U.S. Geological Survey published the first detailed account of the effects of the flood on the Snake River Plain. The name "Bonneville Flood" first appeared in the literature in 1965 (Richmond and others, 1965).

Large rounded boulders of basalt characterize many deposits left by the flood along the Snake River Plain. H. A. Powers, who recognized that these boulders were of catastrophic origin, and Malde applied the name of Melon Gravel to the boulder deposits (Malde and Powers, 1962). They were inspired to use this term after observing a road sign in 1955 that called the boulders "petrified watermelons."

Release of Flood Near Red Rock Pass

The flood left a ground record of its effects in the Snake River Plain by a variety of depositional and erosional features. At Portneuf Narrows, a canyon 45 miles northwest of Red Rock Pass, the flood is estimated to have reached a height of 400 feet.

The release of water from Lake Bonneville was apparently initiated by sudden erosion of unconsoli-

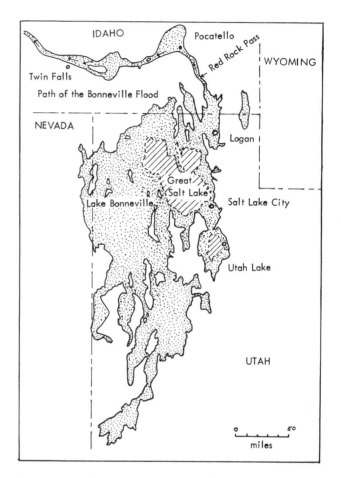

Map showing the maximum extent of Lake Bonneville and the present-day Great Salt Lake and Utah Lake. The path of the Bonneville Flood from Red Rock Pass to Twin Falls is also shown.

dated material on the northern shoreline near Red Rock Pass. Although Malde (1968) originally proposed a flood date of approximately 30,000 years ago, he has subsequently revised this age to 15,000 years ago.

Size of the Flood

Malde (1968) estimated that the probable peak discharge of the flood was approximately one-third

— 159 —

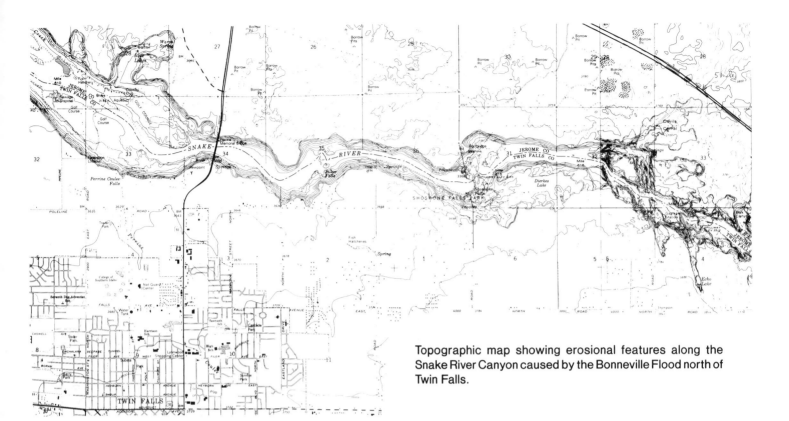

Topographic map showing erosional features along the Snake River Canyon caused by the Bonneville Flood north of Twin Falls.

Arrow points to 15,000 year old shoreline of pluvial Lake Bonneville.

Looking east at the Snake River canyon; note the two large alcoves carved by the Bonneville Flood. Photo taken north of Twin Falls. *Courtesy Lawrence L. Dee.*

cubic miles per hour (15 million cubic feet per second). This is to be compared with a maximum historic discharge in the upper Snake River of 72,000 cfs at Idaho Falls in June of 1894. The total flood volume is believed to be about 380 cubic miles.

The catastrophic flood from glacial Lake Missoula, which swept across northern Idaho, Washington and Oregon, caused far more disturbance than did the Bonneville Flood. When the ice dam failed that contained impounded Lake Missoula, 500 cubic miles of water were suddenly released. This flood escaped at a peak discharge estimated to be 9.5 cubic miles per hour. This rate exceeds that of the Bonneville Flood by 30 times.

Duration of the Flood

Malde (1968) suggested that most of the important despositional and erosional features of the Bonneville Flood were developed in a few days; however, the Snake River sustained a high rate of flow for more than a year.

Melon Gravels

The Melon Gravels deposited by the flood average three feet in diameter, but some well-rounded boulders range up to 10 feet in diameter. These boulders are composed almost entirely of basalt broken from nearby basalt flows. Only several miles of transportation by the flood was sufficient to round the boulders after which they were dumped in unsorted deposits up to 300 feet thick. Melon gravel bars are as much as one mile wide by 1.5 miles long.

Marginal Channels

Many channels were cut by flood waters near the margin of the main channel of the Snake River. These marginal channels were caused by gravel filling the main channel so that the water was diverted

Melon Gravels deposited by the Bonneville Flood west of Twin Falls. Cobbles and boulders of basalt were rounded by action of the flood water.

along a new channel. The channels, which measure several miles long and 150 feet deep, were abandoned when the flood subsided.

Scabland

Bretz (1923) first used the term "scabland" in reference to the eroded surface of basalt flows scoured by the Spokane Flood. This erosion was caused by glacial floods removing soil and rock from the surface. Scabland erosional features include coulees, dry falls (alcoves) and anastomosing channels distributed in such a manner as to cause a bizarre landscape. The area affected by the flood can readily be established by the presence of scabland. Gigantic dry falls and potholes range up to 120 feet in depth. Minor features on the basalt bedrock exposed to the flood include polished and fluted surfaces that indicate the direction of the flow.

Blue Lakes alcove, Devils Washbowl and Devils Corral are alcoves along the north canyon rim of the Snake River several miles north of Twin Falls. They were caused by flow from the Rupert channel along a 10-mile-wide spillway. The basalt was thought to have eroded these alcoves by cavitation rather than by cascading water alone. These alcoves formed tiered sets of abandoned plunge pools by stripping off basalt layers 25 to 50 feet thick so as to cause a stair-cased profile.

Piles of rounded cobbles and boulders (melon gravels) raked from field.

Stratigraphic Relationship between the Bonneville and Spokane Flood

From 20,000 to 16,000 years B.P. (before present), Lake Bonneville rose gradually until it reached the level of an alluvial spillway. The alluvial spillway suddenly collapsed and the water level dropped about 350 feet from the release of about 380 cubic miles of water. The flood is believed to have occurred between 15,000 and 14,000 years ago with the best estimate at about 14,300 years ago (Currey and others, 1983).

The Bonneville flood followed the Snake River Canyon to the Columbia River in Oregon. At several localities such as Tammany Bar near Lewiston, a tributary of the Snake River, deposits of the gigantic floods merged. Deposits from the Spokane Flood were laid by backflood up the Snake River from the easternmost channel of the scabland. The Bonneville flood deposits were placed over about 20 Missoula backfloods or graded flood-laid beds and 21 more Missoula graded beds overlie the Bonneville-flood gravels. Therefore, the Bonneville flood occurred some time in the middle of the 2,000 to 2500 years period during which the 40 plus Missoula floods were released.

THE SPOKANE FLOOD

In 1923, J. Harlon Bretz first proposed that certain erosional features on the Columbia Plateau were caused by the great "Spokane Flood." Though many geologists at the time scoffed at Bretz's proposition, it is now widely accepted that this flood not only occurred some 12,000 to 16,000 years ago during the great iceage, but that it is one of the greatest floods ever recorded by man. Bretz's involvement with the Spokane Flood was initiated in 1923 with his first published paper on the subject which appeared in the *Journal of Geology* and culminated with a final publication in the same journal in 1969 — his many publications on the subject spanned a remarkable 46 years.

The area called the "channeled scablands" is an oval-shaped area of about 15,000 square miles in southeastern Washington. The bedrock of this area is composed of the extensive flows of the Columbia River Basalt erupted during the Miocene Epoch, between 30 million and 10 million years ago. This area has low relief, is situated at an elevation of 2,500 feet and is surrounded by mountains. After the last flow of lava, a blanket of windblown silt or loess accumulated on the lava field. Where these silts still exist west of Moscow, they make up the very fertile soils of the Palouse country of southeastern Washington. This mantle of loess ranges in thickness from less than a foot to several hundred feet and forms many low hills.

The story of the Spokane Flood began about 100,000 years ago when continental glaciers were moving southwest from the great ice fields in British Columbia. The Purcell lobe of the ice sheet moved southward in the Purcell Trench and plugged the Clark Fork Valley. The ice dammed the water of the Clark Fork River near the place where it runs into the Pend Oreille Lake. The impounded water filled many tributary valleys to the east and formed the largest lake in the Pacific Northwest during the great ice age.

Glacial Lake Missoula

Glacial Lake Missoula covered approximately 3,000 square miles and had an estimated 500 cubic miles of water. The lake was about 2,000 feet deep near the ice dam and about 950 feet deep at Missoula. Prominent wave-cut shorelines of glacial Lake Missoula can be easily observed on Sentinal Mountain from the city of Missoula. Wave-cut shorelines are generally not well developed indicating the lake did not remain at any one level for a long time. The successive terraces indicate a gradual filling of the lake. Meltwater from both alpine glaciers and the continental ice sheet fed the lake and raised the lake level.

Release of Flood Waters

When the lake level reached the top of the ice dam it is probable that little time passed before the entire dam was breached. An overflowing stream rapidly cut down through the ice and increased the volume of water and the size of the channel. The ice dam could have been breached and the dam destroyed within a day or two of the first overflow.

When the flood waters were suddenly released, the immense amount of water ran south and southwest out of the mouth of the Clark Fork Valley, through Pend Oreille Lake across Rathdrum Prairie and down the Spokane Valley. Current velocities are calculated to have reached 45 miles per hour in the narrow parts of the Clark Fork Canyon. Calculations also indicate that the maximum rate of flow was 9.5 cubic miles per hour or 386 million cubic feet per second. This rate of flow represents about 10 times the combined flow of all rivers of the world.

The Purcell lobe of the ice sheet probably advanced four to seven times to block the Clark Fork River and impound water. By far the largest lake formed was accomplished 18,000 to 20,000 years ago. The flood from this lake destroyed most of the evidence of all earlier floods.

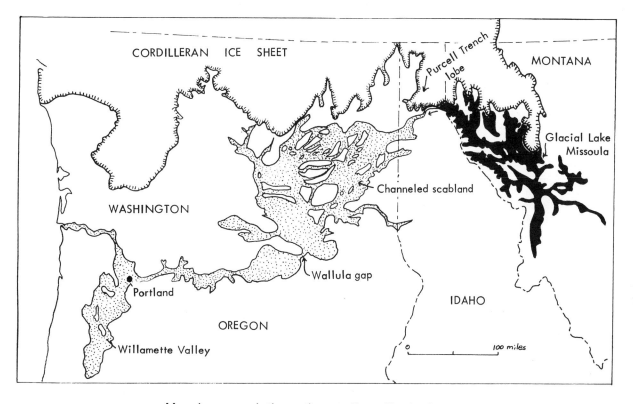

Map shows area in the northwest affected by the Spokane Flood. Maximum area covered by glacial Lake Missoula is shown in black. Stippled area indicates lands swept by flood waters. Modified after Waitt and Johnston (1985).

Giant Ripple Marks

Giant ripple marks can now be found in many places swept by flood waters. These ripple marks are so large that their pattern and shape cannot be detected on the ground; however, aerial photography, which has provided convincing evidence of many flood-caused erosional features, also helped identify the giant ripple marks. The best examples of these ripple marks can be seen on the south side of Markle Pass just north of Perma, Montana. These ripple marks cover a 6-square-mile area and have a relief of 20 to 30 feet. The individual ridges are approximately 2 miles long and 200 to 300 feet apart. Compare these immense features with standard ripple marks one might see in a stream bed or lake shore with ridges measuring less than 1 inch high and separated by several inches.

Channeled Scablands

The large oval-shaped area in southeastern Washington carved by the flood is essentially a large, flat lava field mantled by loess and slightly tilted to the southwest. When the flood moved over the lava field, the huge volume of turbulent water stripped away several hundred feet of loess down to bedrock and carried off blocks of basalt the size of a truck.

The flood carved immense erosional features in the surface of the plain. Canyons more than 200 feet deep and running for many miles were ripped out of the basalt. Plunge pools, cataracts and many other unusual erosional features formed during the flood.

Most of the flood water swept over the lava field in three major rivers: the eastern most river was up to 20 miles wide and 600 feet deep; the middle channel was approximately 14 miles wide; and the western

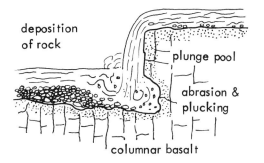

deposition of rock

plunge pool

abrasion & plucking

columnar basalt

Cross section illustrating the formation of falls, under-cutting, and cataract retreat. Water in the plunge pool at the base of the falls undercuts the rock on the upstream side, causing the lip of the falls to collapse and a new lip to form farther upstream.

most and largest river carved the Grand Coulee which measured 50 miles long and 900 feet deep. The Grand Coulee was eroded by a process called cataract retreat. In this process water runs over a cliff into a plunge pool where the turbulent swirling water erodes the rock at the base of the falls and undercuts the rock on the upstream side. This undercutting causes the overhanging wall to cave and collapse thus moving the falls and plunge pool continuously upstream.

Jointing in the basalt greatly enhanced the ability of the flood waters to pluck and remove the basalt. Therefore, as erosion progressed upstream, a series of falls and plunge pools were developed along the way. Dry Falls was the last falls to form at the end of the flood.

The three temporary rivers, along with many interconnected smaller ones, flowed simultaneously across the lava field. At the Pasco Basin in the southwest corner of the lava field, all the flood rivers converged and formed a huge lake that backed up into the Snake River Valley. This lake caused the water at the confluence of the Snake and Clearwater Rivers at Lewiston to be 600 feet deep.

Through Columbia River Gorge to Willamette Valley

All water from this lake was forced to pass through the Wallula Gap and then westward down the Columbia River Gorge to Portland, Oregon. In the Willamette Valley, remnants of the flood waters formed a lake 400 feet deep. When the lake level quickly dropped, large ice bergs rafted from Lake Missoula were emplaced on the shoreline. Melting of the ice left boulders which can still be seen on this ancestral shoreline.

The Spokane Flood covered 550 miles in its traverse across three states. An estimated 500 cubic miles of water was released from glacial Lake Missoula; the water then crossed northern Idaho on its journey to the Willamette Valley in Western Oregon.

Duration of the Flood

Duration of the flood, starting when water was first released from Lake Missoula to the time streams in the flood path returned to normal, is estimated to have been about four weeks. However, most of the water passed in about two weeks. At the ice dam where the flood was released, the maximum rate of flow is estimated to be 9.5 cubic miles per hour. This rate of flow would have drained the lake in two days. Farther along the flood path at Wallula Gap, the maximum rate of flow is estimated at 40 cubic miles per day.

Proposal for Numerous Floods

Waitt and Johnston (1985) have recently proposed that glacial Lake Missoula periodically discharged numerous colossal jokulhlaups (glacier-outburst floods). They published detailed evidence demonstrating that the erosional and depositional features of the Columbia Plateau were not caused by a single flood but rather 40 or more huge floods. In fact, their evidence suggests that the number may be close to 100 floods. Waitt and Johnston (1985) refer to this proposal as the "scores-of-floods" hypothesis.

Graded Beds or Rhythmites

Their hypothesis is primarily based on field evidence that more than 40 successive flood deposited graded beds or rhythymites accumulated in back-water areas. In back-water areas it can be expected that each flood would be represented by a single graded bed. A graded bed or rhythymite is an arrangement of particle sizes within a single bed, with coarse grains at the bottom of the bed and progressively finer grains toward the top of the bed.

Loess and volcanic ash layers separate the rhythymites and represent deposition of material not related to the flood. The more recent the rhythymite, the thinner the bed is and the finer the rhythymite. This indicates that in general the floods were successively smaller and more frequent, possibly because the flood water was discharged at progressively lower lake levels.

Date of Flood

On the basis of radiometric dates of ash deposits and shell material interbedded with the rhythymites, it is estimated that Lake Missoula existed for 2,000 to 2,500 years between 15,300 and 12,700 years B.P. (before present).

Mechanism for Flood

Waitt and Johnston (1985) also gave a convincing explanation as to how each flood occurred. Lake water did not rise to a level allowing it to spill over or around the ice dam. Before the water reached such a level, the ice dam became buoyant and the glacier bed at the seal broke, causing underflow from the lake below the glacial dam. Subglacial tunnels expanded rapidly and a short time later catastrophic discharge occurred. Calculation of the water budget for glacial Lake Missoula indicates that the lake filled every 30 to 70 years.

MOUNT ST. HELENS

Mount St. Helens in southwestern Washington State, situated about 50 miles northeast of Portland, Oregon, is one of many potentially-active volcanoes in the Cascade Range. The Cascade Range extends from Lassen Peak in northern California to Meager Mountain in British Columbia. The volcanoes of the Cascade Range represent a part of the Circum-Pacific "Ring of Fire." It was named in 1792 by Captain Vancouver of the British Navy in honor of Baron St. Helens.

Historic and Prehistoric Activity

Mount St. Helens experienced periodic violent eruptions, particularly between 1831 to 1857. This activity was observed by early settlers and Indians. Since the last steam eruption in 1921, the mountain has been dormant and, until early 1980, was a popular area for outdoor recreation. In the spring of 1980, the mountain came alive with new explosive activity.

The prehistoric eruptive history has been studied by a number of investigators and now a remarkably complete record has been documented. Although Mount St. Helens has a 40,000-year eruptive history, the present cone was formed during the past 2,500 years, making it one of the youngest Cascade volcanoes. It also was formed after the melting of the glaciers during the last ice age — about 10,000 years ago. The slopes of Mount St. Helens have not been eroded by glaciers as have the older volcanoes in the Cascade Range.

Events Leading to the 1980 Eruptions

Before the eruption, many scientists had indicated concern about the possibility of a new eruption. A series of small earthquakes started March 16, 1980. On March 27, 1980, Mount St. Helens experienced its first major eruption in 123 years. Through April 21, 1980 there were intermittent ash and steam eruptions. Visible eruptive activity ceased during late April and early May; however at that time magma was forcefully intruded into the volcano. This caused swelling and cracking of the volcano. The "bulge" caused by the swelling probably started March 27, the day of the first eruption. The bulge raised the surface more than 450 feet. At the same time the bulge was moving horizontally northward at the rate of five feet per day. The magma injected into the volcano increased the volume of the mountain by 0.03 cubic mile prior to the May eruption.

The May 1980 Eruption

Following an earthquake of 5.1 magnitude originating about one mile beneath the volcano, Mount St. Helens finally exploded with a second major eruption on May 18, 1980. The bulge on the north flank collapsed and the catastrophic eruption occurred. Widespread devastation was caused and 60 people lost their lives. This was the biggest volcanic disaster in the United States.

The collapse of the bulge on the north flank represents the longest landslide-debris avalanche recorded in historic time. Three large blocks slid in sequence merging downslope so as to form the debris avalanche. The avalanche moved at speeds of 155 to 180 miles per hour and flowed over a ridge 1,150 feet high. The debris covered a hummocky area of 23 square miles and had a total volume of 0.7 cubic mile.

The landslide opened the volcano so that the pressure could be released explosively in a northward-directed lateral blast of hot gases, rock and ash. This devastated a fan-shaped area 230 square miles to the north of the volcano for a distance of 19 miles from the volcano. The magma in the dome was exposed for the first time by the blast. Initial velocity of the blast was 220 miles per hour with an average velocity of 735 miles per hour.

The blast was heard as far away as British Columbia, Montana, Idaho, and Northern California. However there was a quiet zone 50 to 100 miles from the blast where the eruption could not be heard.

Three concentric zones were identified where the surface was devastated. In the direct blast zone everything was blown away, including trees. In the channelized zone which extended up to 19 miles, everything was flattened; the topography caused channelization of the effects of the blast. In the seared zone, trees were left standing but were seared by the hot gases.

Ash Eruption and Fallout

Ash and steam were exploded vertically shortly after the lateral blast. The ash reached an elevation of 12 miles after the blast. Then it drafted downward in an east-northeasterly direction. Satellite imagery was used to track the advancing ash front. The eruption continued to discharge ash for nine hours. And by May 19, 1980, when the eruption had stopped, ash had spread to the central United States. Within several weeks the finer particles of ash had circled the earth.

Ash falls were observed throughout most of the Rocky Mountain States. In some parts of eastern Washington, as much as two inches of ash accumulated on the ground. During the nine hour eruption, approximately 540 million tons of ash fell over a 22,000 square mile area. This represents a volume of about 0.3 of a cubic mile. Pyroclastic flows, which are material formed by the explosive fragmentation of magma and rock, also occurred. These flows were restricted to small areas north of the cone. Approximately 17 separate pyroclastic flows north of the cone formed after the lateral blast.

Mudflows and Floods

Mudflows or lahars are formed by the mixing of volcanic material and water. They are common on the flanks of newly-formed strato-volcanoes. A strato-volcano or composite volcano is composed of alternating layers of ash, lava flows, mud flows and cinders. These mudflows caused the erosion and dumping of more than 654 million cubic yards of sediment in rivers below. On the upper flanks of the volcano, these mudflows traveled as much as 90 miles per hour.

Damages Caused by the Volcano

The May 18, 1980 eruption of Mount St. Helens caused the loss of 60 lives, destroyed more than 200 homes, devastated tens of thousands of acres of forest land, and killed 7,000 big game animals. Scientists are trying to develop methods to forecast eruptive events several days in advance of the events. Although such a prediction will not save much property or natural resources, it can definitely save lives.

Part 5

FOSSILS

Overview of Hagerman "Horse" Quarry (see arrow) with
town of Hagerman in the background.

INTRODUCTION TO FOSSILS

Paleontology is the study of plant and animal remains. Paleontologists trace the development of life from its forms more than 600 million years ago through its evolution today. Fossils are the remains or evidence of ancient plants or animals that have been preserved in the earth's crust.

Plants and animals have undergone great change through geologic time. The general trend is toward more complex and advanced forms of life. However, some life forms have not changed and others have become extinct. The succession of life indicates that older rocks generally contain the remains of more primitive life forms and the remains of more advanced life forms are confined to the younger rocks.

Most fossils are found in marine sedimentary rocks. Only a very small fraction of prehistoric plants and animals have left a record of their existence. Three requirements must be satisfied for ancient life to be preserved as fossils:

1. the organism generally must have hard parts such as shell, bone, teeth or wood tissue;
2. the remains must escape destruction after death; and
3. the remains must be buried rapidly to stop decomposition.

Very fine-grained sediments are much more proficient in preserving fossils than coarse-grained sediments. Ash-fall tuffs from nearby volcanoes have covered forests near Challis, Idaho. These fossil forests were formed while the trees were still standing.

Fossils are preserved in four basic ways: (1) original soft parts of organisms; (2) original hard parts of organisms; (3) altered hard parts of organisms; and (4) traces of organisms.

Original Soft Parts of Organisms

At death the organism must be buried and preserved in a substance such as frozen soil, ice, oil, saturated soils and amber. The frozen tundra of Alaska and Siberia has preserved large numbers of frozen woolly mammoths. After being frozen for as long as 25,000 years, their bodies are now exposed to the atmosphere due to thawing. The flesh of some of these creatures has been sufficiently preserved to be eaten by dogs. Fossil insects are commonly found in a tomb of amber.

Original Hard Parts of Organisms

Most plants and animals have hard parts capable of becoming fossilized. These include shells, teeth, bones and woody tissue of plants. These hard parts are composed of substances such as calcite, calcium phosphate, silica and chitin which are capable of resisting weathering and chemical action.

Altered Hard Parts of Organisms

The alteration process occurs during and after burial and the results are determined by the composition of hard parts. The following methods are common:

1. *Carbonization* — As the organic material decays after burial, gases and liquids are lost leaving only a thin film of carbonaceous material. Coal is formed in this way. Also fish, graptolites and reptiles are individually preserved in this manner.

2. *Petrifaction* — Fossils are commonly preserved by mineral-bearing ground waters infiltrating porous bone, shell or plant material and converting the material to stone. Calcite, silica and compounds of iron are normally the minerals deposited.

3. *Replacement* — The original hard parts are dissolved and removed by underground water. Simultaneously the original structure may be replaced by substances such as calcite, dolomite, silica and iron compounds.

4. *Traces of Organisms* — Shells, bones, leaves, tracks, burrows and trails are commonly preserved as molds or casts. If a shell or track is pressed down on the ocean bottom while the sediment is still soft, an impression called a mold is left. If this impression is

later filled with another material, a cast is produced.

Fossils Indicate Environment of Deposition

Fossils are used to trace the development of plants and animals through geologic time. We have learned that fossils become progressively complex and more advanced in younger rocks. Fossils are valuable for indicating the environment of deposition of the surrounding sediments. For example, reef corals indicate deposition in warm, shallow salt water. Fossils also indicate the depth, temperature, bottom conditions and salinity of ancient seas.

Correlation of Rocks with Fossils

One of the most important uses of fossils is to correlate or match rock layers separated by many miles. If a similar assemblage of fossils is found in both layers, it may indicate the two layers are related to each other. To be useful for correlation, a fossil should have a very limited vertical range (period of living) and a wide horizontal range (geographic distribution). This means that a fossil lived in a short time in geologic history but was widely distributed during its short life. This type of fossil is called an index fossil or guide fossil.

FOSSILS OF IDAHO

Ted R. Weasma, Geologist

Paleontology and Fossils

Paleontology is the search for knowledge about past life through the study of the evidence (fossils) preserved in the geologic formations of the earth. It is the basis of the geologic time scale and of the correlation of formations on a world wide basis. New methods of dating formations have refined the time scale but have not changed the correlations based on the fossil evidence.

This evidence of life covers all of the five kingdoms presently defined in the study of life. The five kingdom system (monera, protista, fungi, plantae, and animalia) was developed by R. H. Whittaker of Cornell University. This system is generally accepted by biologists today, but is still not perfect. Nature seems to have an aversion to pigeon holes.

The present system, as well as all previous systems, leaves viruses out in the cold even though viruses are definitely organic and contain complex molecules. The new system is still an improvement over the previously used two kingdom system (plants and animals), the three kingdom system (protista, plants and animals, or the four kingdom system (protista, fungi, plants, and animals).

The newest system adds the kingdom Monera. This kingdom includes bacteria and cyanobacteria (blue-green algae). These life forms are biologically unique and did not fit well into the old classification systems. This uniqueness includes the lack of a nuclear envelope and membrane-bound organelles.

Monera are also paleontologically unique as they represent the oldest fossils ever found on the earth and are responsible for our oxygen enriched atmosphere. Evidence of the existence of this simple form of life can be traced back 3.5 billion years. About 10,000 species have been described but some question this and believe that less than 3,000 distinct species actually exist.

The oxygen produced as a waste product by the monera did not become immediately available for use of other types of organisms or for the development of an oxygen enriched atmosphere. The Archean (3.8 to 2.5 bybp) and proterophytic (2.5 to 2.0 bybp) oceans were rich in free iron (bybp means billion years before present). Precipitation of this iron in banded iron formations had to occur before free oxygen could become readily available for other uses. It was not until well into the Proterozoic (2.0 to 0.57 bybp) that changes in the environment allowed the next important advance in life to occur.

The fossil record for the Late Precambrian is very poor. Evidence that is available indicates that the kingdom protista and the kingdom animalia developed during this time period. All of the representatives of the animal kingdom during the Late Precambrian were soft bodied.

The discussion of the various formations in Idaho and their associated fossils comes from a review of many geologic and paleontologic references dealing with Idaho. Those sources reviewed during the preparation of this discussion represent only a small portion of the existing literature.

Many fossil genera and species are not mentioned because the scope of this discussion is not appropriate to a complete listing of all genera and species known from Idaho. A complete listing of all the references reviewed is also inappropriate but will be furnished upon request.

Late Proterozoic

The Late Proterozoic time period lasted for 330 million years (900 to 570 mybp). Multicellular animals such as protomedusae, hydrozoa, anthozoa, octocoralla, and annelida developed in a shallow-water environment. Cyanobacteria continued to be an important life form.

The fossil evidence of monera in Idaho exists in the form of stromatolites. Stromatolites are laminated masses of calcareous rock formed by mat-like communities of cyanobacteria and other monera. Being the only level of the food chain allowed for a tremendous population to develop during the Proterozoic. Unfortunately, there are no published articles dealing specifically with Proterozoic or later monera in Idaho. Those articles that do happen to mention the presence of monera represent passing references to stromatolite structures or beds and their utility or lack of utility in geologic correlations and the study of paleoecology.

Late Proterozoic formations are the oldest fossil-bearing formations in Idaho. The Belt Supergroup of northern Idaho and the Brigham Quartzite of Southern Idaho are the remnants of Precambrian rocks that probably covered the entire state.

Possible worm tracks and worm tubes have been noted in the Brigham Quartzite. Stromatolites, both conical and flat-lying, have been reported in the Gospel Peak area of Northern Idaho. The Lower Wilbert Formation in the Lemhi Range may be Precambrian; however, no fossils have been found.

Cambrian

The Cambrian time period lasted for 65 million years. The moderate to shallow marine waters of the Cambrian System were an excellent environment for a tremendous explosion of life forms. The first sponges, jellyfish, tabulate corals, brachiopods, chitons, gastropods, cephalopods, nautiloids, bivalves, hyolithids, trilobites, crustaceans, ostracods, crinoids, echinoderms, conodonts, graptolites and other marine life forms come from Cambrian deposits.

The Cambrian System in Idaho is represented by formations extending from southeastern Idaho to the Pend Oreille area of northern Idaho. The sediments and the fossils indicate that a broad oceanic shelf existed along the western margin of the existing continent. Idaho was completely underwater during this period.

The northern Idaho Cambrian sediments are

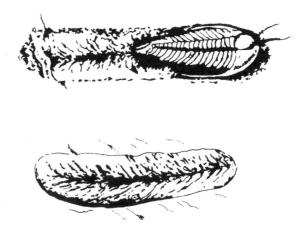

Cruziana (trilobite trace)

metamorphosed and rarely produce good fossils. The Rennie Shale and the Lakeview Limestone have produced identifiable Middle Cambrian fossils. Hyolithids, the crustacean *Agnostus bonnerensis*, various genera and species of trilobites and some brachiopods have been identified. The Lakeview Shale is the main fossil producing formation. Trilobites are the most abundant fossil found.

The southern Cambrian Formations such as the upper Brigham Quartzite, Spence Shale, and the upper Wilbert Formation have produced many identifiable fossils. The Malad, Bear River and Lemhi Ranges yield such fossils as the monera genus *Girvanella*, worm tubes such as *Arenicolites* and *Monocreterion*, trilobite trace fossils *Cruziana* and *Rusophycus*, and trilobites including species of *Albertella*, *Elrathina*, *Glossopleura*, *Idahoia*, *Pagetia* and many more. Brachiopods may also be found, particularly in the St. Charles Limestone.

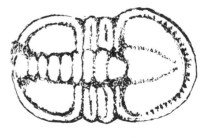

Pagetia clytia

Ordovician

The Ordovician time period lasted for 67 million years. Moderate to shallow water marine environments continued to produce an explosion of new life forms. The greatest diversification was in the invertebrate animal kingdom at the genera and species levels. The first rugose corals, bryozoa, Strophomenide brachiopods, Spiriferide brachiopods, Rhynchenellidae-type brachiopods, starfish and vertebrates show up in the Ordovician along with new cephalopod subclasses, bivalve subclasses and others.

The first vertebrates are placed in the Ordovician because fossil fish of the class agnatha have been found in Ordovician deposits. There is the possibility that conodonts represent the first vertebrates or chordates. Small tooth-like and plate-like calcium phosphate remains are all the evidence we have of the conodonts. Such evidence is inconclusive.

The Ordovician System in Idaho is well represented in the central and southern part of the state. A continuation of the marine shelf environment is indicated. Quartzites, slates, shales, limestones and dolomites have produced identifiable fossils. The quartzites are the least productive. Calcareous algae and fucoid markings have been reported from the Kinnikinic Quartzite. The Swan Peak Quartzite has produced brachiopods and ostracods in the Montpelier region. The Ramshorn Slate has produced crustaceans of the genus *Caryocaris*, graptolites and sponge spicules. The Fish Haven Dolomite has produced corals, brachiopods, gastropods and crinoids in Fish Haven Canyon.

Didymograptus

Shale units and limestones are by far the best-producing units for well preserved fossils. The Garden City Limestone has yielded many fossils. Many brachiopods, including *Dalmanella* and *Strophomena* species, have been found in the Montpelier area. Gastropods including *Maclurea*, *Lophospira*, and *Hormotama* are common. The sponge-like fossil *Receptaculites*, trilobites and the Nautiloid Cephalopod *Endoceras* are also present. Shale, dolomite and limestone units within the Phi Kappa Formation and Saturday Mountain Formation also contain good identifiable fossils. The Saturday Mountain Formation has produced the coral *Columnaria stokesi* and others, graptolites, crinoids, brachiopods, gastropods and the nautiloid cephalopod *Endoceras*. Look near the south side of the Salmon River near Sullivan Hot Springs for these fossils.

The Phi Kappa Formation needs to be especially noted for its fossils. Graptolites first reported by Blackwelder in 1913 are well preserved in this formation. There is a tremendous variety of genera and species many of which can be identified in the field. The Trail Creek area in Custer and Blaine Counties is an exceptional graptolite locality that has been extensively studied. The crustacean *Caryocaris*, sponges and brachiopods are also present. The sequence deposited in this area represents sedimentation from the Ordocician period through the middle of the Silurian period.

The Genera and species of graptolites are too numerous to list completely. Some of the more important Ordovician genera include *Didymograptus*, *Isograptus*, *Glossograptus*, *Climacograptus*, *Pleurograptus* and *Dicellograptus*.

Dalmanella (brachiopod)

Silurian

The Silurian time period lasted for 30 million years. Where life forms expanded into deeper water during the Ordovician as compared to the Cambrian, they began to colonize the land in the Silurian. Most of the major invertebrate life forms are already present. The protista Dinoflagellata and the Pteridophyta and Psilophyte types of vascular plants show up in the Silurian. Hippuritoida mollusca, arachnids, barnacles and terrestrial arthropods also first show up in Silurian deposits along with a great variety of fish.

The Silurian system in Idaho is represented by formations cropping out in the central and southeastern part of the state. The sediments and associated fossils indicate the presence of continued nearshore shelf sedimentation and coral reef building.

The fossiliferous silurian formations include the Roberts Mountain Formation, the Laketown Dolomite and the Trail Creek Formation. Unfortunately none of the new forms of life discussed above have been found in the Idaho formations.

The Roberts Mountain Formation has produced many brachiopods, some gastropods and both tabulate and rugose-type corals in the Challis area.

The Trail Creek Formation produces excellent graptolites in both the Trail Creek area and Malm Gulch. Many species of *Monograptus* and *Crytograptus* have been collected. The type locality in the vicinity of Trail Creek is a continuation of environmental conditions that existed locally for some 60 million years.

Monograptus decipiens

The Laketown Dolomite has produced the greatest variety of fossils of the three above-mentioned formations. The corals *Halysites* and *Cyathophyllum* and some brachiopods have been identified from the Montpelier area. The tabulate corals *Heliolites*, *Favosites*, and *Halysites* have been found in the typical Silurian coral reef-type deposits within the Bayhorse Quadrangle. Brachiopods such as *conchidium* and *plectatrypa* are known as are large crinoid columns.

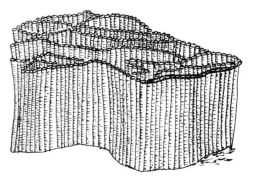

Halysites sp.

Devonian

The Devonian time period lasted for 48 million years. The shelf sea continues to produce a great variety of stromatoporoids, brachiopods, corals, cephalopods and ostracods. The monograptids die out in this period as do most of the trilobites. The first mosses, liverworts, lycopods, ferns and gymnosperms show up in the Devonian. The first terebratulid-type brachiopods, scaphopods, ammoinoids, coleoids (belemnites), mytiloids (mussels), unionoids (fresh water bivalves), brachiopods, hexapods, placoderms, chondrichthyes, and amphibia show up in the Devonian.

Idaho was still under water during the Devonian. We therefore have none of the land forms mentioned above represented in Idaho formations. The Devonian system in Idaho is represented by formations cropping out in the central and southeastern part of the state. Erosion has removed all other traces of this system in Idaho. The sediments that remain indicate moderate to shallow water marine deposition.

There are only six formations in Idaho representing the Devonian. They are the Jefferson, the Grandview, the Three Forks, the Water Canyon, Darby and the lower part of the Milligen. The Three Forks and the Jefferson are the most productive.

The Darby Formation has only produced unidentifiable gastropods whereas the Water Canyon Formation in Bear Lake County has produced a few fish scales and plates as well as *Lingula* brachiopods, pelecypods, gastropods and ostracods. *Psephaspis williamsi, Uranolophus* sp. *Dipterus* sp. and other Lung fish have been identified. The lower part of the Milligen has produced brachiopods including *Cyrtospirifer monticola, Cleiothyridina Devonica* and others. The Grandview dolomite has produced a few poorly-preserved corals, brachiopods and gastropods.

The Jefferson in the aspen range has produced corals and brachiopods. In the Mackay area, the coelenterate *Stromatopora* has been collected. A few disarticulated fish scales and fragments from the Lemhi Range have been identified. The Lungfish *Psephaspis idahoensis, Holonema haiti* and others have been studied. The coral *Favosites,* crinoids, sponges and the coelenterate *Stromatopora* have also been found in the Jefferson.

The three Forks Formation is the most fossiliferous. The Lost River Range between Mackay and Dickey has been highly productive for Devonian fossils. Brachiopods including *Schizophoria striatula, Athyris parvula, Cyrtospirifer whitneyi, Spirifer utahensis* and others have been identified. The gastropod *Euomphalus eurekensis,* bryozoans, pelecypods, crinoids, tabulate corals, rugose corals, cephalopods, conodonts and large fish bones have been found. Worm tracks and algal filaments have also been noted in Devonian formations.

Mississippian

The Mississippian or Early Carboniferous time period lasted for 40 million years. The marine environment continues to produce a great variety of life during this period. The increase in the diversity of life occurs to the greatest extent at the genera and species levels. Conifers, Heterocorallia-type corals, Myoida-type bivalves and reptiles first show up in carboniferous rocks.

Idaho has mostly marine deposits with coral reef faunas well represented. Coarse-grained, distinctive, continentally-derived sediments with associated plant fossils show up in Idaho for the first time during the Mississippian period as a result of the Antler Orogeny. Parts of Idaho were probably not very high above sea level nor were they above sea level for very lng.

The Mississippian system in Idaho is represented by formations cropping out in the central and southern parts of the state. Many formations have been named and renamed. The earlier named Brazer Limestone now includes the Lodgepole, Little Flat, and Monroe Canyon Formations in the Chesterfield Range where the Madison includes the Lodgepole and Mission Canyon in the Garns Mountain area. The White Knob Limestone has been raised to a group status and includes the Middle Canyon, Scott Peak, South Creek and Surrett Canyon Formations. The Milligen, Arco Hills, Bluebird Mountain, Snakey Canyon, Big Snowy, McGowan Creek, Humbug, Copper Canyon and Railroad Canyon Formations have been considered part or wholly Mississippian.

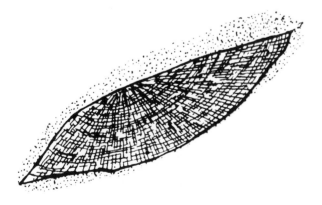

Stromatopora sp.

Sphenophyllum emarginatum

For invertebrate fossils, the Mississippian Formations of Idaho have the greatest diversity and quantity. All of the formations seem to have forams, brachiopods and conodonts. Trace fossils, algae, corals, crinoids, blastoids, bryozoans, gastropods, pelecypods, ostrocods, trilobites, cephalopods, fish fossils and plant remains have also been reported.

The Milligen Formation is the only Mississippian formation with plant remains. The material is poorly preserved and rare. *Sphenophyllum*, fern and possible Lepidodendron fragments have been tentatively identified.

If conodonts are excluded, then fish fossils have only been reported from the White Knob Limestone, the Humbug, The Surrett Canyon Formation and the Scott Peak Formation. The Surrett Canyon and Scott Peak Formations have produced shark teeth.

Many well-preserved fossils can be found in the Lost River Range. The Mackay region is highly fossiliferous. Corals are especially common and diagnostic. Colonial types and horn corals are present and well preserved; however, the honeycomb coral *Favosites* is no longer found.

Pennsylvanian

The Pennsylvanian or Late Carboniferous lasted for 34 million years. Large shallow seas and fresh water swamps created an excellent environment for a great abundance of life. The great swamp forests are todays major coal fields. The plant life was quite diverse and very large when compared to present plant life.

Insects, amphibians and reptiles increased in diversity during this period. Brachiopods, bryozoa and crinoids were abundant. Corals were few and mostly of the solitary type. The blastoids became extinct during this period. An exceptionally large type of foram known as the fussilinid is characteristic of the Pennsylvanian. Trilobites are still around but rare.

The Pennsylvanian system in Idaho is represented by formations in the central and southeastern parts of the state. Tectonic activity during the Pennsylvanian caused uplift and many interruptions of sedimentation. Fossils representing the quality, quantity and diversity of life that existed in the Mississippian were never again repeated in the marine deposits of Idaho. Erosion and metamorphism since the Pennsylvanian has added to the problem of finding good Pennsylvanian fossils.

The lower Wells, lower Snaky Canyon, lower Oquirrh (Manning Canyon), Wood River, upper Amsden, Bluebird Mountain, and Quadrant are the Pennsylvanian formations of Idaho. All have been identified as Pennsylvanian based on fossil evidence, especially the fusilinid-type forams.

The Wells Formation has in some areas produced

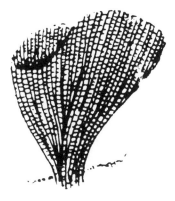

Fenestella (bryozoa)

a good variety of fossils. Forams including *Fusilina* and *Fusulinella* are well preserved. Bryozoans such as *Fenestella*, *Rhombopora*, and *Batostomella*, and Brachiopods including *Lingula*, *Schizophoria*, *Chonetes*, and *Productus* are also found in the Wells Formation. Corals such as *Syringopora* and *Lophophyllum* and the gastropods *Euconospiria* and *Platyceras* are also known. Less common are the scaphopod *Dentalium*, the pectin *Aviculopectin* and the pelecypod *Mucula*. Crinoids are also known as are algae and ostracod fossils.

The Snaky Canyon has produced stromatolites, fusilinid and nonfusilinid-type forams, crinoids, bryozoans, brachiopods, corals and gastropods. The Oquirrh has produced conodonts from the Manning Canyon Shale. Fusilinids include *Wedekindellina*, *Fusulina*, *Fusulinella* and others. These are also found in the Wood River Formation near Hailey. The Oquirrh has also produced the colonial rugose corals *Paraheritschioides grandis* and *Paraheritschioides complexa* from the Deep Creek Mountains. Brachiopods, bryozoans, other corals and gastropods are found in the Oquirrh.

The Wood River has produced algae, fusilinid and non-fusilinid type forams, crinoids, bryozoans, brachiopods and corals. The upper Amsden has produced forams, echinoderms, bryozoans, mollusks, conodonts and hydrozoans whereas the Bluebird Mountain has only had conodonts cited. The Quadrant has stromatolites, bryozoans, brachiopods, corals, crinoids and fusilinids.

Permian

The Permian time period lasted for 41 million years. It was a time of continental-wide tectonic disturbance and climatic changes. The first cycads show up in the Permian. The first Urochordata (sea squirts or tunicates), Archosauria (dinosaurs, crocodiles), Euryapsida (nothosaurs, plesiosaurs, pliosaurs, ichthyosaurs) and the first snyapsida (mammal-like reptiles) show up in the Permian.

The Permian also represents great extinctions. The end of trilobites, conocardiacea-type mollusks, bactritoidea-type cephalopods, rugose corals and hyolithids came during the Permian. All productid brachiopods and most other types also died out as did all of the blastoids and most crinoids.

The Permian System in Idaho is represented by formations in the west and east central areas and the southeast. The formations and fossils indicate a restricted marine environment in the east-central and southeastern parts of the state. The west-central area is characterized by volcanics.

Other major Permian formations in Idaho are the Phosphoria, Park City, Shedhorn and Wells. The Snaky Canyon, Oquirrh, Windy Ridge, Hunsaker Creek, Casto volcanics, upper Wood River and Park City Formations also contain Permian sections.

The Phosphoria is by far the most fossiliferous of the Idaho Permian formations. Sponge spicules, horn corals, bryozoans, brachiopods (including *Lingula*, *Orbiculoidea*, *Cancrinella*, *Productus* and others), pelecypods, pectins, gastropods, belemnite and ammonoid cephalopods, ostracods, conodonts and fish remains including *Helicoprion*.

The large spiral teeth from Helicoprion are the most impressive fish remains from the Paleozoic of Idaho. All of the fish remains reported from earlier formations are isolated teeth, scales, dermal plates and small bones. A recent discovery of a fish cranium in a nodule from the Phosphoria may prove to be an exceptional find. This specimen, found by Dave Hovland and Steve Moore of the Bureau of Land Management, is being prepared for study at the Idaho State Museum of Natural History in Pocatello.

Other Permian formations in Idaho have produced fish remains. These include the Wells which has produced sponges, bryozoans, brachiopods and fish remains; and the Park City which has produced bryozoans, brachiopods, corals, pelecypods, pectins, gastropods, ammonoids, ostracods and fish remains.

In contrast, the Shedhorn, Windy Ridge and Casto Volcanics have not produced any fossils. The Hunsakeer Creek Formation has yielded a few identifiable Permian brachiopods. The Wood River Formation has produced algae, fusulinid-type forams and other forams.

Recent work in the east-central part of the state has brought to light some fossils in the Snaky Canyon Formation that are Permain. These include the Hydrozoan *Palaeoaplysina*, fusulinids such as *Schwagerina*, the rugose corals *Heintzella spitsbergensis* and *Durhamina cordillerensis* and a few crinoids, bryozoans, brachiopods, gastropods and other forams and corals.

The Montpelier Region, Arco Hills, Southern Lemhi Range and southern Lost River Range are the best areas for finding Permian fossils.

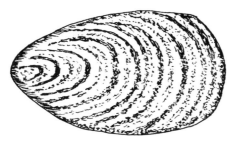

Lingula

Triassic

The Triassic time period lasted for 37 million years. It started out with many unfilled ecological niches due to the extinctions of the Permian. Bivalves, including the unionids and oysters became very diverse in the Triassc. New types of gastropods developed during this period including limpets and periwinkles. The scleratinia-type corals which are the most abundant coral today first showed up in the

Triassic. The first snakes also showed up during the Triassic period.

Especially noteworthy is the development of the first mammals. The mammal record is poor until the Paleocene and the extinction of the dinosaurs. It is, however, evident that by the end of the Triassic, animals with distinctively mammalian oestological features had evolved on the largest single land mass to ever exist.

Very few life forms became extinct during the Triassic. The conodonts, Bellerophon gastropods and the mammal-like reptiles known as paramammals are notable exceptions to the rule.

The Triassic system in Idaho is represented in the western part of the state by the Seven Devils Group, the Martin Bridge Formation and the Hurwal Formation. The Seven Devils Group, which includes the Doyle Creek and Wild Sheep Creek Formations, is known to have ammonites, echinoids, worm-like tubes, corals, gastropods, pelecypods, sponges, bryozoans and brachiopods. The Lewiston area is the best collection locality. The Martin Bridge Formation has produced gastropods, bivalves, corals, echinoderms, spongiomorphs and ammonites. The best collecting is, however, in Oregon. The Hurwal Formation has not produced any fossils.

In the central and eastern parts of southern Idaho, many Triassic formations are exposed. These include the Higham Grit, Ankareh Formation, Dinwoody, Woodside, Thaynes, Timothy Sandstone, Deadman Limestone and Wood Shale.

Many of the formations are fossil poor. The Higham Grit, Deadman Limestone and the Wood Shale have so far been unproductive. The Ankareh Formation has rarely produced any fossils. The Timothy sandstone has only produced minor amounts of coal and unidentifiable plant material.

The Dinwoody and Woodside Formations have been somewhat better sources of paleontologic specimens. These formations, where they are exposed in the Montpelier area, have been considered "one of the finest Triassic columns in the world" (Newell and Kummel, 1941). These formations have produced pelecypods and ammonites. The Dinwoody

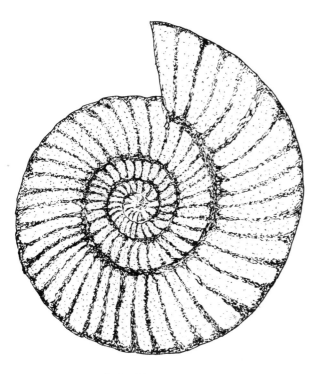

Columbites ornatus

has produced brachiopods including *Lingula* sp. and gastropods including the last known occurrence of the genus *Bellerophon*.

The Thaynes Formation, in contrast to all of the above formations, has been very productive and includes a wide variety of fossils. Many ammonoids have been found in the Thaynes outcrops in the Wasatch Mountains. In the Caribou Range, the Thaynes has produced forams, conodonts, sponge spicules and shark teeth. Near Hot Springs, Idaho, the decapod crustacean *Litogaster turnbullensis* has been found. Cephalopods, including ammonoid and nautiloid types, pelecypods, gastropods, conodonts, and fish remains such as shark teeth and dermal denticles have been found in the Bear River Range. Pelecypods, worm borings and fucoids have been reported in the Garns Mountain area. Crinoids and brachiopods are also known from Thaynes Formation outcrops in Idaho.

The only published record of a genus and species of a Triassic fish from Idaho rocks was recorded in 1904. Herbert Evans described a new species of cestraciontidae *(Cosmacanthus elegans)*. He named the fish from a spine found in Paris Canyon.

Jurassic

The Jurassic time period lasted for 64 million years. It was a time of great evolutionary growth in terrestrial life and a time of expansion for shelf seas. World-wide temperatures were moderate.

Pulmonate mollusks (gill breathers) and coccolithophorida developed during this period. Bivalves, gastropods and crustaceans (ammonites) were the major marine organisms inhabiting the continental shelves. Ammonites became widespread and have proven useful in accurate correlation on a world-wide basis. There are 64 zones used in the study of the Jurassic. One for each million years on average.

Reptiles and land plants became quite diverse and widespread. Mammals continued to develop but remained small. The mammal-like reptiles (paramammals) became extinct during the Jurassic. The flying reptiles reached their peak during this period and the first birds developed.

The Jurassic system in Idaho is represented by formations in the western and eastern parts of the state. Erosion has removed all other traces of Jurassic sedimentation in Idaho.

Jurassic formations in the eastern part of the state include an unnamed formation near mineral, Idaho, the Coon Hollow Formation and the Idorwa Formation. It is possible that they are isolated remnants of a previously continuous sedimentary unit. Fossils are rare in these formations.

Near Mineral, excellent specimens of ammonites, including *kepplerites snugharborensis* and coiled bivalve oysters, including *Gryphaea culebra* have been collected. The Idorwa Formation near the Idaho-Oregon-Washington border has produced a total of 3 ammonites and 1 belemnite fossil. The Coon Hollow Formation has produced 5 specimens of ammonites belonging to the genus *Cardioceras (scarburgiceras)*. No other fossils have been reported from the Coon Hollow Formation.

Gryphaea

Pentacrinus

The eastern side of the state has proved more fruitful. The formations here include the Nugget Sandstone, Twin Creek Limestone, the lower part of the Beckwith (now known as the Preuss Sandstone and Stump Sandstone Formations), and the lower Ephraim Formation of the Gannet Group. No fossils have been reported from the Nugget Formation in Idaho except for one bivalve specimen of the genus *Trigonia*. The Nugget Formation is the oldest Jurassic Formation in the Eastern part of the state.

The next younger formation is the Twin Creek Limestone which is the most fossiliferous Jurassic formation in Idaho. Fossils are generally fairly abundant but rarely well preserved. Crinoids including *Pentacrinus asteriscus* and oysters including *Gryphaea planoconvexa* and *Ostrea strigilecula* have been identified. Bivalves, other than the oysters, include pectins and pelecypods. Brachiopods, ostracods, cephalopods, belemnites, worm burrows, gastropods and a probable hydrozoan have also been reported. The area around Bear Lake seems to be the most productive of identifiable material.

The Pruess Formation is the next younger formation. No fossils have been found in it. The overlying Stump Formation on the otherhand has produced Upper Jurassic fossils including oysters, crinoids, belemnites, corals and sea urchin spines. The lower Ephraim has yielded oysters and belemnites.

Cretaceous

The Cretaceous time period lasted for 79 million years. It was a time of great change for the dinosaurs which reached both their peak and their demise during this time period.

In the protista kingdom at the other end of the scale, life was also changing. Silicoflagellata and Diatomacea began to appear. Diatoms have proven to be very useful for dating later formations. The first angiosperms also appear in Cretaceous times. These flowering plants produce leaves, seeds and pollen. Petrified wood and leaves are the most commonly collected fossil. Fossil seeds are relatively rare. Pollen may be preserved in excellent condition.

The Neogastropoda also developed in the Cretaceous while the Ammonoids which were so widespread and useful during the Jurassic died out. The bivalve order Hippuritoida which developed during the Silurian also passed away by the end of the Cretaceous.

The Cretaceous system in Idaho is only known from the southeastern part of the state. The rest of Idaho was undergoing uplift and erosion during this period.

The Gannet group, which represents the upper part of the previously named Beckwith Formation, is well exposed in Idaho. The formations involved include the Upper Ephraim, Peterson, Bechler, Draney and Tygee (Smoot). The Wayan Formation follows. The Smiths Formation, Thomas Fork, Sage Junction, Cokeville and Quealy have also been described in the Caribou Range. These formations intertongue with the Bear River Formation and the Aspen Formation. The Frontier Formation lies above them and is the youngest Cretaceous formation in Idaho.

The oldest Cretaceous formation in Idaho is the upper Ephraim. Fossil charophyta have been reported from this formation. The Peterson Formation has produced a typical Cretaceous fresh water assemblage. The preservation is not very good and identifications are tentative. They include the pelecyopod *Unio.?*, the gastropods *Viviparus?*, *Planorbis?*, *Goniobasis?*, and two species of *physa*. Ostracods and charophytes from the Peterson Formation have been possitively identified to the species level.

Charophytes are remains of a fresh water algae. The remains represent casts of the plant nucules (female reproductive structure). They are sometimes commonly referred to as stoneworts.

The next younger formation in the Ganett group is the Bechler. The Bechler has been unproductive but may in the future be found to have some fossil content. The overlying Draney Limestone has a fossil content similar to the Peterson Limestone. This includes unfortunately the same poor preservation of charophytes, ostracods, *Unio?* and Goniobasis?.

The sandstone unit above the Draney has been called the Tygee or the Smoot. It is not at this time known to have any fossils preserved in it.

The Wayan Formation is the most fossiliferous Cretaceous formation in Idaho. The only known dinosaur fossils from Idaho occur in the Wayan. The fossil evidence is, sad to say, very sparse and poor. The material collected represents at least two types of crocodile, an iguanodontid dinosaur (*Tenontosaurus* sp.), indeterminate Ankylosaurian dinosaur material, indeterminate ornithischian dinosaur material, possible gastroliths and egg shells. *Unio* sp. pelecyopod; gastropods, including *Viviparus, Limnaea* ? and *Goniobasis?*; turtle shell; and plant remains including pollen, coal, leaves and petrified wood are also known from the Wayan Formation.

Pollen samples have shown that the tree ferns *Taurocusporites spackmani* and cf. *Ver-*

Tempskya sp.

ricosisporites obscurilaesuratus grew in Idaho during the Cretaceous. The coal deposits have not produced identifiable material. Some indeterminate dicotyledonous leaves have been noted. Nicely preserved silicified wood has been known from the Wayan Formation for over half a century. These remains are sections of the trunk of the tree fern Tempskya. *Tempskya minor* and *Tempskya knowltoni* have been identified. These tree ferns were columnar, unbranched, and stood up to 20 feet high with diameters up to 16 inches. Most of them were less than 15 feet high with a diameter of 8 to 10 inches.

Almost all of the Tempskya material from Idaho has come from the Wayan Formation in the Ammon and Wayan areas. The Aspen Shale Formation is the only other known Idaho source.

The remaining Cretaceous formations of Idaho have so far been poor sources of fossils. The lower Bear River or its equivalent has produced ostracods and charophytes. The Thomas Fork Formation has been reported to contain some dinosaur eggshell fragments.

Palegene (Paleocene, Eocene and Oligocene)

The Paleogene time period includes the Paleocene, Eocene and Oligocene epochs. It lasted for 43 million years. Many important changes in life occurred during the Paleogene, especially in terrestrial life.

The great Cretaceous extinctions made room for a great expansion of the survivors. This expansion generally started out slowly in the Paleocene but by the Oligocene had gained a good momentum. The complexity of this radiation, the voluminous literature associated with it, and the lack of evidence in the Idaho fossil record precludes much of a discussion of it here.

Idaho has been a land mass since at least the Early Cretaceous. Except for fresh water and volcanic deposition, Idaho has been eroding throughout the Cenozoic.

The earliest record of fossil remains from the Paleogene of Idaho, which I have been able to find, is a plant record. Angiosperms which include Monocots and Dicots possibly began in the Jurassic. They are definitely known from the Cretaceous and by the end of it are undergoing a significant expansion. Much of the work by early paleobotanists identified fossil leaves using the well-known geologic principle of "the present is the key to past." Early angiosperms, however, may not have modern keys. Identification made on the gross characteristics of specimens that do not have the fine venation patterns preserved are open to question. Most of the work published before the 1970's suffers from this problem.

Paleogene formations in Idaho include the Eocene Challis volcanics which have fossil plant remains at Salmon, Germer, Thunder Mountain, Democrat Creek and Bullion Gulch reported by Axelrod in

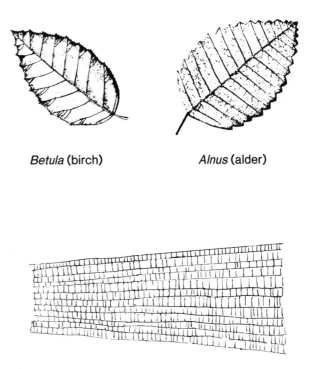

Betula (birch) *Alnus* (alder)

Typha sp.

1968. The Middle Eocene Salmon flora is located along the Salmon River near the city dump. It represents a cool-temperature climate. *Acer* (maple), *Alnus* (alder), Amelanchier (service berry), *Betula* (birch), Glyptostrobus (water pine), Metasequoia (dawn redwood), Salix (willow), sequoia (redwood), Typha (cattail), and other plant remains have been identified. There is no other fossil-bearing Paleogene formation known in Idaho.

Neogene (Miocene, Pliocene)

The Neogene time period includes the Miocene and Pliocene Epochs. It has lasted for 18.4 million years. Life through this period became increasingly similar to presently-living species. Most of the genera still exist today as do many of the species.

Modern carnivores, rodents and ungulates have gone through a period of expansion during the Neogene of North America. The primitive mammalian forms were increasingly headed towards extinction.

Angiosperms were still expanding out into new genera and species. Grasses developed and spread out into savannah lands during this period. Conifer forests, however, have declined in diversity and areal extent.

The Neogene of Idaho is represented in the north-central and southern parts of the state. There are more published acounts of fossils from the Neogene of Idaho than there are for any other time period. A complete listing of all the general and species identified has not been made but would contain representatives of all the kingdoms of life. The record is especially good for Miocene plants, Pliocene gastropods and Pliocene vertebrates.

Miocene

Important outcrops in the northern part of the state include various Latah flora localities and the Clarkia localities of Miocene age. The Latah flora localities have been known since the 1920's. The Clarkia fossil area of northern Idaho was not discovered until 1972. The Clarkia is especially noteworthy for the excellent preservation of leaves. Fossil evidence of all the kingdoms of life including bacteria, algae, fungi, leaves, insects, mollusks and fish has been collected from Clarkia localities.

The east-central section of Idaho north of the Lemhi River and Leadore has been studied for many years by Ralph Nichols. Mr. Nichols has reported a diverse Miocene vertebrate fauna from this area.

The Salt Lake Group of southeastern Idaho is in part Miocene. This is based on a *Merychippus* horse skull found in 1932. *Merychippus* material has been collected by Ralph Nichols in the Lemhi area and by Howard and Darlene Emry in the Coal Mine Basin area of southwestern Idaho.

I might digress here a bit to say that the Emry family has been exceptionally helpful to the Idaho Museum of Natural History. Their work as unpaid field associates for the museum has led to the recovery of many excellent vertebrate specimens from Idaho that would probably have been lost to science if not properly collected and turned in to professional paleontologists.

Other Idahoans have also recognized that vertebrate fossils are important to science. Mr. Mark Hoagland discovered vertebrate fossils in the Reynolds Basin area of Owyhee County and donated them to the museum. His find represents the only vertebrate fossil locality known from this area. Proboscidian, camel, rhino, horse, beaver and rodent material has been found. The closest vertebrate fossil localities are in the younger Miocene sediments of the Poison Creek and Chalk Hills Formations which crop out to the north and east of Reynolds Basin.

Most of the Miocene localities of Idaho are known from fossil leaf localities. These include the Payette Formation flora, Trapper Creek flora, Thorn Creek flora, Succor Creek flora and those mentioned above.

Pliocene

The Pliocene of Idaho is not specifically known for its flora although it does contain fossil wood localities, fossil cones, pollen and some leaf impressions. Vertebrate fossils by the thousands have come from the Pliocene of Idaho. The Glenns Ferry Formation of southwestern Idaho has been the major source. New important finds continue to be made. The Tyson Family of Murphy Idaho has recently discovered a very rich area near their property which has kept Museum of Natural History assistants quite busy. Mastodont, *equus* sp., camel, cervid, *canis* sp., beaver and possibly felid material has been found and saved thanks to the Tyson family.

I can not emphasize how important it is to insure that vertebrate fossils are properly handled. The information associated with a vertebrate fossil can be easily lost if it is not properly collected. Locality data can be a significant part of the information. A specimen that is picked up and removed from a site needs to have accurate locality information written down so that a professional paleontologist can gain information on the stratigraphic position of the specimen. Taphonomic information is also lost unless it is written down.

The specimen itself can be very fragile and so be easily destroyed. I therefore strongly urge those that find vertebrate fossils to contact professionals about

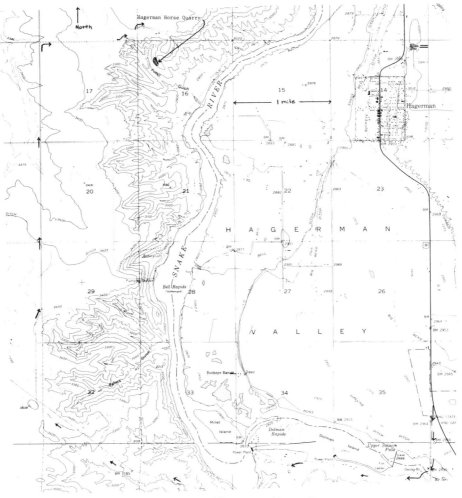

Location map to Hagerman Horse Quarry.

any discovery that is made. Any professional geologist or paleontologist in the state should be able to help you or put you in contact with someone that can. Be patient but persistent. Work schedules do not always allow immediate response.

A fine example of someone who recognized the above principles was Elmer Cook of Hagerman, Idaho. Elmer discovered some fossil bones in the early 1920's while working his cattle. It was not until 1928 that he found a geologist to tell about it. The geologist, Harold T. Stearns of the U.S. Geological Survey, sent some of the material to the Smithsonian Institu-

tion. The Smithsonian followed up by sending out a field party in 1929.

The Hagerman fauna sites have proven to be the richest and most important Pliocene locality in the world. The years following the original discovery have continued to be fruitful. The area has been set aside as the Hagerman Fauna Sites National Natural Landmark. Vertebrate studies, mollusk studies and recently plant (pollen) studies have created a Pliocene species list unmatched by any other Pliocene Blacan locality in the world. The area has a tremendous potential for continued research and interpretation.

Quaternary

The Quaternary time period includes the Pleistocene and Holocene Epochs. It represents 1.6 million years of geologic time from the beginning of the Glacial Epoch to the present. We have made a distinction between the last ten thousand years and the Pleistocene. This distinction may not be justified. The accuracy of dating earlier periods has not allowed us to define them to so fine a distinction. We may be in an interglacial period of minor importance in terms of geologic time. Life is still adjusting to the last ice advance and retreat. It may have to adjust to a new one.

Pleistocene

Life in the Pleistocene was very similar to the life of the present. Some species have either died out completely or have moved out of North America and continued to evolve. We no longer have any native proboscidians, rhinocerases, camels, llamas, horses or sloths in North America. The mammoths, wooley rhinocerases and ground sloths have passed on forever.

Pleistocene fossils have been found throughout the state. Not all areas are very productive. The only Pleistocene fossil record that I have found for northern Idaho refers to a single horse tooth found at Moscow in the "Palouse" Formation. I would be happy to hear from anyone who may have Pleistocene fossils from northern Idaho. Almost all of the Idaho Pleistocene localities are either related to the Snake River Plain or are found in Late Pleistocene cave and archeological sites. Because archeological materials and vertebrate fossils are important to science, they are not open to collecting without a permit. This insures that collection and curation are performed professionally.

The best known Pleistocene locality in the state is American Falls Reservoir. The best collection in the world of the giant horned *Bison latifrons* comes from sites at the reservoir. The major part of the collection at the Idaho State Museum of Natural History in Pocatello, Idaho comes from American Falls. This fine collection has been preserved thanks to the collecting efforts of Darlene and Howard Emry and family.

Jaguar Cave in upper Birch Creek valley has had an extensive Pleistocene fauna found in it. Other caves that have been open since the Pleistocene have also been natural animal traps. This kind of fossil preservation is quite unique as caves commonly contain complete fossilized skeletons. Such discoveries are not common as any animal that dies and is not immediately buried is torn apart by carnivores, attacked by bacteria and subjected to the stresses of heating and cooling.

Thanks to fast burial by the Bonneville Flood, a series of articulated vertebra with the spinal processes intact, a tusk and a humerous of a proboscidian was preserved northeast of Glenns Ferry near Sugar Bowl Hill. This find was saved thanks to the efforts of George Drewery of Glenns Ferry. George spent three years talking to archeologists. He was finally able to get a hold of a geologist. The fossils were collected and preserved shortly thereafter.

In a gravel deposit near Grandview, Idaho, mammoth and bison bones were found some 20 years ago by workers on site. Mr. George Eddins of Nampa, Idaho has turned in what he found. The bones were fairly broken up but, through the efforts of Greg McDonald and Winston Lancaster of the Idaho Museum of Natural History, they have been reassembled into two large pelvis sections. The fact that Mr. Eddins saved these bones from going through the rock crusher is deeply appreciated.

Holocene

The Holocene or Recent time in Idaho covers the last 10,000 years. Deposits containing preserved evidence of past life include swamps, caves, archeological sites and lake bottoms. A rare occurrence of preservation of bones in a talus deposit has been found near Challis, Idaho. This unqiue find was discovered by Nancy Anderson of Salmon, Idaho. A very good collection of rodent bones has been recovered from this site.

Part 6

MINERAL AND GEMSTONE DEPOSITS

Panning for gold

MINERAL DEPOSITS

Idaho has excellent examples of many diverse types of mineral deposits; however the classic lode and placer deposits tend to dominate. A lode deposit is a tabular-shaped deposit between definite boundaries. A lode may consist of several veins spaced closely together. A vein is a fissure or crack in a rock filled by minerals which were transported in by fluids. A placer deposit is one where gold or other heavy minerals are concentrated in a gravel deposit.

The purpose of this chapter is to explain how the common types of mineral deposits form and describe the types and availability of minerals that may be of interest to the recreational collector. Particular emphasis is on gold and gem minerals. Gold, in both lode and placer sources, is abundant in Idaho. Numerous gemstones such as sapphire, topaz, garnet, zircon, opal, jasper, aquamarine and many others have been found in both lode and placer deposits.

Mining began in Idaho about 1852 and continued on a small scale using mostly hand methods until the 1880s. Later, development of the lead-silver lodes began on a large scale. The initiation of large-scale placer mining using hydraulic mining and dredges resulted in a huge increase of gold production. Placer mines outnumbered lode mines until World War II put a temporary stop to gold mining.

Hydrothermal Deposits

A hydrothermal deposit is one precipitated from a high temperature solution. As hot water with minerals in solution rises towards the earth's surface, the lower temperature and pressure near the surface cause the minerals to precipitate out of solution. Molten rock or magma below the surface supplies the hot fluids which travel upwards along the pressure gradient. Magma is 3 to 8 percent water by weight and lavas contain about 4 percent water.

Preparation of Rocks for Mineralization

Several processes must affect the rock in order to

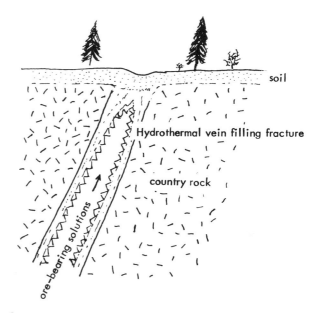

Cross section showing ore-bearing solutions filling an open fracture. The ore minerals migrate toward the surface and precipitate on the walls of the fracture.

make it more receptive to mineralization. The rock must become more permeable and brittle. Rocks are hardened by silica, then shattered by faulting so as to increase permeability. Broken silica causes clean fractures with little or no powder so that fluids may move easily through the rock. Typically rocks with a high porosity such as sandstones and conglomerates also have a high permeability. Shales, on the other hand, have a high porosity but a low permeability. Consequently, shale beds may confine and trap a mineral deposit rather than allow it to pass through. Joints and contraction cracks in igneous rocks make excellent channelways for fluids. Vesicular layers and interbeds between lava flows also provide very good permeability.

Mineral veins and faults

Faults are fractures along which displacement has occurred. A shear zone is a highly-fractured zone with closely-spaced, subparallel fault planes. It is normally a very permeable zone; however, the presence of clay zones called gouge (finely-ground rock) greatly reduces permeability. The greater the displacement, the more gouge forms. Therefore, small faults with slight displacement are the most favorable locations for ore deposits. Brittle quartzites make either clean breaks or shattered zones, whereas shales and many igneous rocks make tight fractures with much gouge, so they have a low permeability. Faults formed near the surface are generally more open and consequently have higher permeability. Thrust faults are caused by compression and typically have a fault plane that dips 30 degrees to horizontal. Thrust faults have tight fractures containing much gouge, low permeability and are poor for mineralization. Gravity or normal faults are caused by extension; they tend to be open, permeable and excellent for mineralization. The fault planes of normal faults tend to dip 40 to 70 degrees.

Mineralized faults generally occur where more than one fault is involved. Typical configurations include (1) subparallel groups of faults, (2) one fault intersected by another fault (the zone of intersection is very commonly mineralized), (3) faults that branch like the limbs of a tree, and (4) a zone of intersecting faults called stockworks. Stockworks generally have a cylindrical or pipelike shape and are caused by shattering of igneous rocks.

Ore Fluids

As hot fluids are discharged from magma, they circulate through huge volumes of shattered rock dissolving a variety of minerals. After taking minerals in solution at high temperatures and pressures, the fluids move towards the surface along permeable channels such as fracture zones. When the temperature and pressure drops sufficiently, minerals will begin to precipitate along the walls of the fractures.

Classification of Hydrothermal Deposits

A widely-used classification of hydrothermal mineral deposits is based on the temperature of formation:

Hypothermal: 300° to 500° C (deep deposits)
Mesothermal: 200° to 300° C (medium deposits)
Epithermal: 0 to 200° C (shallow deposits)

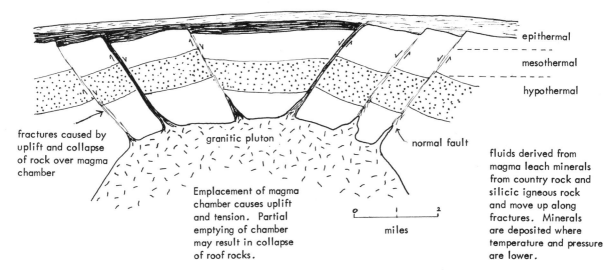

fractures caused by uplift and collapse of rock over magma chamber

granitic pluton

normal fault

Emplacement of magma chamber causes uplift and tension. Partial emptying of chamber may result in collapse of roof rocks.

miles

epithermal

mesothermal

hypothermal

fluids derived from magma leach minerals from country rock and silicic igneous rock and move up along fractures. Minerals are deposited where temperature and pressure are lower.

Generalized cross section shows the relationships among a magma chamber, tension faults and hydrothermal mineral deposits.

White quartz vein about one foot thick in dark country rock.

Epithermal Deposits

Epithermal deposits are an important source of lode gold deposits in Idaho. They are formed at less than 3000 feet from the surface and at low temperatures ranging between 50 to 200 degrees centigrade. Mineralization occurs by open-space filling with such textures as drusy (crystal lined) cavities, symmetrical banding and comb structures. The fissures may open at the surface as hot springs. Epithermal

veins are typically related to Tertiary plutons and volcanism.

Mineralogy of Lode Gold Deposits

Lode gold deposits are formed by hydrothermal solutions precipitating such minerals as quartz, barite, carbonate minerals, flourite, gold, gold tellurides and silver. Many of these deposits have yielded much more silver than gold.

Host Rock

Host rocks are typically found in altered volcanic rocks of Tertiary age, and to a much lesser extent they occur in granitic rocks of Late Cretaceous to Early Tertiary age.

Gold Content

The epithermal gold-quartz lodes have been referred to as "bonanza" lodes because they tend to be much richer than the other types of lodes. Although the ore grade commonly ranges to one ounce of gold per ton, ore can carry up to 20 ounces of gold per ton.

Quartz Veins and Gossans

Only a small percentage of vein quartz will contain gold. "Bull quartz" is a term for a glassy quartz that is generally barren of gold. Gold below the oxide zone is generally associated with sulfides. Sulfide gold includes pyrite, chalcopyrite, arsenopyrite and galena; however gold may also exist in a free state below the oxide zone. Iron streaks and vugs lined with rusty crystals in quartz veins are promising for gold. If gold is present in such veins, it may be possible to see it with a hand lens or the naked eye. Commonly gold is the only valuable mineral left in a gossan. A gossan (iron hat) is a porous, rusty capping on a sulfide deposit. Any outcrop or float of iron-stained, light-colored igneous rock, fractured and recemented with silica, should be carefully examined.

Predicting Gold Value with Depth

Gold is an inert, insoluable mineral and is not susceptible to leaching. As a result, the gold content of the rock may decrease with depth. Another depth problem occurs if the gold is contained in sulfides. In such a case, free gold is only available in the zone of weathering above the water table.

Linear Features

Major linear features may be used to find mineral deposits. Linear features are topographic features such as ridges and canyons that follow a straight line and are probably the surface expression of a fault. Satellite imagery and high altitude aerial photography are useful for this purpose. Mineral deposits tend to be aligned along linear features. The intersection of linear features are an excellent place to prospect. Lineaments may represent deep fractures which could provide access to ore fluids.

Deposits Formed from Secondary Enrichment

Some mineralized vein deposits are enriched at or below the water table by a process called supergene enrichment. Surface water moving along the fractures above the water table in the zone of oxidation dissolves minerals and carries them in solution down

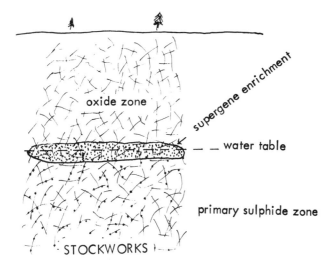

The original primary sulphide zone that once existed above the water table in this deposit is now oxidized. The mobile metallic minerals went into solution and were transported to the water table where they were precipitated as new ore minerals by a process called supergene enrichment.

to the water table. At the water table, secondary minerals are deposited which are generally much richer than primary minerals originally deposited in veins. For example, a typical primary sulfide mineral is calcopyrite with 34.5 percent copper. If this mineral is taken into solution and carried down to the water table, the copper may again be deposited in the form of bornite (63 percent copper), covellite (66 percent copper) or chalcocite (80 percent copper). The following minerals are commonly found in gossans or oxidized upper portions of veins:

Iron minerals – rusty brown, yellow, red
Copper minerals – blue, green
nickle ores – pale green
Cobalt – pink, red color
Molybdenum – pale yellow
Manganese – sooty black
Uranium – bright orange, yellow, green

Contact Metamorphic Deposits

After intrusion, a magma gives off heat and fluids. These hot fluids migrate upwards towards low temperature and pressure. New minerals and textures form along the contact of the pluton and the country rock. Minerals grow larger and grain size increases. If the country rock is a limestone, it is recrystallized into a marble. The intruded magma supplies valuable metals and silica. Silica precipitates in the pores of sedimentary rock as a quartz cement. Silica also reacts with chemicals in the country rock to form silicate minerals. Hot solutions leach out portions of the country rock and in its place silica and other minerals are deposited. Deposition occurs in permeable beds along bedding planes, cavities and fractures. Metals are very mobile and tend to be driven out of the magma and localized in the roof of the magma chamber.

Skarn minerals are formed at the contact between a granitic pluton and a carbonate-rich rock such as a limestone. Skarn minerals desirable for collecting include garnet, mica, corundum, quartz, diopside, tremolite, spinel, epidote, wollastonite, flourite, tourmaline and topaz.

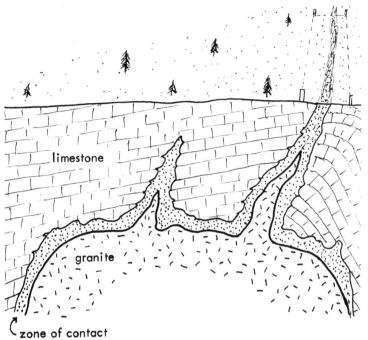

Cross section of a contact metamorphic deposit. This type of deposit tends to form at the contact between a limestone country rock and a granitic intrusion.

Pegmatites

Pegmatites are very coarse-grained igneous or metamorphic rocks. Igneous pegmatites form from residual volatile-rich fractions of the magma; whereas, metamorphic pegmatites are formed by mobile constituents that concentrate during metamorphic differentiation. Pegmatites have a tubular or dike-like shape or may be lensoid masses. They are generally small with a thickness from several feet to more than 100 feet and may have a length measured in tens or hundreds of feet.

Most pegmatites in Idaho have a silicic to intermediate composition; however, some mafic pegmatites are known. Pegmatites are generally found in and near the roofs of large plutons. Most pegmatites in Idaho have a very simple mineralogy. Typical minerals include quartz, orthoclase feldspar and mica. Small red garnets and black tourmaline are also common as small disseminated crystals. Many valuable economic minerals as well as crystal specimens are recovered from pegmatites. These minerals include quartz, feldspar, micas, chalcopyrite, molybdenite, sphalerite, beryl, apatite, tourmaline, monazite, topaz, garnet, spodumene, cassiterite and lepidolite. Rare earth minerals found in pegmatites include tantalum, niobium, beryllium, lithium, cesium, uranium, cerium and thorium. Most pegmatites are characterized by a crude zoning. This happens because a pegmatite crystallizes somewhat like a geode, from the outside towards the center. Pegmatites typically have a quartz core because quartz is generally one of the last minerals to crystallize.

Some pegmatites have a gas cavity at the center of the pegmatite. These cavities range from several inches to more than a foot in length and often contain large crystals with fully-developed crystal faces. Gem minerals such as amazonite (green microcline), topaz, beryl (aquamarine in Idaho plutons) and smoky quartz are common in Idaho pegmatites.

Prospecting for Pegmatites

One of the best ways to find pegmatites with pockets or cavities in which crystal specimens may be found is to carefully examine the float. Float is a term used to describe fragments of the pegmatite deposit that might be detached and moved downslope. Look for large pieces of quartz with attached crystals of amazonite and tourmaline. Also large pieces of feldspar and mica indicate a pegmatite. Crystals with faces are especially diagnostic because they indicate a pocket exists in a pegmatite where other crystals may be found. Pegmatites form low areas because they tend to weather relatively quickly; as a result, vegetation may thrive over pegmatites. However, the quartz core is more resistant that the surrounding minerals and will stand out in high relief. This quartz may be rose, gray, smoky or amethyst capped. Pegmatites generally do not occur as a single dike but rather as a group of dikes. So if you find one, there will most likely be more within 50 to 100 feet.

Geologist reveals large orthoclase feldspar crystal in center of pegmatite dike. Photo taken in Quiet City of Rocks area.

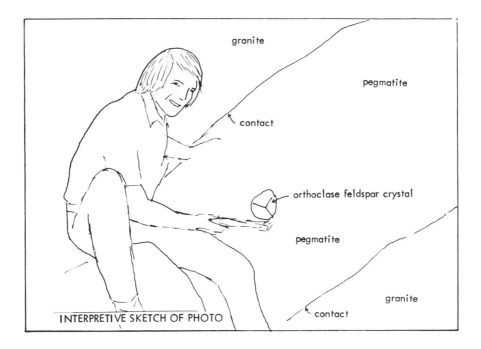

granite

pegmatite

contact

orthoclase feldspar crystal

pegmatite

granite

contact

INTERPRETIVE SKETCH OF PHOTO

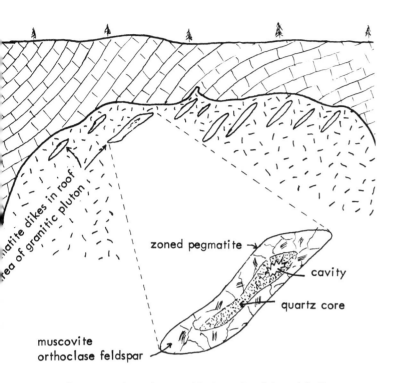

Cross section of a granitic intrusion (pluton) in limestone. Pegmatite dikes tend to occur near the roof of the pluton.

Labels in figure: matite dikes in roof of granitic pluton; zoned pegmatite; cavity; quartz core; muscovite orthoclase feldspar

Mineral Identification

Books of white mica called muscovite are very common in pegmatites. These books tend to increase in size towards the centerline of the pegmatite body. Pink, lithium-rich mica is called lepidolite. Orthoclase feldspar is very commonly found as large flesh-colored crystals. Beryl crystals are generally found imbedded in quartz; they tend to range from pale green to blue in color. Tourmaline occurs as long, black rod-like crystals which generally point towards the center. Translucent white quartz typically forms in the core of pegmatites.

Beryl in Idaho Pegmatites

Beryl-bearing pegmatites are associated with the Kaniksu Batholith in the vicinity of Priest Lake. Most localities are west of the lake. In eastern Latah County near Avon, a muscovite-rich pegmatite with beryl, tourmaline and garnet is exposed. The beryl crystals reportedly range up to 18 inches in length. Blue to bluish-green beryl is found in the Sawtooth Range near Glenn Peak and Mount Everly; some of this beryl is gem-quality aquamarine and is accompanied by flourite. Beryl-bearing pegmatites in a Tertiary granitic pluton are found in the Cathedral Rocks area of Lemhi County. Gem-quality blue beryl has also been found in granitic rock in the Boise Basin area. Pegmatite mining in Idaho began in 1888 for minerals such as mica, feldspar and beryl.

Coeur d'Alene District

The Coeur d'Alene district in northern Idaho is one of the major lead-zinc-silver producing areas of the world. Since mining began in the early 1880s, mines in the 300-square-mile district have produced more than 2.89 billion dollars worth of silver, lead, zinc, copper and gold.

The country rock (host rock) consists of six formations of the fine-grained, siliceous, Precambrian Belt Supergroup. The sediments are intruded by several types of small stocks and dikes. The structural geology of the area is complicated by a variety of folds and faults of diverse ages and movements. The district is at the intersection of the west-northwest-trending Osburn fault and a north-trending anticlinal uplift. Six periods of mineralization, ranging in age from Precambrian to Tertiary have been identified. The main period of mineralization probably occurred during the Late Cretaceous. The productive veins, apparently controlled by deep fractures, trend northwesterly. Although many veins crop out at the surface, some apex several thousand feet below the surface. Depth appears to have had little effect on the occurrence or type of ore.

DeLamar Silver Mine in Southwestern Idaho

Gold was discovered in the DeLamar area in 1863; however, production, primarily by underground mining, terminated in 1914. The exploration phase for the DeLamar mine began in 1969 and by 1977 open pit mining was started.

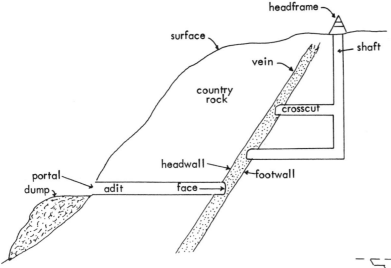

Cross section of underground mine workings.

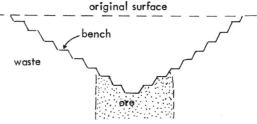

Cross section of an open-pit mine.

In 1986, ore reserves totaled approximately 11 million tons, averaging 1.8 ounces per ton of silver and 0.023 ounces per ton of gold. Approximately 27,000 tons of ore and waste are moved each day, of which 3,300 tons are ore. Current production includes about 1.6 million ounces of silver and 29,000 ounces of gold annually.

Silver and gold mineralization occurs in Tertiary silicic volcanic rocks at the DeLamar Silver Mine. The silicic volcanics and subsequent mineralization were controlled by large normal faults. Ore-grade mineralization is best developed in porphyritic rhyolite domes overlying basalt flows.

Thompson Creek Molybdenum Mine

The Thompson Creek Molybdenum Mine, owned by Cyprus Mining Company, is located about 40 miles southwest of Challis. Although the most important use of molybdenum is as an alloy to enhance the strength and durability of steel, it has many other uses.

Exploration of the mine began in 1967 and continued for 14 years. In 1978 the decision was made to develop the property. The ore body consists of an igneous granitic stock of Late Cretaceous age intruded into argillites of Mississippian age. The intrusive and sedimentary rocks are overlain by Challis volcanics of Eocene age. The molybdenite occurs primarily in veins and veinlets disseminated throughout the deposit. The ore body has an estimated 181 million tons of reserves, averaging 0.18 percent molybdenite. Actual mining and ore processing began in 1983, more than 17 years after Cyprus staked its claims. This mine, with associated facilities and equipment, is one of the most modern large open pit mines in the western United States.

PLACER DEPOSITS

Placers are mineral deposits in which heavy valuable minerals are concentrated by water, gravity or wind action. Minerals must have a high density to be concentrated; they must also be resistant to weathering and mechanical wearing during transportation. Placers consist primarily of unconsolidated to semi-consolidated sand and gravel with several pounds of heavy minerals to the ton. Heavy minerals found in Idaho placers include garnet, magnetite, corundum (sapphire), diamond, hematite, rutile, gold, cassiterite, platinum and monzonite.

Placer deposits are of particular interest to the inexperienced prospector of limited means because they are relatively easy to find and easy to work. Placer deposits have probably contributed a little over one-fourth of all gold ever produced, or almost one billion ounces. The United States has produced about 114 million ounces of placer gold. Major production of U.S. placer gold includes the following:

1. Sierra Nevada of California – 68 million ounces
2. Fairbanks, Alaska – 7.2 million ounces
3. Nome, Alaska – 3.5 million ounces
4. Virginia City, Montana – 2.5 million ounces
5. Boise Basin, Idaho – 2.3 million ounces

Stream Load

The stream load includes all the material moved by a stream. Materials are moved in four ways:

1. Traction load – the largest particles are pushed by the current.
2. Suspension load – the particles are small enough to stay off the stream bed because of turbulent forces.
3. Saltation load – particles are of intermediate size and bounce along the bottom.
4. Solution – particles are soluble and go into solution.

The manner in which a particle is transported down stream depends on its size, shape and specific gravity. Large particles may be too large to move under most conditions. Well-rounded particles are more easily moved by traction, whereas flaky particles tend to be moved by suspension. Specific gravity is the most important factor in movement. Minerals with a high specific gravity, such as gold, are the most difficult for a stream to move.

Types of Placers

Residual placers are those where valuable minerals are concentrated at or near the source and the valueless lighter minerals are transported away by erosive forces such as wind, water and gravity.

Eluvial placers are generally found as a concentration of gold on a hillside slightly below a vein source. The lighter surface material may be removed by surface wash and wind. This type of placer generally occupies a very small area.

Gulch or stream placers are situated in or near active streams. They are characterized by steep gradients and poorly-sorted material with large boulders. Gold is coarse and concentrated on bedrock.

River placers exist in or near rivers with fairly broad valleys. The gravels of river placers tend to be much smaller in size than those of creek placers. The gold of river placers is fine and tends to be concentrated on bedrock.

Bench placers are remnants of deposits left on a terrace or hillside when a stream occupied a higher level than it does at present. There may be several sets of benches. If water problems can be solved, these deposits offer some of the best potential for Idaho gold placers.

Flood gold deposits carry very fine gold picked up and redeposited during floods. The classic locality for flood-gold deposits is the Snake River in Idaho. In deposits of the Snake River the particles of gold are so fine that it may require several hundred colors to be worth one cent. Flood gold tends to be concentrated in the upper few inches of the gravel and at the up-

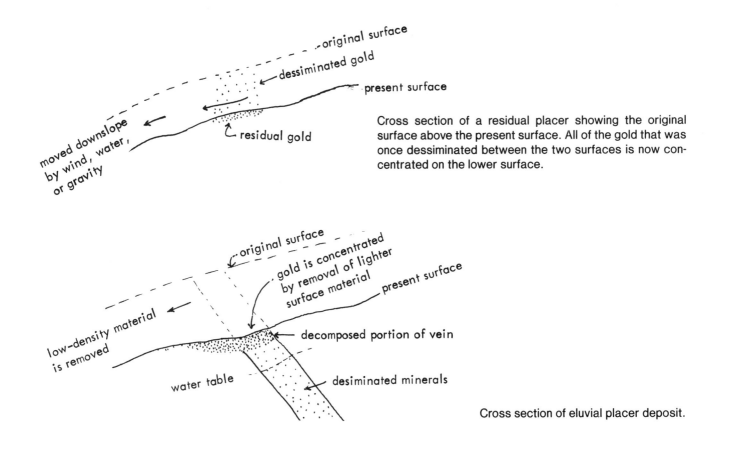

Cross section of a residual placer showing the original surface above the present surface. All of the gold that was once dessiminated between the two surfaces is now concentrated on the lower surface.

Cross section of eluvial placer deposit.

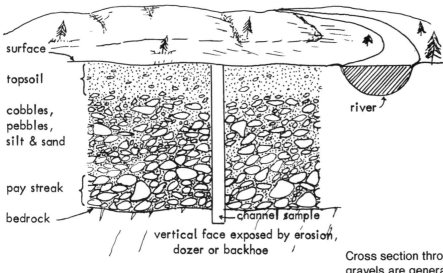

Cross section through typical stratified river gravels. River gravels are generally evaluated by taking vertical channel samples from the surface to bedrock.

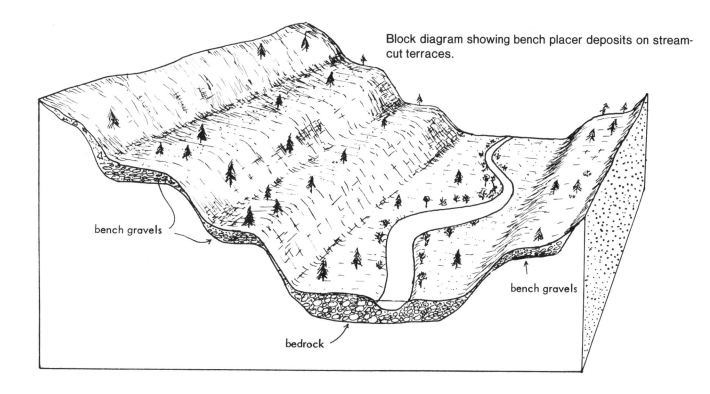

Block diagram showing bench placer deposits on stream-cut terraces.

bench gravels

bench gravels

bedrock

stream point of the bar. Although a few operations on the Snake River have been profitable for a short duration, there has been no sustained or significant production since such mining started in the 1860s. Flood gold gets its name because the fine gold can be transported long distances during flood conditions.

Desert placers are formed by the removal of lighter material from the surface leaving the surface layer enriched in gold. Concentration of placer gold is erratic and unpredictable because much debris moves off hillsides due to gravity, wind and sheet wash. Desert streams generally are violent in nature and move down gullies during infrequent rain storms. Such infrequent and sporadic water movements are ineffective in concentrating gold. The deposits tend to be small and rest on false bedrock such as caliche layers. Some enrichment is due to removal of lighter material from the surface by wind and water.

Tertiary gravels generally refer to the large gold-bearing gravels deposited about 50 million years ago. Many are lithified and buried by hundreds of feet of more recent gravels or volcanic rocks. Tertiary grav-

els have been mined effectively by drift and hydraulic mining.

Glacial placers are formed by glaciers scraping off material from mountainous areas. Gold-bearing vein material is removed along with huge amounts of barren material. During this process, gold is mixed indiscriminantly with large amounts of glacial debris. However, glacial streams working through the glacial till have the capacity to sort the rock and mineral fragments according to size and specific gravity and concentrate any gold contained in the till.

Eolian placers form in desert regions where wind action removes lighter material and enriches the surface in gold. Such deposits have been worked profitably by dry rockers.

Hidden or buried placers are formed where a placer deposit is buried by younger rock. A classic example of this type of deposit occurs between Idaho City and Boise. In this area, a basalt flow covered stream placer deposits of Mores Creek when the creek occupied a higher level than it does at present. Mores Creek has since cut down through the basalt,

— 199 —

Looking south at "fossil" stream channel cut in sandstone bedrock. The lowest part of the channel is the most likely place to find gold. Photo taken on 8th street in the foothills north of Boise.

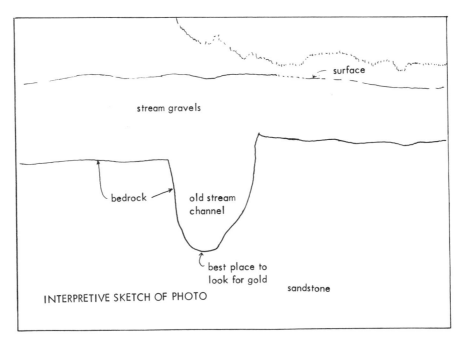

INTERPRETIVE SKETCH OF PHOTO

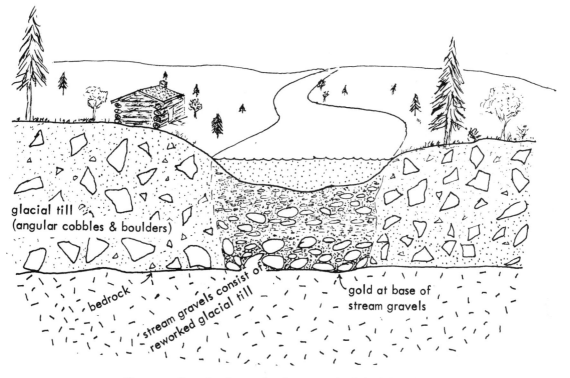

Cross section of a stream that has reworked glacial till. The action of the stream has stratified the underlying gravels so that heavier minerals were moved downward to bedrock. Pebbles and cobbles were also rounded by stream action.

through the underlying buried gravels and then cut into the granite below. Now in several localities one can see the placer gravels of ancient Mores creek sandwiched between the overlying basalt flow above and the underlying granite of the Idaho Batholith.

Sources of Placer Minerals

Sources of placer minerals include veins or lodes, preexisting placer deposits, alluvial material with no placer concentration and sedimentary rocks such as conglomerate.

Lodes

The lode that supplied the placer minerals may no longer exist because of erosion. Several or many veins may have supplied the gold to one placer deposit. Any one of the source veins may not be rich enough to sustain a mining operation.

Preexisting Placers

Preexisting stream placers are constantly being reworked by running water. The new placers may or may not be richer than the original.

Bedrock

Rocks that have steeply-inclined bedding, fractures or cleavage, such as slates and schists, are effective at trapping gold. The bed of the Salmon River in the vicinity of Riggins has a bedrock with steeply-dipping cleavage. Rocks such as clay, volcanic tuffs and decomposed granite provide effective bedrock. If the bedrock is too smooth or flat, it will be ineffective because an irregular surface is necessary to trap the gold. In hard rocks, the gold works into fractures and crevices; whereas, in softer materials such as decomposed granite, it works into the bedrock. This is why the top several feet of bedrock should be removed when cleaning bedrock. As a rule-of-thumb, approximately 90 percent of all gold in a placer deposit is concentrated within one foot of bedrock — either above or below.

Paystreaks

Paystreaks are narow, elongate-shaped bodies containing higher gold concentrations than surrounding materials. They represent the original stream floor where gold was concentrated. The form is irregular and the enriched material may or may not have a different appearance than the surrounding material.

Evolution of Placer Deposits

Placer deposits are formed gradually over a long period of time, and as long as they are subject to agents of erosion, they are under constant change. Such change may not only lead to greater concentration but also to deterioration.

Prospecting for Placer Gold in Idaho

If you wish to prospect for placer gold in Idaho, you are more likely to be successful working bench placers than active stream placers. If you are prospecting with hand tools in a foot or two of water in an active stream, you will find it is very difficult to get through several feet of stream gravels to reach bedrock.

However, if you are prospecting bench gravels, particularly along highways that follow streams, it is fairly easy to find road cuts that expose the contact between terrace or bench gravels and the underlying bedrock. Having found the gravel-bedrock contact, you then look for the lowest point along the contact, which under the most fortunate circumstances, would be the cross section of an ancient river channel. Then take your sample from gravels on the lowest point of bedrock, using a shovel and canvas so as not to let small particles of gold escape.

Geology of Placer Deposits

Placer gold is derived from chemical and mechanical weathering of rock containing gold, generally in veins. Upon disintegration of the host rock, the free gold is transported by running water. As rock fragments are transported downstream, they are broken into smaller particles and additional gold is released. Water saturates all the sedimentary material in the stream bed. The turbulence and movement of water then allows the gold to work down to bedrock. Sedimentary materials tend to stratify according to density so that the minerals with the highest specific gravity (gold is about 7 times quartz and feldspar) quickly move through the sediment until trapped within or on bedrock. Minerals with a lower specific gravity move faster and farther downstream than mineral particles with a higher specific gravity.

Bench Gravels

Once gold is discovered in stream placers, one should investigate bench gravels above the stream for remnants of earlier stream gravels deposited before the stream cut to its present level. This type of deposit is often overlooked and represents a fruitful area for prospecting. Bench gravels may or may not lie on a terrace. In some cases bench or terrace gravels may be found by inspecting aerial photographs or topographic maps.

Stream Gradient

The upper portion of streams do not generally contain placer gold because the gradient is too steep; however some coarse gold may be found in bedrock crevices. A steep gradient occurs where the stream drops 100 feet per mile or more. The best placers are developed where the gradient is 25 to 50 feet per mile or just downstream from the steep gradient. Only very fine gold particles can be found where the gradient is low. Topographic maps, prepared by the U.S. Geological Survey, are excellent for determining the gradient of a stream.

Stratification and Sorting

Coarse gold is typically found with gravel-sized or larger sedimentary material; whereas, fine gold is found in silt, sand and pebble-sized material. Stratification and sorting are valuable indicators of how

Collecting sample of placer gravels at bedrock. The shovel points towards bedrock.

promising a placer is. Poorly-sorted and stratified material such as glacial deposits generally are not gold bearing. There must be stratification or sorting of the material so that concentration can occur.

Stream Placers

In terms of past production, gravels in stream placers are important. The stream may be intermittent or permanent. Gold occurs in crevices, potholes and in small "pay streaks" in gravel lenses or bars.

Bars

Bars form in streams at places of relatively low velocity such as at or near the convex bank or the inside meander of a stream. Most of the gold and other material in a stream is moved during the flood stage so it is important to realize when prospecting stream gravels, that the position of a pay streak is established during the flood stage.

Buried Placers of Old Tertiary Channels

Many ancient stream channels are buried and cannot be discovered except by indirect evidence. If the base level of a stream is raised, gravels will prob-

Cross section of stream gravels showing the relationship of gold to stratification and bedrock.

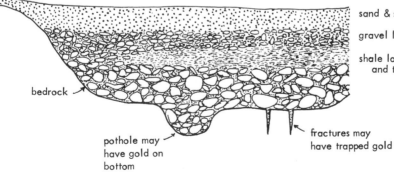

Cross section of stream

sand & silt layer may have fine gold

gravel layer may contain coarse gold

shale layer may act as false bedrock and trap gold on upper surface

bedrock

pothole may have gold on bottom

fractures may have trapped gold

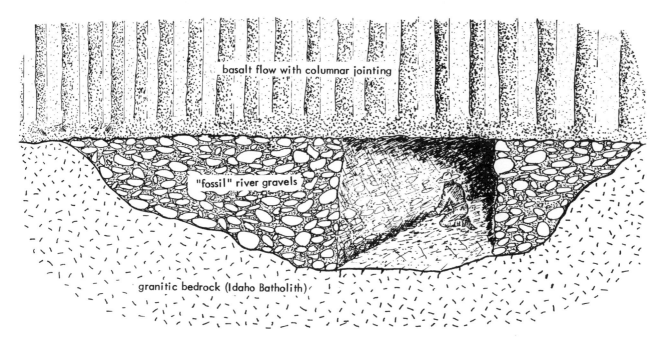

basalt flow with columnar jointing

"fossil" river gravels

granitic bedrock (Idaho Batholith)

Buried placer deposit may be seen along Highway 21 between Boise and Idaho City. Fossil river gravels lie on the Cretaceous Idaho Batholith and are covered by the much younger canyon-filling basalt. A miner is shown working on bedrock in the mine adit.

ably be covered by renewed sedimentation of finer material, slumps and gravity flows of earth material. Volcanic flows and tuffs have covered many placer deposits in Idaho. In many cases the old gravels are consolidated by cementation or compacted by the weight of overburden. These gravels are commonly mined by underground "hardrock" methods. Miners followed the old streams channels with adits (horizontal underground workings).

Bedrock Concentration of Gold

A stream may cut down through thousands of feet of rock as it works its way to bedrock. All during this time gold is continuously concentrated on bedrock as a steam continues to cut downwards. A stream performs like a sluice box, trapping the gold on the stream bed and allowing the stream to carry the valueless, lighter materials on downstream. When base level is reached, the stream begins to widen its valley

so that a narrow, rich belt of gold-enriched bedrock meanders through a wide valley. The bordering bedrock may have a concentration of gold, but it will be less than the narrow, rich belt or "pay streak." In order to find the higher gold values on a stream bed, you should cut a trench to bedrock across the stream. Then take vertical channel samples incrementally along the trench.

Gold Concentrations above Bedrock

Gold is rarely uniformly disseminated or distributed throughout a placer deposit. However, fine gold in silt and sand deposits may come closest to approaching a disseminated deposit. If there is a continuing source of gold, the overlying alluvium will contain disseminated gold.

Gold Panning

Although there are numerous descriptions avail-

River gravels "sandwiched" between granite below and basalt flow above. Photo taken at roadcut on Highway 21 between Boise and Idaho City.

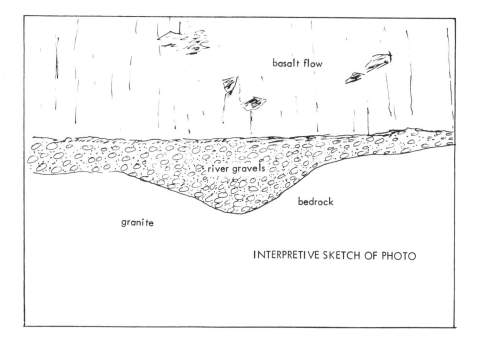

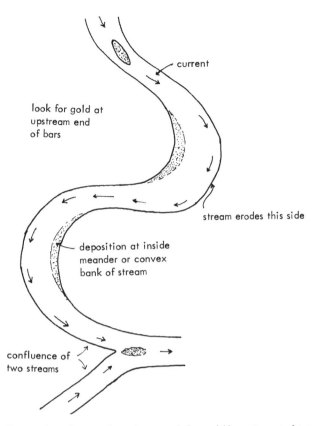

Illustration shows where to search for gold in a stream. As a general rule, the farthest upstream portion of a gravel bar is the best place to search for gold.

extremely important to remove all grease from the inside surface. Heating at a sufficiently high temperature (500 degrees fahrenheit) not only burns off the grease but also has the added advantage of turning the pan blue. Gold, being light yellow, shows up much better with a blue or black background. Plastic gold pans in black and green also work quite well. In fact a pie tin will work if you have nothing else.

Procedure for Panning

1. First fill the pan level full or slightly heaping with placer material.
2. Submerge the pan in water, preferably still water 6 to 10 inches deep.
3. Carefully and slowly stir the contents of the pan with both hands so as to totally saturate the material with water. It is extremely important at this stage to break up all dirt clods and dissolve the clay.
4. While the pan is held in a flat position under water, shake the pan in a circular or back-and-worth manner. The purpose of the shaking is to stratify the contents of the pan in layers so that the heavier minerals are concentrated on the bottom and the lighter material moves upwards.
5. A 16-inch pan full of water-saturated gravel may weigh as much as 30 pounds or more. For this reason the work can be lightened if the pan is worked under water.
6. The pan is tilted so that the less dense material can be floated over the edge of the pan.
7. The gold and other heavy minerals will work downward and concentrate at the edge of the flat pan bottom.
8. Continue to shake the pan in a circular motion under water or with water in it. Then repeat the tilting action so as to wash or float off the light surface layers.
9. Finally the pan contents are reduced to the heavy mineral concentrates and any gold present can readily be seen.

Many beginners worry that their style is faulty and that they are losing gold; however, if normal

able on how to pan gold, washing gold by panning is such a simple process that with very little experience a panner can recover almost all the gold from a pan. By following the basic principles discussed below, anyone can develop his or her own technique. Experience generally improves speed and efficiency rather than percent of recovery. The object is to process the material as rapidly as possible while at the same time retaining as much gold as practical. The extra time spent trying to recover the very fine gold is generally not worthwhile.

The standard gold pan is 16 inches in diameter, 2½ inches deep and made of sheet iron. However, smaller 8 to 14 inch pans are much easier to use, particularly for the beginner. Before using an iron pan, it is

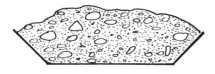

Gold pan is heaped full
of placer gravels.

Place pan under water to
breakup dirt clods and
remove pebbles.

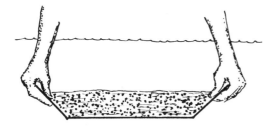

Shake pan with a circular
motion to stratify material.
This allows minerals with a
relatively higher specific
gravity to work towards the
base of the pan.

While pan is submerged in water,
work low density material over
the edge of pan. Then repeat the
action in the preceding illustration.

The series of illustrations above show how to pan for gold.

amounts of heavy minerals or black sands are recovered, then it is quite likely that the gold which has a much higher density would also be saved.

Capacity of the Gold Pan

Panning is the most arduous and lowest capacity method that may be used to wash gold from placer gravel. Because an accomplished panner can only wash 8 to 10 pans per hour, the method is not suitable for anything but high-grade gravels. Such high-grade material generally occurs only at bedrock or in crevices.

A 16-inch gold pan level full of dry gravel will weigh approximately 22 pounds. However the weight may be more or less depending on the amount of moisture and the size and type of material. Typically, one cubic yard of bank gravel weighs 3300 pounds. Depending on the type of placer material, 150 to 180 pans are normally equivalent to one cubic yard. If a person is able to pan at the rate of 10 pans per hour, it is possible to pan about ½ cubic yard per day. Under exceptional conditions, such as an experienced panner working with clean gravel, it is possible to pan up to one cubic yard in a day.

Separation of Black Sands from Gold

Nuggets and small particles of gold of sufficient size should be picked out with tweezers and placed in a vial. There are several different methods or combinations of methods for separating the remaining fine gold from the black sand concentrate. Transfer the concentrates to a smaller pan and continue to manipulate the pan in the manner described above until the black sands are separated. This procedure should be done above another pan so that if gold is lost, it can be recovered. If the concentrates are dried, the black sands can be separated either by a magnet or by blowing. Magnetite commonly represents up to 90 percent of the heavy mineral concentrate. Several drops of mercury can be placed in the concentrates and the remaining fine gold amalgamated. If the colors are very fine, the added time and effort to recover them may not be worthwhile. For example, the Snake River gold in southern Idaho is so fine that

several hundred colors may only be worth one cent.

Pans with copper bottoms may be used for the amalgamation process. First the copper bottom is abraded with emery paper and then, using a device other than your hand, coated with a clean shiny surface of mercury. Gold in the concentrates is picked up by contact with the mercury surface. Only fine material should be used in the pan as coarse concentrates will grind off the mercury. As amalgam collects on the bottom of the pan, it should be scraped off with a scraper made of iron. You should always use extreme caution when working with mercury. Take particular care not to touch mercury with your hands or breath its vapors.

Amalgamators

Rusty gold or gold partly coated by iron oxide does not amalgamate completely because the mercury cannot make complete contact with the gold. To remedy this problem, the heavy mineral concentrates with the gold must be agitated to clean the gold. Mechanical amalgamators are normally used to treat rusty gold. Most amalgamators consist of a cast iron container in which the concentrates are placed. A rock tumbler will work well for small samples. Water, one or two percent mercury, caustic soda and steel balls are combined with the concentrates. As the container is turned slowly for several hours, the steel balls provide a grinding action to clean the gold. Finally the gold, amalgam and mercury are recovered by panning.

A small concrete mixer serves very satisfactorily as an amalgamator. Such a device can handle 50 to 100 pounds of concentrate, one or two pounds of mercury and a few cobbles or steel balls together with water. Generally about an hour is sufficient to complete the amalgamation process.

Cleaning Amalgam

Amalgam is first separated from the black sands by carefully washing with a gold pan. The amalgam or impure mercury is then squeezed manually through a tight cloth such as canvas, chamois skin or buckskin. The process is best done under water to

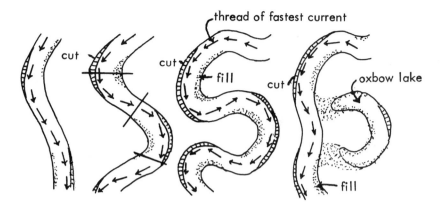

Meander development as a stream progresses through its life cycle.

avoid losing mercury. The cleaned mercury still contains a small amount of gold which will increase its reactivity with gold. After squeezing, the stiff, pasty amalgam may still contain up to 75 percent mercury with the balance in gold and silver.

Separating Gold from Amalgam

Gold may be recovered from amalgam by several different methods. The selection of a particular method is based on convenience or the need to recover the mercury. If it is unnecessary to recover the mercury, the simplest method is to volatize the mercury by heating the amalgam. In this method, the mercury is placed on a clean iron surface and heated to 675 degrees fahrenheit, a temperature at which mercury vaporizes. Mercury vapor which may appear as a heavy white vapor, is extremely dangerous and should not be inhaled.

Potato Method

The potato method is commonly used by prospectors because it is both simple and allows part of the mercury to be recovered. The following procedure is used:

1. A large potato is cut in half.
2. On one half, a recess is hollowed out which is larger than the amount of amalgam.
3. The amalgam is placed on a clean sheet of iron such as a pan suitable for heating.
4. The potato is placed over the amalgam and then heat is applied below the sheet of iron.
5. After 15 to 20 minutes of heating, the mercury will be driven off into the potato and the gold will be left in the hollow of the potato.
6. The mercury can then be recovered by crushing and panning the potato.

Nitric Acid Method

The amalgam is placed in a beaker with a 1 to 1 solution of nitric acid and water which is heated until the mercury is dissolved. After the mercury is dissolved, the gold sponge can be washed in water. Finally the gold may be annealed in a porcelain crucible.

Retorting

Retorting of amalgam to recover gold requires the most elaborate equipment but allows all the mercury to be saved. A retort is basically a pipe-shaped device in which the amalgam is placed in the end that is heated to vaporize off the mercury. The mercury vapor then moves through a condenser pipe where it cools and condenses back to liquid mercury.

SAMPLING AND EVALUATION OF GOLD PLACERS

One cannot overstate the necessity of proper sampling and evaluation of a mineral deposit before committing labor and money into a mining venture. This is true whether the deposit of interest is placer or lode. Thousands of mining operations have failed because mining costs exceeded the value of production. At best, a mining venture is risky; however, through proper sampling and evaluation, it is possible to predict with a reasonable degree of accuracy the potential success of an operation. The standard methods of sampling placers include panning gravel, drifting, test-pitting, trenching, drilling and shaft sinking.

Weight Versus Volume of Placer Material

While evaluating a placer gravel deposit, it is generally necessary to convert bank (in place) volume to loose volume or to convert to tonnage. The degree of compaction of placer material has a great bearing on the weight per unit volume. For example, bank or in place placer material may expand or swell more than 50 percent in volume when excavated and placed in a loose state. Thus, the weight of a given volume of placer material depends on many variables, including size of particles, shape of particles, degree of compaction, amount of moisture, specific gravity of each particle and porosity. It is always important to indicate whether the volume is bank or loose. If the placer material is measured in its loose state, it should be converted back to bank measurement for the purpose of computing value per cubic yard and reserve data.

Map Geology before Sampling

Before making a detailed sample survey, it is generally desirable to work out and map both the bedrock and alluvial geology of the area of interest. Of course substantial information on the geology of the area will also be obtained during the sampling process.

Sampling

Panning along a stream bed is an excellent method to establish the existence of gold; however, it is not a reliable quantitative method for determining the value of the placer deposit. Sampling placer deposits is generally difficult and time consuming. Every placer deposit is different and during the sampling process one must carefully follow these practices: (1) sample in a manner that will relate to the most likely method of mining; (2) establish the depth to bedrock at as many points as possible; (3) sample incrementally to determine relative values of each layer; this is important in designing the mining plan; and (4) take vertical channel samples from the surface to bedrock and make the samples as large as possible. It is not necessary to sample a portion of the overburden if that overburden will not be processed. For example, in drift or tunnel mining the valueless overburden can be avoided; whereas, in surface hydraulic mining all material above bedrock must be either stripped or processed.

Sampling Equipment

Standard sampling equipment includes a gold pan, small shovel, pick, sample bags or buckets, sample tags, field notebook, pencils and sample location map. Other useful, but less essential equipment includes camera, scale, hand lens, small broom, chisels, ruler, rock hammer, tape and compass.

Sample Density and Spacing

The more closely spaced the sample sites, the greater the accuracy of the sample results. However placer sampling is almost always difficult and is subject to many constraints. Generally it is desirable to have uniformly-spaced sample points, but barren spots, large boulders, water and other obstacles may preclude uniform sampling. The assay value of placer samples varies widely from site to site even if separated by only several feet. This is particularly true of coarse material with a large percentage of pebble size or larger.

Sample Depth

The sample should be taken vertically from the surface to bedrock. The upper few inches of bedrock should also be taken if possible. Unfortunately, it is almost always difficult to sample down to bedrock whether using hand labor or mechanized equipment. In a typical placer, more than 50 percent of the gold will be found at or near bedrock, so the importance of sampling to bedrock is obvious.

Bedrock and False Bedrock

The term "bedrock" where used in connection with placer or alluvial mining means a hard-surface below which there is no valuable placer material. Bedrock can be represented by a great variety of rock types including granite, basalt, sandstone, schist, gneiss, quartzite, shale and conglomerate. Even a poorly-consolidated clay or sand layer can be considered bedrock. Generally bedrock within a given placer mining area consists of a single rock type. Normally bedrock will carry the greatest values in its depressions and cracks. During the sampling process it is unlikely that one of these rich or hot spots would be sampled unless the bedrock is exposed.

False Bedrock

False bedrock can be a problem both during sampling and mining. False bedrock is simply a hard surface of dense material that is suspended above true bedrock. False bedrock can be very deceiving because it can consist of the same material as the true bedrock. Problems connected with false bedrock include inaccurate sample results and obscuring the potentially higher valued gravels. By utilizing drilling and seismic reflection methods, it is sometimes possible to ascertain the depth of true bedrock. A seismic record can provide a continuous profile across the deposit.

Sampling Procedure

If you wish to sample a stream bank or sample in a trench or pit prepared by hand or equipment, you can follow the procedure below. Prepare a vertical face from the surface to just below bedrock. Make certain that the face is freshly cleaned and trimmed before sampling. Carefully place a canvas or plastic tarp at the base of the face and bring the edge up as closely to the lowest edge of the face as possible. The canvas is used to collect the sample material removed from the channel. Use care that no material is lost while transferring the sample from the tarp to the sample container. Take as large as sample as possible under the circumstances; normally a one cubic foot sample is adequate. If possible, you should acquire sample buckets that are one half cubic foot in size for easy measurement. In general the larger the material size, the larger should be the sample. Where large boulders are present, it is almost impossible to get a representative sample.

Typically gold in a deposit is erratically distributed along bedrock, false bedrock and in pay streaks. Large samples and incremental sampling may improve results. Sticky clay, a high water table and tree roots are common obstacles to sampling and mining.

Salting of Samples

Salting or taking a sample that is artificially high may occur either deliberately or through poor sampling procedure. Deliberate salting may be done to sell a property at an inflated price or to patent a claim. Such samples may be salted by gold placed in gravels before the sample is cut or placed in containers or equipment during processing.

Failure to include large boulders in a sample, will result in a salted or inflated sample value. Another type of indeliberate salting occurs where assay value is computed on the basis of weight or volume of the concentrates rather than the weight or volume of the original sample.

IDAHO GEMSTONE DEPOSITS

Although Idaho has a variety of gem mineral deposits including rock crystal and amethyst, jasper, chalcedony, agate, agatized wood, opal, garnet, aquamarine, topaz and zircon, only a few of the nationally-significant Idaho deposits are discussed in this chapter.

Old Mine Dumps

Old mine dumps are an excellent place to search for crystal and mineral specimens. Every year weathering and erosion break down these old mine-waste materials and new specimens are exposed to the view of the collector.

Garnets

Garnets occur throughout the State of Idaho in a variety of rock types, including pegmatites, garnetiferous schists and other metamorphic rocks. On the East Fork of Emerald Creek in northern Idaho, gem-quality almandite garnets are found in placer gravels of the stream bed. These purple to red garnets are significant for the asterism or stars caused by inclusions aligned in layers. Emerald Creek garnets are formed in a mica schist by metamorphism. Through the processes of weathering and erosion, the garnets are freed from the mica schist matrix. The high specific gravity of almandite garnets allows them to be concentrated on the bedrock of Emerald Creek in placer deposits. Collectors recover this gem by digging to bedrock and using screens to recover the garnets.

Bruneau Jasper

The most famous jasper in Idaho is the "Bruneau Jasper," a red and green gem-quality stone. The Bruneau jasper deposits are, for the most part, covered by unpatented mining claims and are situated approximately 50 road miles south of Bruneau in Owyhee County.

At the Bruneau-Jarbidge eruptive center, 8 to 10 large rhyolite flows fill a structural basin. These flows average about 320 feet thick and several exceed 650 feet thick.

Gas cavities are abundant in the upper zones of the rhyolite flows but are fairly uncommon in the lower zones. They range in size from small vesicles to large cavities more than three feet in diameter. Some cavities are spherical, but most are irregular due to stretching while the rhyolite was still hot and plastic. Typically, those of similar size tend to occur together in horizontal zones. Some flows have abundant cavities, whereas others are nearly devoid of them.

Fractures, gas cavities, spherulite shrinkage cavities and openings around breccia fragments serve as sites of deposition for secondary silica. Silica occurs in various forms, including opal, chalcedony and red and brown jasper. As the flow cools, silica is leached from it and then redeposited in cavities when the silica-bearing fluids cool sufficiently.

The Bruneau jasper deposit is a zone of jasper-filled sperulite shrinkage cavities. There are two small fractures in the upper zone of the Bruneau Jasper rhyolite flow in the Indian Hot Springs area. The deposit which is several hundred meters across has been commercially exploited. The Bruneau Jasper flow is the most silica-rich rhyolite flow in the area and is the source of silica that resulted in the predominantly red and brown jasper.

Spencer Opal Deposit

The Spencer opal deposit is located about 5 miles east-northeast of the town of Spencer. The best access to the deposit is by driving east from Spencer on the Spencer-Kilgore county road for approximately 5 miles, then turning left (north) on a dirt road and continuing 2 miles to the mine site. Many opal prospects lie on the south side of Opal Mountain; however, most of these deposits are covered by patented or unpatented mining claims.

Opal occurs in a Tertiary-age rhyolite flow. As the

Inspecting lithophysae (gas cavities) in rhyolite flow for crystals.

rhyolite was extruded from deep within the crust, the sudden release of pressure caused gas to separate from the fluid magma and form large vesicles or cavities. The opal was later deposited in the cavities by hot water percolating through the silica-rich rocks. As the hot water moved through the rocks, it took silica into solution and then redeposited the silica as opal in the cavities and fractures.

The nodules, which are mineralized with opal, range in size from less than an inch to more than a foot in diameter. Opal occurs in the nodules as stratified cavity filling or closely-spaced layers, generally less than 0.1 inch thick. Where the silica is precipitated as microscopic spheres in an orderly arrangement, the entering light is refracted through the opal layers causing bands of "fire" with colors of green, yellow, pink, blue and red.

Opal consists of noncrystalline (amorphous) silicon dioxide (SiO_2) and up to 20 percent water. The best quality opal contains less than 10 percent water. Exposure to sunlight will cause dehydration and fading of the colors. Consequently, the stone must be maintained so as to prevent water loss. Opal-filled nodules are disseminated through thick zones in the rhyolite.

Mining of the nodules is accomplished with a large dozer or by setting off small explosives. The opal-filled nodules can then be extracted by hand methods.

One of the best deposits in the area is the well-known Deer Hunt Mine. The mine was reportedly discovered in 1948 by two deer hunters who were lost in a storm. The Deer Hunt Mine is open to rock hounds interested in digging the opal for a set price per pound. People from all over the world visit this mine every year to mine the popular opal gemstone.

Corundum

The mineral corundum is composed of aluminum oxide and is second only to diamond in hardness. Corundum occurs in a variety of colors. The transparent red corundum is the gemstone ruby; the transparent blue variety is the gemstone sapphire. All of the Idaho deposits of gem-quality corundum are found as placer deposits rather than in the original rock where the gems were formed. Most of these alluvial placer deposits yield dull-gray corundum which is not considered to be gem quality. Crystals have been found at the following localities:

1. Gravel bars along Rhodes and Orofino Creeks in Clearwater County near Pierce.
2. Placer deposits of the Stanley Basin in Custer County.
3. In the Gold Fork tributary of the Payette River in Valley County.
4. Between McCall and New Meadows on the headwaters of Goose Creek is a collecting area known as Rocky Flat.

Corundum concentrates in placer deposits along bedrock similar to gold and garnet because of a high specific gravity. Consequently, gem corundum is recovered in the same manner as placer gold. A screen is generally used to separate the course material containing valuable crystals from finer dirt and sand.

LOCATING MINING CLAIMS IN IDAHO

Minerals Locatable Under the Mining Laws

The Federal mining laws (30 USC §22) state: "Except as otherwise provided, all valuable mineral deposits in lands belonging to the United States, both surveyed and unsurveyed, shall be free and open to exploration and purchase."

The above definition of a locatable mineral is somewhat vague but undoubtedly could be applied to almost any mineral with sufficient value that it could be extracted and marketed at a profit. There is no such thing as a list of locatable minerals because of the requirement for value. For example, some deposits of gold, uranium and gemstones are valuable, whereas other deposits are not. Whether or not a particular mineral deposit is locatable depends on such factors as quality, quantity, minability, demand, marketability, etc.

Minerals Not Locatable

Rather than attempting to establish what minerals are locatable, it may be more practical to discuss what minerals are definitely not locatable. The number of locatable minerals authorized by the 1872 Mining Law has been substantially reduced by several subsequent Federal laws. The Mineral Leasing Act of 1920, as amended, authorized that deposits of oil, gas, coal, potassium, sodium, phosphate, oil shale, native asphalt, solid and semisolid bitumen and bituminous rock including oil-impregnated rock or sands from which oil is recoverable only by special treatment after the deposit is mined or quarried and deposits of sulphur in Louisiana and New Mexico may be acquired only through a mineral leasing system. The Materials Act of July 31, 1947 (61 Stat. 681) amended by the Act of July 23, 1955 (69 Stat. 367) excluded common varieties of sand, stone, gravel, pumice, pumicite and cinders. However, uncommon varieties of sand, stone, gravel, pumice, pumicite and cinders are locatable. The Act of September 28, 1962 (76 Stat. 652) removed petrified wood from the locatable mineral category.

Minerals Never Locatable

Even before the Materials Act of 1947 and the Act of July 23, 1955 were enacted, many mineral materials were never locatable even though they could be marketed at a profit. In fact the Materials Act of 1947 was enacted to provide a means to dispose of them. Material in this category includes ordinary deposits of clay, limestone, fill material, etc. Non-locatable minerals generally have a normal quality and a value for ordinary uses.

Lands Open to Location

Mining claims may be located on unreserved, unappropriated lands administered by the Bureau of Land Management, U.S. Department of the Interior and the unreserved, unappropriated public domain land in the National Forests administered by the Forest Service, U.S. Department of Agriculture.

Lands patented under the Stockraising Homestead Law or other land disposal laws that reserved locatable minerals to the United States may be subject to mineral location. The effect of the mineral reservation in the patent is to segregate the land into a surface estate and a mineral estate. The mineral estate may be subject to location under the general mining laws in the same manner as are vacant, unappropriated public lands. However, the surface owner is entitled to compensation for any damages resulting from exploration or mining.

Lands Closed to Location

The national parks and most national monuments are closed to mining location; however, valid mining claims existing at the date a national park or monument was established are entitled to certain grandfather rights. Indian reservations, military reservations, most reclamation projects, Federal wildlife refuges, and land segregated under the Classification and Multiple Use Act are generally closed to mining location.

A great variety of withdrawals or land classifications have served to segregate the public lands from mineral location and entry. Prior to locating a mining claim, the public land records of the Bureau of Land Management should be examined to determine if the area of interest is available for mineral location. A mineral location on lands segregated from mineral entry would not only be a waste of time and money but would also be an unauthorized trespass.

Qualifications of Locators

Mineral locations may be made by citizens of the United States or persons who have declared their intention to become citizens. Minors and corporations organized under the laws of any state are eligible to make mining locations. Agents are allowed to make locations for qualified locators.

Lode Mining Claims

Lode mining claims may be located upon discovery of a vein or lode "of quartz or other rock in place bearing gold, silver, cinnabar, lead, tin, copper or other valuable deposits" (30 USC §23). A lode claim shall not exceed 1,500 feet in length along the course of the vein or lode. Also a claim must not extend more than 300 feet on each side of the middle of the vein at the surface. Thus, the dimensions of a lode mining claim must not exceed a parallelogram 1,500 feet in length by 600 feet in width. Federal law also requires that the end lines of each claim must be parallel to each other.

Federal regulations (43 CFR 3841-5) specify that certain information must be contained in the location notice. The course and distance from the discovery shaft on the claim to some permanent, well-known object, such as stone monuments, blazed trees, confluence of streams, intersection of roads and prominent mountains, should be described as accurately as practicable. Survey monuments such as brass cap section corners are excellent, especially since the

Federal law (30 USC §23) requires that the location of the claims shall be designated with reference to the lines of the public survey if such claims are situated on surveyed lands.

Placer Mining Claims

Placer claims may be located for "all forms of deposit, excepting veins of quartz or other rock in place" (30 USC §35). All placer mining claims must conform as near as practicable with the United States system of public land surveys and the rectangular subdivisions of such surveys, even though the claims are located on unsurveyed lands. If the claims conform to such legal subdivisions, no further survey or plat shall be required for patent. On unsurveyed land and in certain situations, placer claims may be located by metes and bounds.

No location for a placer claim can exceed 20 acres for each individual participating. However, an association of two locators may locate 40 acres; three may locate 60 acres, and so on. The maximum area that may be embraced by a single placer claim is 160 acres and such a claim must be located by an association of at least eight persons. Corporations are limited to 20-acre claims. A 20-acre placer claim might be described as being in N½ NE¼ NW¼, Sec. 5, T. 5 N., R. 3 W., Boise Meridian.

Uncommon varieties of building stone may be located with placer-type claims pursuant to the Act of August 4, 1892 (27 Stat. 348; 30 USC §161). The law requires that building-stone placers may be located only on lands "that are chiefly valuable for building stone."

Tunnel Sites

Tunnel locations are made by erecting a substantial post or monument at the face or point where the tunnel is started. Stakes or monuments should be placed along the line of the tunnel at appropriate intervals to a distance of 3,000 feet from the point of commencement. The owner of a mining tunnel shall have the possessory right to 1,500 feet of any blind lodes cut, discovered, or intersected by such tunnel. This gives the locator of the tunnel exclusive right to prospect an area 3,000 feet by 3,000 feet, while work on the tunnel is being prosecuted with reasonable diligence. Claims staked by other parties after commencement of the tunnel for lodes not appearing at the surface, within the area claimed by the tunnel locator, are invalid. The miner is entitled to locate lode claims to cover the veins intersected by the tunnel. However, failure to prosecute work on the tunnel for six months shall be considered as an abandonment of all rights to undiscovered veins on the line of the tunnel.

A notice of location must be posted on the monument at the point of entry of the tunnel and filed in the county recorder's office of the county in which the tunnel is located. The notice of location shall include the following information: (1) names of the locators; (2) the actual or proposed direction of the tunnel, including the height and width of the tunnel; and (3) the distance from the face or point of commencement to some established survey monument or well-known permanent object.

A sworn statement must be attached to the copy of the location notice filed in the county court house. The sworn statement must describe the extent of the work performed and the amount expended by the locators and their predecessors on the tunnel. The locators must also demonstrate that there is a bona fide intent to prosecute work on the tunnel with reasonable diligence so as to discover a vein or lode.

Mill Sites

The Federal requirements for mill sites are set forth in 30 USC §42 and CFR 3844. Mill site locations shall not exceed 5 acres in size. The land under location must be nonmineral and not contiguous to the vein or lode. Although a mill site may adjoin the sidelines of a lode mining claim, it is unlikely that lands adjoining the endlines would be either nonmineral or not contiguous to the vein.

The Federal law authorizes three general categories of mill sites:

1. A mill may be located if needed by the owner of a lode mining claim for mining and milling purposes.

2. The Act of March 18, 1960 authorized the location of a mill site if needed by the owner of a placer claim for mining, milling, processing, beneficiation, or other operations in connection with such a claim.

3. A mill site may be located for the purpose of establishing and maintaining a custom or independent quartz mill or reduction works. The owner of such a mill need not own a mine in connection with the mill.

On surveyed lands mill sites should be located by legal subdivision, regardless of whether they are dependent mill sites in connection with lode or placer claims or independent mill sites. Dependent mill sites must be used or occupied for mining or milling purposes. Independent mill sites must be used or occupied for milling purposes.

Location Procedure

The first step before locating a claim is to verify that the lands of interest are open to mineral location. This is accomplished by examining the land status maps and records at the land office of the Bureau of Land Management. Unpatented claims are recorded in the county recorder's office in the county in which the claim is located. There are three basic steps to location procedure:

(1) discovery of a valuable mineral deposit;

(2) marking the boundaries of a claim on the ground; and

(3) posting and recording the location notice with the county recorder and the BLM.

Marking Claim Boundaries

Federal law requires that "the location must be distinctly marked on the ground so that its boundaries can be readily traced" (30 USC §28). The State of Idaho has detailed statutory requirements for marking claim boundaries. It requires that a monument be placed at each corner of the claim. Placer claims located by legal subdivision also require corner monuments. Materials used for monuments include posts, blazed trees and piled rocks; however, by far the most common monument is the 4-inch-square post.

It is very important to clearly mark the claim boundaries by durable monuments because the position of the monument on the ground will generally prevail over the recorded description. The more difficult it is to move or destroy a monument, the less likely the claim will be overstaked. It is preferable to slightly overlap claims than to inadvertently omit desired land.

Monumenting a Claim

State law requires the locator to mark the boundaries of his mining claim by placing a monument or post at least four feet in height and four inches square or in diameter at each corner of the claim. Each post or monument shall be marked with the name of the claim, the position or number of the corner and the direction of the boundary lines. A witness monument may be erected if it is not possible to place a monument on the actual claim corner.

Location Notice

The location notice is the basic title document showing ownership to a mining claim. State law requires the following information be contained in the location notice:

1. The name of the locator or location.
2. The name of the claim and whether located as a lode mining claim or as a placer mining claim.
3. The date of the location and the mining district, if any, and the county in which the claim is located.
4. The directions and distances which describe the claim.
5. The direction and distance from the corner where notice is posted to such natural object or permanent monument, if any such there be, as will fix and describe in the notice itself the site of the claim.

After completion of the location notice, at least three copies should be made. One is posted on the number 1 corner monument of the claim; a second is recorded with the county recorder in the county in which the claim is situated; a third is recorded with the Bureau of Land Management, 3380 Americana Terrace, Boise, Idaho 83706 within 90 days after the location date of the claim; and a fourth is retained for personal records. Failure to file a notice of location with both the Bureau of Land Management and the county recorder constitutes an abandonment of the claim.

It is extremely important for the recorded location notice to have an accurate description of the location of the claim. Many claims have such a vague description that they could exist anywhere over a large area.

Assessment Year

The Federal statute requires that not less than $100 worth of labor be performed on each lode or placer claim during each year in order to hold possessory right or maintain title. The Act of August 23, 1958 (72 Stat. 829) changed the period for doing assessment work so that each assessment year begins at noon September 1 instead of noon July 1. Assessment work is not required during the assessment year the claim is located. For example, if a claim were located November 10, 1972, the first assessment work would be required for the assessment year beginning September 1, 1973 and ending September 1, 1974.

The *Idaho Code* requires that an affidavit of assessment work must be filed with the county recorder within 60 days after September 1 of each year.

Federal Requirements for Recordation of Assessment Work

Section 314 of the Federal Land Policy and Management Act of 1976 (also see 43 CFR 3833) requires that on or before December 30 of each year following the calendar year in which the claim was located and every year thereafter, one of three documents must be filed with the state office of the Bureau of Land Management: (1) evidence of annual assessment work; (2) a detailed report of geological, geochemical or geophysical surveys; or (3) a notice of intent to hold the claim. The claimant may select any one of the three types of filings; however, if assessment work is done, an affidavit of assessment should be filed.

GLOSSARY

aa A lava flow with a rough, spiny surface.

adit A nearly horizontal passage from the surface by which a mine is entered. In the United States an adit may be called a tunnel; however, strictly speaking, a tunnel is open at both ends.

alluvial fan A fan-shaped deposit of sand and gravel deposited by a stream at the base of a mountain.

alpine glaciation Glaciation of a mountainous area.

andesite Fine-grained igneous rock with composition intermediate between a rhyolite and a basalt.

apex The highest portion of a vein; it may or may not reach the surface.

anticline An arched fold in which the rock layers dip away from the fold axis.

aplite A light-colored, fine-grained granitic rock.

apophyses An offshoot of a larger pluton.

aquifer A porous water-bearing rock or sediment through which water can move rapidly.

arete A sharp ridge that separates adjacent glacially-carved valleys.

argillaceous Clayey

assessment work At least $100 worth of work must be performed annually on unpatented mining claims in order to maintain a possessory right.

ash Volcanic fragments the size of dust blown into the air during an eruption.

asterism Star-shaped figure of light displayed by some crystals when viewed in reflected light.

asthenosphere The layer of the earth extending from 60 miles below the surface to 150 miles; it behaves plastically.

augen gneiss Shear resistant minerals in metamorphic rocks; they appear as large rounded grains or eyes.

bajada An apron at the foot of a desert mountain range formed from lateral coalescing of alluvial fans.

basalt A dark volcanic rock with fine-grained texture; it is composed of ferromagnesium minerals and calcium-rich plagioclase feldspar.

base level A theoretical depth limit for stream erosion.

batholith A large discordant pluton with an exposed surface area of at least 40 square miles.

bedding planes A nearly flat surface separating two beds of sedimentary rock.

bedrock Solid rock forming the earth's crust, generally covered by overburden.

block faulting A type of faulting in which the crust is broken into a number of subparallel blocks.

breccia Rock composed of angular or broken fragments.

caldera A large, basin-shaped depression formed by the collapse of a volcano.

caliche A hard, thick calcareous crust.

cementation The chemical precipitation of material in the pore spaces separating mineral grains and binding the grains into a hard rock.

chlorite A grass-green to blackish-green hydrous silicate; occurs in thinly banded masses.

chert A dense, hard silica with microscopic-size quartz grains.

cinder cone A volcano constructed of loose rock fragments ejected from the central vent.

cirque A horseshoe-shaped, steep-walled glaciated valley head.

clastic sedimentary rock A sedimentary rock composed of fragments of preexisting rocks.

clay size A term used to designate the particle size of a sediment as very fine, and smaller than silt.

cleavage The ability of a mineral to split along preferred planes.

col A saddle-like gap across a ridge or between two peaks.

composite volcano See strato volcano.

conglomerate A sedimentary rock composed of gravels cemented together.

continental crust The thick, granitic crust under continents.

country rock A loose term to describe the general mass of rock adjacent to an ore body, as distinguished from the vein or ore deposit.

crater A basin-like depression over a vent at the summit of a volcanic cone.

craton Portion of a continent that has been structurally stable for a long period of time.

creep A very slow, continuous downslope movement of soil or debris.

cross bedding The original layering of sedimentary rocks in which the layers are inclined at an angle to the horizontal.

crust The outer layer of the earth.

crystal A homogenous solid with an orderly internal atomic arrangement.

decollement An overthrust sheet.

detrital Composed of mineral or rock fragments.

development The preparation of a proven deposit for mining.

diabase Generally coarse-grained variety of basalt in which plagioclase occurs in an interlocking network of crystals and grains of pyroxene.

diatomite A siliceous deposit composed of the remains of microscopic plants called diatoms.

dike A tabular rock body, generally igneous in origin; cuts across surrounding rock strata.

diorite A coarse-grained plutonic rock with a composition midway between granite and gabbro.

dip The angle at which a vein or bed is inclined from the horizontal, measured at right angles to the strike.

dolomite A carbonate mineral with the composition of Ca Mg $(CO_3)_2$.

drumlin A long, streamlined hill made of glacial till.

earthquake A shaking of the ground caused by a sudden release of energy stored in the rocks below the surface.

end moraine A ridge of till piled up along the front edge of a glacier.

eolian Pertaining to the wind.

epicenter The point on the earth's surface directly above the focus of an earthquake.

epicontinental Situated on the continental shelf.

epithermal A hydrothermal deposit formed at low temperature and pressure generally within 0.5 mile of the earth's surface.

epizone The uppermost depth zone of metamorphism characterized by low temperature and pressure.

erosion The physical removal of rock by an agent such as running water, glacial ice or wind.

erratic An ice-transported boulder that was not derived from bedrock near its present site.

esker A long sinuous ridge of sediment deposited by glacial melt water.

eugeocline A term used to describe Lower Paleozoic silicic assemblage rocks that may be continental rise deposits.

euhedral A mineral grain completely bounded by its own crystal face.

exfoliation The process by which concentric layers form at the surface of bare rocks.

extrusive Any igneous rock that forms at the earth's surface.

facies change A lateral or vertical change in rock characteristics.

fault A break in the earth's crust caused by forces which have moved or displaced the two sides relative to one another.

fissure A large crack in the earth's surface.

felsic rocks Igneous rocks containing a large proportion of feldspar and silica.

float Isolated, displaced fragments of a rock, especially on a hillside below a vein.

flute cast A raised bulge on the underside of a sedimentary bed showing current direction.

flysch Rapid erosion of an adjacent rising mountain belt yields sediments that are thin bedded, graded deposits of sandy and calcareous shales and muds rhythmically interbedded with conglomerates and coarse sandstones.

foliation Parallel alignment of tectural and structural features of a rock.

footwall The underlying surface of an inclined fault plane.

foreland A stable area marginal to an orogenic belt toward which the rocks of the belt were thrust or overfolded.

formation A lithologically distinctive rock unit or deposit with an upper and lower boundary that is large enough to be mapped.

fossil The remains or traces of organisms buried by natural causes and preserved in the earth's crust.

fracture The way a substance breaks where not controlled by cleavage.

frost heaving The lifting of a rock or soil by the expansion of freezing water.

gabbro A mafic, coarse-grained igneous rock composed predominantly of ferromagnesium minerals and calcium-rich feldspar.

geocline Related to a geographic transition.

glacier A large long-lasting mass of ice, formed on land by the compaction and recrystallization of snow, which moves because of its own weight.

gneiss A metamorphic rock composed of light and dark layers.

gossan An iron-bearing weathered product overlying a sulfide deposit.

gouge A thin layer of ground rock.

graben A long narrow block that has been dropped down between two faults.

gradient The slope of a stream bed, generally expressed in feet per mile.

granite A granular igneous rock composed mostly of quartz, feldspar and commonly mica or hornblende.

granodiorite A granitic rock with characteristics of diorite.

gravity fault A fault in which the hanging wall has moved down with respect to the footwall.

ground moraine A blanket of till deposited beneath a glacier.

hanging wall The rock or wall on the upperside of an inclined vein or inclined mine opening.

hoodoo A fantastic column, pinnacle, or piller of rock produced by differential weathering or erosion of layers of varying hardness.

horn A sharp peak attributed to cirques cut back into a mountain on several sides.

horst A block that has been raised between two faults.

hydrothermal Pertaining to hot water.

hypothermal A mineral deposit formed at great depth and in the temperature range of 300 to 500° C.

igneous rock Rock formed from solidification of magma.

intermediate magma Rocks with a chemical composition between felsic and mafic compositions.

intrusive rock Rock that crystallized from magma emplaced in rock below the surface.

island arc A curved line of volcanic islands.

isoclinal fold A fold in which the limbs are parallel to one another.

isotope Atoms of the same element that have different numbers of neutrons but the same number or protons.

jasper A variety of chert colored red, blue, green or yellow by iron-oxide impurities.

joint A fracture in a rock along which no displacement has taken place.

kettle a basin-shaped depression in glacial drift, formed when buried blocks of glacial ice melt.

kipuka An area surrounded by a lava flow.

lacustrine deposits Deposits formed on the bottom of lakes.

lahar A mudflow on the flanks of a volcano.

landslide A relatively rapid movement of soil and rock downslope.

lateral moraine A ridge of debris that continually accumulates along the side of a glacier.

lava Molten rock upon the surface of the earth.

limestone A sedimentary rock in which calcium carbonate predominates.

listric fault A curved fracture that is concave upward with the lower portion almost horizontal.

lithification The consolidation of sediment into sedimentary rock.

lithosphere The rigid outer shell of the earth, approximately 60 miles thick.

load cast A depression in a sedimentary bed caused by unequal settling and compaction and the partial sinking of overlying material into the depression.

locatable minerals Minerals that may be acquired under the Mining Law of 1872, as amended.

location Perfecting the right to a mining claim by discovery of a valuable mineral, monumenting the corners, posting a notice of location and recording the claim.

lode A tabular-shaped deposit of valuable minerals between definite boundaries; a lode may also include several veins spaced closely together so that they may be mined as a unit.

loess Wind-deposited silt.

maar A low-relief volcanic crater formed by multiple shallow eruptions.

mafic rocks Igneous rocks containing a relatively high content of magnesium, iron and calcium.

magma Molten rock material beneath the earth's surface from which igneous rocks are formed.

magma chamber A cavity beneath the earth's surface surrounded by solid rock and containing magma.

magnetic anomaly Any departure from the normal magnetic field of the earth.

magnetite A black, strongly-magnetic iron oxide mineral.

mantle A thick shell of rocks that separates the earth's crust from the core below.

mantle plume A narrow column of hot mantle rock that rises and spreads radially outward.

marble recrystallized limestone or dolomite.

mass movement The movement of rock material downslope through the direct pull of gravity.

matterhorn A glacial horn resembling the matterhorn.

medial moraine A moraine in the middle of a glacier formed by the merging of the lateral moraines of two coalescing valley glaciers.

mesothermal Hydrothermal mineral deposit formed at a temperature range of 200° to 300°C.

mesozone Intermediate depth zone of metamorphism.

metamorphism The transformation of preexisting rock into a distinct new rock as a result of high temperature, high pressure or both.

metasediments A sediment or sedimentary rock that shows evidence of having been subjected to metamorphism.

meteoric Ground water derived primarily from precipitation.

miarolitic cavaties Irregular cavities in igneous rocks.

migmatite Mixed igneous and metamorphic rock.

mill site Nonmineral public lands to be used as a mill site under the Mining Law of 1872, as amended, for the processing of ore for the development of a claim.

mineral deposit Any occurrence of minerals, in or on the earth; the deposit may or may not be profitable to mine.

mineralization The deposition of minerals in a rock.

mineral rights ownership of all minerals including all those rights necessary for access, exploration, development, mining, processing and transportation.

mining The extraction of ore.

mining claim A claim in which an individual, by the act of valid location under the mining laws, has obtained a right to remove and extract minerals from the land, but where full title has not been acquired from the U.S. Government.

miogeocline A prograding wedge of shallow-water sediment at the continental margin.

moraine An accumulation of rock materials carried and deposited by a glacier.

normal fault See gravity fault.

obsidian Volcanic glass.

oceanic crust The thin basaltic crust under the oceans.

ophiolite rocks An association of mafic rocks largely altered to serpentine which appears to have formed initially at or close to an oceanic ridge.

ore A mineral deposit than can be mined at a profit under existing economic conditions.

orogeny An episode of intense deformation of the rocks in a region, generally accompanied by metamorphism and plutonic activity.

outwash plain Flood plains formed by streams draining from the front of a glacier.

pahoehoe lava A type of solidified lava characterized by a smooth, ropy or billowy surface.

paleontology The science that deals with the study of fossils.

pay streak A limited horizon within a placer deposit, containing a concentration of values or made up of material rich enough to mine. Gold tends to concentrate at or near bedrock.

pediment An erosional bedrock surface that slopes away from a desert mountain range.

pedis possessio A claimant in actual occupancy of a mining claim, even if he did not have a discovery, could hold against anyone who had no better title, so long as he was diligently engaged in seeking a discovery.

pegmatite Extremely coarse-grained igneous rock.

permeability The capacity of a rock to transmit a fluid.

phenocrysts Large crystals surrounded by smaller crystals in an igneous rock.

phreatic explosion A volcanic eruption caused by heating and expansion of ground water.

phreatomagmatic A volcanic explosion that extrudes both magmatic gases and steam; it is caused by the contact of magma with water.

phyllite A low-grade metamorphic rock, with a well-developed rock cleavage; it contains minute, aligned mica flakes on the cleavage surface which gives it a lustrous sheen.

physiography A description of the natural features of the earth's surface.

placer A place where gold is obtained by washing; an alluvial or glacial deposit, as of sand or gravel, containing particles of gold or valuable mineral.

plankton aquatic organisms that drift, or swim weakly.

plate tectonic theory The theory that the earth's surface is divided into a few, large thick plates that are slowly moving.

playa lake A shallow temporary lake on a flat valley floor in a dry region.

pluton An igneous body that crystallized deep underground.

porosity The percentage of the total volume of a rock that is occupied by open spaces.

porphyritic rock An igneous rock in which large crystals are enclosed in a matrix of finer-grained minerals or glass.

pressure ridge An elongate uplift of the congealing crust of a lava flow, probably caused by the pressure of underlying still-flowing lava.

pumice A frothy, porous volcanic glass that has a rhyolitic composition.

pyrite A hard, brass-yellow mineral compound of iron sulfide; also known as "fools gold."

pyroclastic rocks Rocks formed from material thrown out of volcanoes.

quartz diorite A quartz-rich diorite.

quartz monzonite A coarse-grained, quartz-rich granitic rock.

quartzite A rock composed of sand-sized grains of quartz that have been welded together during metamorphism.

radiometric date The age of a material as determined through the measurement of radioactive decay.

recessional moraine An end moraine built during the retreat of a glacier.

recrystallization The growth of small grains into larger ones.

recumbent fold A fold in which the axis of folding is more or less horizontal.

reverse fault A fault in which the hanging-wall block moved up relative to the footwall block.

rhyolite A fine-grained, felsic igneous rock composed mostly of feldspar and quartz.

rift A large crack in the earth's crust, generally of tensional origin.

ring fracture A steep-sided fault that is cylindrical in outline and associated with cauldron subsidence.

ripple marks Small ridges formed on sediment surfaces exposed to moving wind or water.

rock glacier A tongue-shaped, slow-moving mass of rocks and ice in high country.

rock slide Rapid sliding of a mass of bedrock along an inclined surface of weakness.

salable minerals Minerals such as common varieties of sand, stone, gravel, cinders, pumice, pumicite and clay that may acquired under the Materials Act of 1947, as amended.

saline Salty.

sand dune A ridge or hill or sand caused by wind.

sandstone A sedimentary rock formed by the cementation of sand grains.

schist A metamorphic rock characterized by coarse-grained, platy minerals with parallel orientation.

scoriaceous mafic volcanic rock which is frothy and cellular.

sediment Material that has been deposited by settling from a transportation agent such as water or wind.

sedimentary rock Rocks formed by the lithification of sediments.

seismic refraction The bending of seismic waves as they pass from one material to another.

seismic waves A wave or vibration produced by an earthquake.

shaft A vertical or inclined opening giving access to an underground mine.

shale A fine-grained laminated sedimentary rock composed of clay and silt.

shearing Movement in which parts of a rock slide relative to one another and parallel to the forces.

shelf, continental That part of the continental margin between the shoreline and the continental slope.

shield volcano A shield-shaped volcanic cone built almost entirely of fluid lava.

silica An oxide of silicon (SiO_2).

sill A tabular intrusion concordant to the layering in the country rock.

skarn Lime-bearing silicates occurring at granite-limestone contacts.

slate A fine-grained, compact metamorphic rock which splits readily into sheets.

slope, continental That part of the continental margin that is seaward of the continental shelf; it has a slope of 3 to 6 degrees.

slump The movement of rock material downslope as a unit along a concave-upward slip plane.

spatter cone A small, steep-sided cone built from lava spattering out of a vent.

spherulite A spherical mass of crystals radiating from a central point.

stalactites An icicle-shaped deposit formed by evaporation of solutions dripping from the roof of a cavern.

stalagmites A cone-shaped mass of dripstone formed on cave floors, generally directly below a stalactite.

stock A small discordant pluton with an outcrop area of less than 40 square miles.

stratigraphy The science of dealing with the definition and interpretation of stratified rocks.

stratovolcano A steep volcano consisting of alternating layers of lava and pyroclastic materials.

strike The direction of the line of intersection of a dipping, planar feature, such as as a fault, vein or bed, with a horizontal plane.

strike-slip fault A fault in which the movement is parallel to the strike of the fault system.

subduction The sliding of the seafloor beneath a continent or island arc.

supergene enrichment A mineral deposit formed and enriched by descending solutions.

surface rights Rights to land exclusive of mineral rights.

syncline A downfold of rocks or a fold in which layered rock dips toward an axis.

Tailings Material rejected from a mill after the recoverable valuable minerals have been extracted.

talus An accumulation of broken rock at the base of a cliff.

tectonism Forces generated within the earth that result in uplift, movement or deformation of part of the earth's surface.

tephra Fragments of rock produced by volcanic explosions.

terminal moraine An end moraine marking the farthest advance of a glacier.

thrust fault A reverse fault in which the dip of the fault plain is at a low angle to the horizontal.

till Material deposited by glacial ice.

topography The configuration or relief of the land surface.

transcurrent fault See strike slip fault.

transform fault A fracture zone in the ocean basin along which ridges are offset and lateral movement occurs.

tsunami A giant ocean wave generated by a submarine earthquake.

tuff A rock formed from volcanic ash.

vein A well-defined zone or belt of mineral-bearing rock confined between nonmineral rock, typically tabular in shape.

vent An opening in the earth's surface through which a volcanic eruption takes place.

vesicle A cavity in a volcanic rock caused by gas in a lava.

vitric Glassy.

volcanic bombs Irregular to spindle-shaped air-borne blocks of lava hurled from a volcanic vent during an eruption.

water table The upper surface of ground water.

weathering The mechanical disentegration and chemical decomposition of rocks.

welded tuff A pyroclastic rock whose particles have been fused together by heat still contained in the deposit.

xenolith A foreign inclusion in an igneous rock.

REFERENCES

Armstrong, R. L., 1974, Precambrian (1.5 x 10 year old) rocks in central and south-central Idaho – the Salmon River arch and its role in Cordilleran sedimentation and tectonics: Am. Jour. Sci., v. 275-A, p. 437-467.

Armstrong, R. L., 1975, The geochronometry of Idaho: Isochron west, no. 14.

Armstrong, R.L., Leeman, W. P., and Malde, H.E., 1975, K-Ar dating, Neogene volcanic rocks of the Snake River Plain, Idaho: Am. Jour. Sci., v. 275, p. 225-251.

Armstrong, R. L., Taubeneck, W. H., and Hales, P. O., 1977, Rb-Sr and K-Ar geochronometry of Mesozoic granitic rocks and their Sr isotopic composition, Oregon, Washington, and Idaho: Geol. Soc. Am. Bull., 88, p. 397-411.

Armstrong, R. L., Harakal, J. E., and Neill, W. M., 1980, K-Ar dating of the Snake River Plain (Idaho) volcanic rocks – new results: Isochron / West, no. 27, p. 5-10.

Axelrod, D. I., 1968, Tertiary floras and topographic history of the Snake River basin, Idaho: Geol. Soc. Am. Bull., v. 79, p. 713-734.

Bennett, E. H., 1980, Granitic rocks of Tertiary age in the Idaho Batholith and their relation to mineralization: Economic Geology, v. 75, p. 278-288.

Bennett, E. H., 1984, The Trans-Challis fault zone: A major crustal discontinuity in central Idaho: Geol. Society of America Abstracts with Programs, v. 16, p. 442.

Bennett, E. H., 1986, Relationship of the trans-Challis fault system in central Idaho to Eocene and Basin and Range extension: Geology, v. 14, p. 481-486.

Berry, G. W., Grim, P. J., and Ikelman, J. A., 1980, Thermal springs list for the United States: U.S. National Oceanic and Atmospheric Administration Key to Geophysical Records Documentation No. 12.

Bhattacharyya, B. K. and Mabey, D. R., 1980, Interpretation of magnetic anomalies over southern Idaho using generalized multibody models: U.S. Geological Survey Open-File Report 80-475, 48 p.

Bonnichsen, Bill, 1982, The Bruneau-Jarbidge eruptive center, southwestern Idaho, in Bill Bonnichsen and R. M. Breckenridge, editors, Cenozoic Geology of Idaho: Idaho Bureau of Mines and Geology Bulletin 26, p. 237-254.

Bonnichsen, Bill and G. P. Citron, 1982, The Cougar Point Tuff, southwestern Idaho, in Bill Bonnichsen and R. M. Breckenridge, editors, Cenozoic Geology of Idaho: Idaho Bureau of Mines and Geology Bulletin 26, p. 255-281.

Bretz, J. H., 1923, The channeled scablands of the Columbia Plateau: Journal of Geology, v. 31, p. 617-649.

Brooks, H. C., and Vallier, T. L., 1978, Mesozoic rocks and tectonic evolution of eastern Oregon and western Idaho, in Howell, D. G., and McDougall, D. A., eds., Mesozoic paleogeography of the western United States: Society of Economic Paleontologists and Mineralogists, Pacific Section, Pacific Coast Paleogeography Symposium 2, p. 133-146.

Camp, V. E., Hooper, P. R., and Wright, T. L., 1982, Columbia River basalt in Idaho: physical and chemical characteristics, flow distribution, and tectonic implications, in Bill Bonnichsen and R. M. Breckenridge, editors, Cenozic Geology of Idaho: Idaho Bureau of Mines and Geology Bulletin 26, p. 55-75.

Cathcart, J. B., Sheldon, R. P., and Gulbrandsen, R. A., 1984, Phosphate-rock resources of the United States: U.S. Geological Survey, Circular 888, 48 p.

Christiansen, R. L., 1982, Late Cenozoic volcanism of the Island Park area, eastern Idaho, in Bill Bonnichsen and R. M. Breckenridge, editors, Cenozoic Geology of Idaho: Idaho Bureau of Mines and Geology Bulletin 26, p. 345-368.

Crone, A. J., Machette, M. M., Bonilla, M. G., Lienkaemper, J. J., Pierce, K. L., Scott, W. E., and Bucknam, R. C., 1985, Surface faulting accompanying the Borah Peak earthquake, central Idaho, in Stein, R. S., and Bucknam, R. C. (eds.), 1985, Proceedings of Workshop XXVIII on the Borah Peak, Idaho earthquake, v. A: U.S. Geological Survey Open-File Report 85-290, p. 43-58.

Currey, D. R., Oviatt, C. G., and Plyler, G. B., 1983, Stansbury shoreline and Bonneville lacustral cycle: Geological Society of America Abstracts with Programs, v. 15, p. 301.

Evans, H. M., 1904, A new Cestraciont spine from the Lower Triassic of Idaho: Univ. of Calif. Pubs., Bull. of the Dept. of Geol., v. 3, no. 18, p. 397-407.

Gulbrandsen, R. A., and Krier, D. J., 1980, Large and rich phosphorous resources in the Phosphoria Formation in the Soda Springs area, southeastern Idaho: U.S. Geological Survey Bulletin 1496, 25 p.

Gastil, R. G., 1979, A conceptual hypothesis for the relation of differing tectonic terranes to plutonic emplacement: Geology, p. 542.

Greeley, Ronald, 1982, The style of basaltic volcanism in the eastern Snake River Plain, Idaho, in Bill Bonnichsen and R. M. Breckenridge, editors, Cenozoic Geology of Idaho: Idaho Bureau of Mines and Geology Bulletin 26, p. 407-421.

Hamilton, Warren, 1963, Metamorphism in the Riggins region, western Idaho: U.S. Geological Survey Prof. Paper 436, 95, p.

Hamilton, Warren, Myers, B. W. b., 1962, Menan Buttes, cones of glassy basalt tuff in the Snake River Plain, Idaho: Short Papers in Geology, Hydrology, and Topography, U.S. Geological Survey Prof. Paper 450-E, p. 115-118.

Hardyman, R. F., McIntire, D. H., and Ekren, E. B., 1985, Eocence volcanism and the western Snake River Plain: Geological Society of America Abstracts with Programs, v. 17, no. 4, p. 223.

Harrison, J. E., 1972, Precambrian Belt Basin of northwestern United States: its geometry, sedimentation and copper occurances: Geol. Soc. Am. Bull., v. 83, p. 1215-1240.

Harrison, J. E.; Griggs, A. B., and Wells, J. D., 1974, Tectonic features of the Precambrian Belt basin and their influence on post-Belt structures: U.S. Geological Survey Professional Paper 866, 15 p.

Heller, P. L., Bowdler, S. S., Chambers, H. P., Coogan, J. C., Hagen, E. S., Shuster, M. W., Winslow, N. S., Lawton, T. F.; 1986, Geology, v. 14, p. 388-391.

Hooper, P. R., 1984, Physical and chemical constraints on the evolution of the Columbia River Basalt: Geology, p. 494.

Hooper, P. R., 1982, Structural model for the Columbia River basalt near Riggins, Idaho in Bill Bonnichsen and R. M. Breckenridge, editors, Cenozoic Geology of Idaho: Idaho Bureau of Mines and Geology Bulletin 26, p. 129-136.

Hovland, R. D., 1981, Geology of the northwest part of the Lower Valley Quadrangle, Caribou County, Idaho (M.S. thesis): San Jose, California, San Jose State University, 108 p.

Hyndman, D. W., 1985, Source and formation of the Idaho Batholith: Geological Society of America Abstracts with Programs, v. 17, no. 4, p. 226.

Keefer, D. K.; Wilson, R. C.; Harp, E. L., and Lips, E. W., 1984, Landslides in the Borah Peak, Idaho earthquake of 1983, in Reaveley, L. D., (ed.), The Borah Peak earthquake, October 28, 1983: Earthquake Engineering Institute Reconnaissance Report on the Borah Peak Earthquake.

Killsgaard, T. H.; Freeman, V. L. Coffman, J. S., 1970, Mineral Resources of the Sawtooth Primitive Area, Idaho: Geological Survey Bulletin 1319-D.

Kimmel, P. G., 1982, Stratigraphy, age and tectonic setting of the Miocene-Pliocene lacustrine sediments of the western Snake River Plain, Oregon and Idaho, in Bill Bonnichsen and R. M. Breckenridge, editors, Cenozoic Geology of Idaho: Idaho Bureau of Mines and Geology Bulletin 26, p. 423-437.

King, J. S., 1982, Selected volcanic features of the south-central Snake River Plain, Idaho, in Bill Bonnichsen and R. M. Breckenridge, editors, Cenozoic Geology of Idaho: Idaho Bureau of Mines and Geology Bulletin 26, p. 439-451.

King, P. B., and Beikman, H. M., 1974, Geologic map of the United States: U.S. Geological Survey, scale 1:2,500,000.

Kuntz, M.A., Champion, D. E., Spiker, E. C., Lefebvre, R. H., and McBroome, L. A., 1982, The Great Rift and the evolution of the Craters of the Moon lava field, Idaho, in Bill Bonnichsen and R. M. Breckenridge, editors, Cenozoic Geology of Idaho: Idaho Bureau of Mines and Geology Bulletin 26, p. 423-437.

Lachenbruch, A. H. and Sass, J. H., 1980 Heat flow and energetics of the San Andreas fault zone: Journal of Geophysical Research, v. 85, p. 6185-6222.

Leeman, W. P., 1982, Development of the Snake River Plain-Yellowstone Plateau province, Idaho and Wyoming: an overview and petrologic model, in Bill Bonnichsen and R. M. Breckenridge, editors, Cenozoic Geology of Idaho: Idaho Bureau of Mines and Geology Bulletin 26, p. 155-177.

Lund, Karen, 1984, The continent- island arc junctures in west-central Idaho – a missing link in Cordilleran tectonics: Geological Society of America Abstracts with Programs, v. 16, no. 6, p. 580.

Lund, Karen, and Snee, L. W., Structural and metamorphic setting of the central Idaho Batholith: Geological Society of America Abstracts with Programs, v. 17, no. 4, p. 253.

Mabey, D. R., 1982, Geophysics and tectonics of the Snake River Plain, Idaho, in Bill Bonnichsen and R. M. Breckenridge, editors, Cenozoic Geology of Idaho: Idaho Bureau of Mines and Geology Bulletin 26, p. 139-153.

Mabey, D. R., 1983, Geothermal resources of southern Idaho: U.S. Geological Survey Circular 866.

Mabey, D. R., Peterson, D. L., and Wilson, C. W., 1974, Preliminary gravity map of southern Idaho: U.S. Geological Survey Open-File Report 74-78.

Malde, H. E., 1968, The catastrophic late Pleistocene Bonneville flood in the Snake River Plain, Idaho: U.S. Geological Survey Professional paper 596, 52 p.

Malde, H. E., and Powers, H. A., 1962, Upper Cenozoic stratigraphy of the western Snake River Plain, Idaho: Geological Society of America Bulletin, v. 73, p. 1197-1220.

Maley, T. S., 1974, Structure and petrology of the lower Panther Creek area, Lemhi County, Idaho: Unpublished Ph.D. Dissertation, University of Idaho, 130 p.

Maley, T. S., 1975, An occurrence of orbicular rocks near Shoup, Idaho: Geological Society of America Abstracts with Programs, v. 7, no. 5, p. 626.

Maley, T. S., 1975, Structural facies in the augen gneiss of northwestern Lemhi County, Idaho: Geological Society of America Abstracts with Programs, v. 7, no. 5, p. 626-627.

Maley, T. S., 1976, Structural history of the Salmon River Mountains, east-central Idaho: Geological Society of America Abstracts with Programs, v. 8, no. 3, 392-393.

Maley, T. S., 1977, Idaho Mining Laws: Northwest Mining Associations Second Annual Service Directory, p. 143-148.

Maley, T. S., 1984, Mineral Title Examination, Mineral Land Publications, Boise, Idaho, 396 p.

Maley, T. S., 1985, Mining law — from Location to Patent, Mineral Land Publications, Boise, Idaho, 597 p.

Mansfield, G. R., 1927, Geography, geology, and mineral resources of part of southeastern Idaho: U. S. Geological Survey, Profession Paper 152, 453 p.

Moore, S. W., and Hovland, R. D., 1984, Idaho earthquakes: Your Public Lands, U.S. Bureau of Land Management, v. 34, no. 4, p. 19-20.

Muffler, L. J. P., 1979, Assessment of geothermal resources of the United States – 1978: U.S. Geological Survey Circular 790.

Newell, N. D., and Kummell, Bernard, 1941, Permo-Triassic boundary in Idaho, Montana and Wyoming: Am. Jour. Sci., v. 239, no. 3, p. 204-209.

Oberlindacher, Peter, 1983, Geology of the southern part of the Wooley Range, Caribou County, Idaho (M.S. thesis): San Jose, California, San Jose State University, 110 p.

O'Neill, J. M., and Lopez, D. A., 1985, Character and regional significance of the Great Falls tectonic zone, east-central Idaho and west-central Montana: American Association of Petroleum Geologists Bulletin, v. 69, p. 437-447.

Reid, R. R., Greenwood, W. R., and Morrison, D. A., 1970, Precambrian metamorphism of the Belt Supergroup in Idaho: Geological Society of America Bulletin, v. 81, no. 3, p. 915-917.

Reid, R. R., Morrison, D. A., and Greenwood, W. R., 1973, The Clearwater orogenic zone: a relict of Proterozoic orogeny in central and northern Idaho, in Belt Symposium, v. 1: Idaho Bureau of Mines and Geology, p. 10-56.

Richmond, G. M., Frywell, R., Neff, G. E., And Weiss; P. L., 1965, The Cordilleran ice sheet on the northern Rocky Mountains, in The Quaternary of the United States: Princeton, New Jersey, Princeton University Press, p. 231-242.

Ross, C. P., and Forester, J. D., 1958, Outline of the geology of Idaho: Idaho Bureau of Mines and Geology, Bulletin No. 15, 74 p.

Ross, S. H., and Savage, C. N., 1967, Idaho Earth Science: Idaho Bureau of Mines and Geology.

Ruppel, E. T., 1975, Precambrian and Lower Ordovician rocks in east-central Idaho: U.S. Geological Prof. Paper 889.

Ruppel, E. T., 1973, Precambrian sedimentary rocks in east-central Idaho, in Belt Symposium: Idaho Bureau of Mines and Geology, no. 1, p. 78-79.

Ruppel, E. T., 1982, Cenozoic block uplifts in east-central Idaho and southwest Montana: U. S. Geological Survey Prof. Paper 1224, 24 p.

Ruppel, E. T., and Lopez, D. A., 1984, The thrust belt in southwest Montana and east-central Idaho: U.S. Geological Survey Prof. Paper 1278, 41 p.

Spear, D. B., and King, J. S., 1982, The geology of Big Southern Butte, Idaho, in Bill Bonnichsen and R. M. Breckenridge, editors, Cenozoic Geology of Idaho: Idaho Bureau of Mines and Geology Bulletin 26, p. 395-403.

Stein, R. S., and Bucknam, R. C., 1986, Quake replay in the Great Basin: Natural History, v. 6, p. 29-34.

————, (eds.), 1985, Proceedings of Workshop XXVIII on the Borah Peak earthquake, v. A and B: U.S. Geological Survey Open-File Report 05-290, 686 p. (v. A), 23 p. (v. B).

Stewart, J. H., 1972, Initial deposits in the Cordilleran Geosyncline: Evidence of a late Precambrian (<850 m.y.) continental separation: Geological Society of America Bull., v. 83, p. 1345-1360.

Sutter, J. F., and Lund, Karen, 1984, Metamorphic, plutonic, and uplift history of a continent-island arc suture zone, west-central Idaho: Geological Society of America Abstracts with Programs, v. 16, no. 6, p. 670-671.

Toth, M. I., 1985, Petrology and evolution of the bitterroot lobe of the Idaho Batholith: Geological Society of America Abstracts with Programs, v. 17, no. 4, p. 269.

Toth, M. I., and Stacey, J. B., 1985, Uranium-lead geochronology and lead isotope data for the bitterroot lobe of the Idaho Batholith: Geological Society of America Abstracts with Programs, v. 17, no. 4, p. 268.

Vallier, T. L., 1967, Geology of part of the Snake River Canyon and adjacent area in northeastern Oregon and Idaho (Ph.D. thesis): Corvallis, Oregon State University, 267 p.

Vallier, T. L., 1977, The Permian and Triassic Seven Devils Group: U.S. Geological Survey Bulletin 1437, 58 p.

Waitt, Jr., R. B., and Johnston, D. A., 1985, Case for periodic colossal jokulhlaups from Pleistocence glacial lake Missoula: Geological Society of America Bulletin, v. 96, p. 1271-1286.

Waring, G. A., 1965, Thermal springs of the United States and other countries of the world – a summary: U.S. Geological Survey Professional Paper 492.

White, D. E., and Williams, D. L., eds., 1975, Assessment of geothermal resources of the United States – 1975: U.S. Geological Survey Circular 726.

Womar, M. B.; Greeley, Ronald, and King, J. S., 1982, Phreatic eruptions of the eastern Snake River Plain of Idaho, in Bill Bonnichsen and R. M. Breckenridge, editors, Cenozoic Geology of Idaho: Idaho Bureau of Mines and Geology Bulletin 26, p. 453-464.

Wood, S. H., Wurts, C. N., Lane, T., Ballenger, N., Shaleen, M., and Totorica, D., 1985, Hydrologic effects of the October 28, 1983 earthquake, in Reaveley, L. D., (ed.), Earthquake Engineering Research Institute Reconnaissance Report on the Borah Peak Earthquake, 16 p.

Yates, R. B., 1968, The trans-Idaho discontinuity: International Geological Congress, 23rd, Prague 1968, Proc., v. 1, p. 117-123.

INDEX